Exodus

Exodus

THE PATH OF DELIVERANCE
FROM WASTELAND
TO GRACE LAND

J. D. Walt

ZONDERVAN REFLECTIVE

Exodus

Published by Zondervan, 3950 Sparks Drive SE, Suite 101, Grand Rapids, MI 49546, USA. Zondervan is a registered trademark of The Zondervan Corporation, L.L.C., a wholly owned subsidiary of HarperCollins Christian Publishing, Inc.

Requests for information should be addressed to customercare@harpercollins.com.

Zondervan titles may be purchased in bulk for educational, business, fundraising, or sales promotional use. For information, please email SpecialMarkets@Zondervan.com.

ISBN 978-0-310-17168-3 (audio)

Library of Congress Cataloging-in-Publication Data

Names: Walt, J. D. (John David) author
Title: Exodus : the path of deliverance from wasteland to grace land / J. D. Walt.
Description: Grand Rapids, Michigan : Zondervan, [2026] | Series: Daily seeds
Identifiers: LCCN 2025029461 (print) | LCCN 2025029462 (ebook) | ISBN 9780310171607 paperback | ISBN 9780310171614 ebook
Subjects: LCSH: Bible. Exodus—Meditations | Spiritual exercises | LCGFT: Meditations
Classification: LCC BS1245.54 .W35 2026 (print) | LCC BS1245.54 (ebook) | DDC 222/.1207—dc23/eng/20250904
LC record available at https://lccn.loc.gov/2025029461
LC ebook record available at https://lccn.loc.gov/2025029462

HarperCollins Publishers, Macken House, 39/40 Mayor Street Upper, Dublin 1, D01 C9W8, Ireland (https://www.harpercollins.com)

Cover design and illustration: Nate Farro
Series design: Derek Thornton / Notch Design
Interior design: Denise Froehlich

Printed in the United States of America

25 26 27 28 29 LBC 5 4 3 2 1

Contents

Week 4: Exodus 11:6–14:4

Week 5: Exodus 14:5–28

Week 6: Exodus 14:29–15:27

Week 7: Exodus 16:1–30

Week 8: Exodus 16:31–18:12

Week 9: Exodus 18:13–20:11

Week 10: Exodus 20:12–23:30

Week 11: Exodus 24:1–32:6

Week 12: Exodus 32:7–33:23

Week 13: Exodus 34:1–40:38

Preface

What are the two most important words of the day? I'm glad you asked. My take: the first word and the last word. Who gets the first word in your day? Who gets the last word? I have a confession: I have realized my slow drift into giving Instagram the first word of my day. It was simple and benign—just a quick scroll through the photos my friends posted over the last half day or so. Then this realization: Netflix was getting the last word of my day. Before drifting off to sleep, I would watch the next episode of some show that had caught my attention along the way. First word: *Instagram*. Last word: *Netflix*.

Days become weeks. Weeks become months. Months become years. And days, weeks, months, and years become us. Our lives consist not in the big decisions and banner events dotting our calendars, but in the little things we consistently do day after day after day. We are what we do . . . every single day.

Each one of us has within our stewardship the ability to decide who will get the first and last words in our life. You know where this is headed. But first let me tell you what happened with my Instagram-Netflix ways. The problem is that I want to make Instagram and Netflix the problem when they aren't the problem. The problem is with me and the misspent priority of my own heart. So I didn't decide to delete Instagram and swear off Netflix. Instead, I decided I would shift the priority of my heart. I determined to give the Word of God the first word and the last word of my days.

Though my day may be filled with a thousand distractions and a hundred course corrections, it is now determined—my day will be framed by, surrounded with, enclosed in the Word of God. First Word. Last Word. God's Word.

> The grass withers and the flowers fall,
> but the word of our God endures forever. (Isaiah 40:8)

Consider the stark simplicity and brazen boldness of this word from the prophet Isaiah. Everything is ephemeral. Only one thing is eternal—the Word of God.

Next to the front door of our home, the one we enter and exit through almost every time, is a chalkboard. And on the chalkboard are written those words. I read that verse at least once every single day. I say it aloud so my ears can hear it. Can I possibly be reminded enough that everything around me is passing away save one thing—the Word of God? Can I possibly be encouraged enough to come to Jesus and have him build my life on the singular enduring reality of the Word of God? First Word. Last Word. God's Word.

I offer you an invitation through this book to journey with me and others to shift the priority of your heart and mind. Each day we will gather around a biblical text. We will invite the text of Scripture to speak both the first and the last word of our day. Write some of the text for the day in a journal or on a note card, a whiteboard, or a chalkboard, and make it a simple act of worship to read it aloud each morning as the first word of the day and also at the close as the last word of the day.

Along the way, we will reflect together on how to increase the priority, prominence, and integration of the Word of God in our everyday lives. If we will give ourselves to the gentle work of this way of walking together, I suspect we will find pathways of delight and devotion winding through the wilderness of this world and the sanctuaries of our own souls that we never imagined existed. And something tells me these First-Word-Last-Word-God's-Word paths will find their way into tomorrow and next week and next month and onward, until they have become our lives.

Now I'm going to say, "The grass withers and the flowers fall," and you are going to say, "But the word of our God endures forever."

J. D. Walt

How This Works

This is a different kind of Bible study. The Bible is both the source and the subject. And you will learn information about the Bible along the way, such as its history, context, original languages, and authors. The goal is not educational in nature, but transformational. We will focus more on knowing Jesus than on knowing *about* Jesus.

To that end, each reading begins with the definitive inspiration of the Holy Spirit, the ongoing, unfolding text of Scripture. Following that is a short and hopefully substantive insight into the text and some aspect of its meaning. For insight to lead to deeper influence, we turn the text into prayer. Finally, influence must run its course toward impact. This is why you will find questions at the end of each chapter. These questions are designed not to elicit information but to crystallize intention.

Discipleship always leads from inspiration to attention, from attention to intention, and from intention to action.

Committing to Everyday Reading and Prayer

While Scripture always addresses us personally, it is not written to us individually. The content of Scripture cries out for a community of listeners and readers. This resource is designed for discipleship in community. You could read this like a traditional book—a few pages or chapters at a time. You could cram the readings the night before a group meeting. Those ways of reading are not the intention of this book. Keep in mind, Daily Seeds is not called *Daily* Seeds for kicks. We believe Scripture is worthy of our most focused and consistent attention. Every day. We all have misses, but let's make everyday reading and prayer more than a noble aspiration; let's make it our covenant with one another.

This discipleship tool will create spiritual habits of individual reading and of praying the biblical text—six days on your own and one day with others.

How to Use with Small Groups

Daily Seeds is a proven discipleship resource that works in a variety of contexts—from churches studying a book of the Bible together to small groups to Sunday school classes to virtual meetings. Assuming your group meets weekly, group and class members should read one chapter every day. You will notice there is not an assigned reading for the seventh day. On the seventh day, meet with your group to share, pray, and encourage one another with insights or struggles that the text brought up in you during the previous six days. Use the following guidelines to help structure your group meetings as you allow Scripture to transform you in community.

The guidelines for using Daily Seeds in small groups or class settings are meant to be simple. Perhaps share the responsibility of leading group meetings. Remember that the goal is transformation.

1. Hearing the Text

Invite the group to settle into silence for a period of no less than one and no more than five minutes. Ask an appointed person to keep time and to read the biblical text covering the period of days since the last group meeting. Allow at least one minute of silence following the reading of the text.

2. Responding to the Text

Invite anyone from the group to respond to the reading by answering these prompts: What did you hear? What did you see? What did you otherwise sense from the Lord?

3. Sharing Insights and Implications for Discipleship

Moving in an orderly rotation (or free-for-all), invite people to share insights and implications from the week's readings. What did you find challenging, encouraging, provocative, comforting, invasive, inspiring, corrective, affirming, guiding, or warning? Allow group conversation to proceed at will. Limit to one sharing item per turn, with multiple rounds of discussion.

4. Shaping Intentions for Prayer

Invite each person in the group to share a single discipleship intention for the week ahead. It is helpful if this goal for growing in discipleship can also be framed as a question the group can use to check in from the prior week. At each person's turn, they are invited to share how their intention went during the previous week. The class or group can open and close the meeting according to its established patterns.

Introduction

I took my four adult children on a vacation to the mountains of Colorado. Some friends generously offered us the use of their vacation home in the beautiful mountain town of Frisco. We opted for a summer visit so we could ride bikes, take hikes, and do other activities impossible to enjoy during snow season. After a couple of easy hikes, we decided to tackle more of a real mountain—at least to us. It was not technical climbing but a well-worn trail. All told it came to about ten thousand feet to the summit.

It started out well enough, but it didn't take long for the incline to steepen, and our legs began to weaken. Every five to ten minutes, we would cross paths with climbers on their way back down the mountain. Being a "that dad" kind of a father, I began asking each of the descending climbers a burning question: "How much farther?"

Their answers varied from "Not much farther" to "You're not even half way yet!" to a range of other vague responses somewhere between discouraging and indifferent. Couldn't they see the exhaustion on our faces? Didn't they notice that I was on the brink of a mutiny as my kids sat on the trail contemplating turning back and aborting the mission? I expected encouragement and hoped for hope from these fellow trail-blazing strangers.

As we begrudgingly continued our weary ascent, we started setting a timer; adopting a kind of pomodoro technique—we would climb for ten minutes and rest for five. Soon we were climbing for five minutes and resting for ten. You get the point. These ever-extending breaks gave us a chance to talk about what we were experiencing with comparisons to Mount Everest and beach vacations. We explored our motivations for choosing this daunting excursion instead of the all-you-can-eat pancake buffet in the village. Mainly, we discussed what we most wanted to hear from the descending climbers in response to my incessant question, "How much farther?" We arrived at a consensus. We didn't really want to know how long or how far or how hard it would be. We just wanted to be encouraged. We decided we wanted to hear two things and in this order: (1) "You're going to make it!" and (2) "It's going to be worth it!"

We determined—should we be graced to reach the summit—on our descent we would greet every ascending passerby, bidden or not, with these words: "You're going to make it, and it's going to be worth it!" We did it, and you should have seen the look on their faces as they palpably felt the encouragement of our good news. It brought new meaning to the old Christmas hymn "Go Tell it on the Mountain."

In retrospect, upon further reflection, this was not a mountaintop story, but rather a wilderness story. With every struggling step of ascent, we wanted to be delivered to the top of that mountain, and with every gleeful yet even more perilous step of descent, we wanted to be delivered back to the bottom of the valley. A wilderness story always turns out to be a deliverance story. And this is the story of the book we call Exodus—a wilderness story meets a deliverance story.

Perhaps that's why this devotional journey chooses to begin not at the beginning but fifteen verses in. By the time we get to the fifteenth verse of the first chapter, we've already forgotten the incredible story of God's faithfulness to Joseph through the extraordinary wilderness journey that was his life. We've already forgotten all the fledgling origins of the twelve tribes who first settled in this land of refuge. We've already forgotten the name of the Pharaoh who arose, of whom it was famously said, "He knew not Joseph." It took only fourteen verses to turn the flourishing refuge of salvation into a forsaken land of slavery.

Yes, the story of Exodus begins in the wilderness and yet on the doorstep of deliverance, with a king speaking to midwives and the hope of the world riding in a tiny baby in an ark of reeds pushed into a flooding river. Soon the wilderness road will lead us to a burning bush and the king of the universe speaking to this once tiny baby now become an old man, a hireling shepherd and a forgotten exile. This Moses would become God's agent of deliverance; his hand of guidance through the long wilderness journey—indeed, the very emissary of the exodus.

And God said, "I will be with you. And this will be the sign to you that it is I who have sent you: When you have brought the people out of Egypt, you will worship God on this mountain" (Exodus 3:12).

Who knew Exodus would be a long, slow, often steep and always winding ascent to the top of a mountain? Here's the forty-chapter book summary. It will take twenty chapters to get to the top of the mountain, followed by another twenty chapters to descend back to the bottom of the valley.

In no time, the Israelites would be asking, "How much farther?" while making plans to turn back. And the God of the exodus would answer again and again, "I will be with you." Translation: (1) "You're going to make it," and (2) "It's going to be worth it."

God led them with a cloud by day and fire by night; fed them with manna in the morning and quail in the evening; and supplied them with water from a rock and healing from a snake as the wilderness story turned into a deliverance story and became our exodus story.

I commissioned my son David, whom I write about in entry 75 and refer to as a modern-day Bezalel, a skilled artisan and craftsman, to tell the story of Exodus through a single painting. Can we just say he understood the assignment? He titled the piece *Ex Deus*. Upon seeing it, I immediately noted how he had misspelled Exodus. He replied, "Dad! It's Latin. It means, "From God."

I have included a grayscale rendition of the piece on the following page. It is presented in color and is available for purchase at seedbed.com/exodusprint. I must warn you before you press forward of a spoiler alert. In the interest of discovering one's own joyful epiphanies through the exploration of art, the curious traveler may elect to forgo the artist's dad's interpretive description to follow. If that is you, skip to the end.

I hoped you would join me. There is so much to notice and appreciate. In the foreground to the right is the classic memento mori marker, which means, "Remember, you must die." Just across in the left foreground we behold the mystery manifested by ten words: "The bush was on fire. It did not burn up." The stark contrast between the two images implies a choice between them. Upon further reflection, the deeper wisdom of the Son of God whispers, "Whoever wants to save their life will lose it, but whoever loses their life for my sake will find it." The life on fire yet not consumed may only be accessed by passing through the memento mori. The secret to life is to die before you die. It reminds us of the Desert Fathers and Abbot Lot's burning question, "What more must I do?" and Abbot Joseph's illuminated reply, "Why not be completely changed into fire?" Juxtaposed between the two ancient signs appears another sign—a more modern sign—yes, a street sign. It reveals the intersection of two unnamed streets, as if to invite the pilgrim to identify the choice before them in the present wilderness season. Is it the intersection of faith and fear, of hope and doubt, of good and best, or perhaps of the pained past and the possible future? And after all of this, we still find ourselves in the foreground of the wilderness journey.

As we step onto the path, we face a long and winding, wandering and weaving road ahead. As our eye follows the path to the horizon line, our eyes are lifted to the sky where we discover the mirrored path of the pillar of cloud. The meandering journey through the wilderness of this earth turns out to be the willed path of heaven—even the plan of God. We are reminded of the wise words of the Danish theologian Søren Kierkegaard's famous dictum, the wisdom of the wilderness: "Life can only be understood backwards, but it must be lived forwards."[1]

There's even more to notice in the transforming color from the land to the sky and the movements from darkness to light and from arid desert to green pasture. Perhaps the most curious feature of *Ex Deus* is the triangular trinity of telephone poles connected by a wire. For my money, this typifies and incarnates the ancient tabernacle of the unseen triune God with which the book of Exodus ends. No wire proceeding to or from the triangle points to the uncreated, self-contained transcendence of the Godhead. The wires strung between them signal the mysterious divine interpersonal communion of prayer. That the poles are grounded on the path and not somehow suspended in the sky exemplifies the invitation to pilgrims to come within and join the conversation. Finally, and most serendipitously, the three telephone poles turn out to be the crosses of Calvary, foreshadowing the long and winding road to "on earth as it is in

1 Jack Maden, "Kierkegaard: Life Can Only Be Understood Backwards, but It Must Be Lived Forwards," Philosophy Break, March 2020, https://philosophybreak.com/articles/kierkegaard-life-can-only-be-understood-backwards-but-must-be-lived-forwards/.

heaven," as if to complete the passover through final perdition and pave the path to ultimate redemption.

Be encouraged pilgrim. No matter what wilderness within which you now find yourself, be assured of these two things: (1) You are going to make it, and (2) it is going to be worth it.

All of it is coming to you as gift—*ex Deus*—from God the Father through God the Son and by God the Holy Spirit.

> Glory be to the Father and to the Son and to the Holy Ghost.
> As it was in the beginning, is now and ever shall be.
> World without end. Amen! Amen!

—John David (J. D.) Walt Jr.
Ash Wednesday 2025

Ex Deus by David Walt

1 WEEK

Exodus 1:15–3:1

1

Exodus 1:15–21

Plan B?

The king of Egypt said to the Hebrew midwives, whose names were Shiphrah and Puah, "When you are helping the Hebrew women during childbirth on the delivery stool, if you see that the baby is a boy, kill him; but if it is a girl, let her live." The midwives, however, feared God and did not do what the king of Egypt had told them to do; they let the boys live. Then the king of Egypt summoned the midwives and asked them, "Why have you done this? Why have you let the boys live?"

The midwives answered Pharaoh, "Hebrew women are not like Egyptian women; they are vigorous and give birth before the midwives arrive."

So God was kind to the midwives and the people increased and became even more numerous. And because the midwives feared God, he gave them families of their own.

Consider This

I was having lunch with a dear friend recently. It was the ten-year mile marker of the day he found his forty-year-old son dead of a heart attack. He told of how this tragedy led to the rapid decline and death—six years later—of his otherwise healthy wife of fifty-two years. He shared the burden of his ensuing sadness and loneliness in the four years since. Then, with tears forming in his eyes, he said, "Plan B." I asked what he meant, and he said, "I guess my life is now on plan B."

I can't stop thinking about it. "I guess my life is now on plan B." It's probably how I feel about my own life. Plan A had a marvelous forty-five-year run and then a ten-year-long trainwreck brought on by our experience with mental illness, leading to the devastation of an unwanted divorce and the death of a family's future never to be. I guess *my* life is on plan B too.

How's that for a welcome to Exodus?

Only fifteen verses into the epic story of Exodus we get these words:

> The king of Egypt said to the Hebrew midwives, whose names were Shiphrah and Puah, "When you are helping the Hebrew women during childbirth on the delivery stool, if you see that the baby is a boy, kill him; but if it is a girl, let her live."

When the unnamed king of Egypt called a meeting with the named Hebrew (slave) midwives, that signified a plan B situation was underway.

> If you see that the baby is a boy, kill him.

Yep, that's definitely plan B.

Everything seemed to be going well enough for the Israelite people in Egypt:

> Now Joseph and all his brothers and all that generation died, but the Israelites were exceedingly fruitful; they multiplied greatly, increased in numbers and became so numerous that the land was filled with them. (Exodus 1:6–7)

Doesn't that sound like plan A? Sounds like it's straight out of Genesis 1: "God blessed them and said to them, 'Be fruitful and increase in number; fill the earth and subdue it'" (Genesis 1:28).

Plan B entered the picture when a new king, to whom Joseph meant nothing, came to power in Egypt. "Look," he said to his people, "the Israelites have become far too numerous for us. Come, we must deal shrewdly with them or they will become even more numerous and, if war breaks out, will join our enemies, fight against us and leave the country" (Exodus 1:8–10).

Plan B is always driven by fear, scarcity, and self-preservation and is fueled by the projection of unlikely worst-case scenarios. Watch where it leads:

> So they put slave masters over them to oppress them with forced labor, and they built Pithom and Rameses as store cities for Pharaoh. (Exodus 1:11)

Plan B is cruel, oppressive, destructive, and devastating. It saps faith and slays freedom. But can we be honest about something? Plan B didn't start with the king of Egypt. It began much earlier. It was conceived all the way back in the beauty of the garden known as Eden (a.k.a. plan A). Plan B entered the world at Genesis 3:1 with three fateful words: "Now the serpent. . . ."

> If you see that the baby is a boy, kill him.

He's been stealing and killing and destroying ever since. Consider Joseph, son eleven of twelve, whose brothers hatched plan B to throw him into the bottom of a well and then relented to sell him as a slave to a band of Ishmaelites heading to Egypt (see Genesis 37:12–28).

In the midst of a plan B reality, God always has a plan A story.

Joseph, all the way back through his favored life as "the dreamer" was an agent of plan A. And all the way forward, through the tortuous path of his future—from favored son to forgotten slave to falsely accused to wrongly imprisoned and onward to becoming the hand of the king and the deliverer of those who betrayed him—Joseph was God's secret agent of his unstoppable plan A.

In the midst of a plan B reality, God always has a plan A story.

Back in Exodus, Shiphrah and Puah were lifting the torch as the secret agents of plan A:

> The midwives, however, feared God and did not do what the king of Egypt had told them to do; they let the boys live.

We must not resign ourselves to plan B. Why? Because God never gives up on plan A.

As Joseph the dreamer said so well to his brothers who betrayed him: "You intended to harm me, but God intended it for good to accomplish what is now being done, the saving of many lives" (Genesis 50:20).

Buckle up! The story of Exodus; indeed, of the whole Bible, is the story of how the plan A God of heaven and earth winds his way into and through plan B—crushing the serpent underneath his feet, redeeming, restoring, and renewing his people and the whole creation; displacing darkness by light, desecrating sin by righteousness, destroying death by resurrection, and crushing chaos by new creation.

Plan B? I guess my life is no longer on plan B.

What if the time for your exodus has come? That knocking you hear at the door? Plan A is back!

The Prayer for Deliverance

Lord Jesus, you are my Deliverer. I hear you decree a season of exodus over me, over my family, and over my church. I receive it. And as you decree it, I declare it. Prepare my heart, mind, soul, and strength for the deliverance that comes with exodus. Now let it be as you decree—for my good, for others' gain, and for your glory.

Glory be to the Father and to the Son and to the Holy Ghost.
As it was in the beginning, is now and ever shall be.
World without end. Amen! Amen!

The Questions

Have you felt resigned to the ravages of plan B in your life? Are you ready to get back on board with plan A? What might that mean? Do any Bible stories or particular texts come to mind along these lines? Consider writing them in your journal.

2

Exodus 2:1–4

Plan B vs. Plan C and the Fallacy of Lesser Evils

Now a man of the tribe of Levi married a Levite woman, and she became pregnant and gave birth to a son. When she saw that he was a fine child, she hid him for three months. But when she could hide him

> *no longer, she got a papyrus basket for him and coated it with tar and pitch. Then she placed the child in it and put it among the reeds along the bank of the Nile. His sister stood at a distance to see what would happen to him.*

Consider This

In yesterday's devotional, I failed to note the last line of Exodus 1: "Then Pharaoh gave this order to all his people: 'Every Hebrew boy that is born you must throw into the Nile, but let every girl live'" (v. 22).

Get a picture in your mind of hundreds of young men carrying their infant sons in their arms, walking out to the bank of the Nile, and throwing their sons into the river to drown (see Acts 7:19). Forgive me for asking you to see such a sight. Sadly, this is the world we live in.

It is a choice of evils. Do the parents suffer the death of their child, or should they risk being caught (at which point they would lose not only the child but perhaps the mother and father too as a punishment; or maybe even the rest of the children)? That would be plan C. We are dealing with pure evil here.

One of the most successful and seductive strategies of plan B is to convince us we have no other choice but plan C, an even worse version of plan B. This is the strategy of sin, darkness, death, and evil—to convince us we must choose between the lesser of two evils. I struggle to admit it because I know just how real the choice of evil dilemmas can be, but to choose the lesser of two evils is still to choose evil.

I believe the choice-of-evils defense (so called because it is a way of defending an evil choice) is not so much a logical fallacy for Christians as it is a theological fallacy. Why? Because with God, there must always be another option. It's always plan A. To our thinking, while plan A may not always seem like a good alternative (because it often involves a cross), it is always a non-evil option. That's what we see in today's text.

> When she saw that he was a fine child, she hid him for three months.

This mother saw the inestimable potential in the life of a child given by God. Something in her knew this child belonged to God. But doesn't every parent see a fine child when they look at a newborn? Something about the vision of this mother was different. It's a good word to us parents—we must ask God to grant us the vision to see our children as he sees them. She refused to kill her baby boy. She knew there must be another way.

> But when she could hide him no longer, she got a papyrus basket for him and coated it with tar and pitch. Then she placed the child in it and put it among the reeds along the bank of the Nile.

This choice was mortifying, yet it was creative and full of love and care. Moses's mother's choice created the possibility of something different happening; something new and unexpected. Sure, it was fraught with peril, but it was not a lesser-of-evils choice. It was a choice of greater faith—one that extended life as far as she possibly could—a choice creating the opportunity for all the unpredictable possibilities of God to work.

One of the dark strategies of the spirit of the age of the great confusion in which we live is to bully God-fearing citizens of the kingdom into an ever-evolving choice-of-evils dilemma. We must come to grips with the truth. Beneath the choice-of-evils scenario is a choice of fears. Who will we fear more: God or evil? When we fear evil, we invariably resort to choosing the lesser of evils (plan B or plan C). When we fear God, we resist evil and we choose the way of greater faith—the way most often invisible to the naked eye—plan A.

Note the plaque on the wall of the celebrated Hall of Faith: "By faith Moses' parents hid him for three months after he was born, because they saw he was no ordinary child, and they were not afraid of the king's edict" (Hebrews 11:23).

Plan A is always more creative, always more costly, always riskier, and always more faith-full.

Let's pause here on the bank of the Nile as the tiny ark of faith floats into the water's current, holding an infant slave condemned to death; a baby boy carrying all the hopes of the future of the kingdom of God.

> His sister stood at a distance to see what would happen to him.

Let's take big sister's hand as we together behold plan A unfold.

The Prayer for Deliverance

Lord Jesus, you are my Deliverer. I hear you decree a season of exodus over me, over my family, and over my church. I receive it. And as you decree it, I declare it. I receive your deliverance from evil and the evil one and into the creative, costly, faith-filled possibilities of plan A. Prepare my heart, mind, soul, and strength for the deliverance that comes with exodus. Now let it be as you decree—for my good, for others' gain, and for your glory. Grant me courage, Lord, not only to resist evil but to rebuke the ever-so-reasonable invitation to choose evil under the auspices of it somehow ever being lesser. This seems impossible in this world, and yet nothing is impossible with you. I know the choice of greater faith will come at a cost to myself, my reputation, and my respectability. I declare in faith that I fear no evil. I fear God. And, even more, I love you, God. Come, Holy Spirit, and train me to be such a person of faith. I am praying in Jesus's name, the Master of plan A.

> Glory be to the Father and to the Son and to the Holy Ghost.
> As it was in the beginning, is now and ever shall be.
> World without end. Amen! Amen!

The Questions

What do you see as we watch this scene on the bank of the Nile unfold? What must it have been like to be Moses's mother and father? Are you ready to forsake plan B and its ever-evolving choice-of-evils dilemma? Where does your mind run in a practical way as it comes to being pressed into choosing the lesser of two evils? Can you see where you have succumbed to it in the past? What will it take to leave that whole paradigm behind and shift into the choice of the greater alternatives of faith?

3

Exodus 2:5–10

The Way Back to Plan A—from Weak Resignation to Deep Surrender

Then Pharaoh's daughter went down to the Nile to bathe, and her attendants were walking along the riverbank. She saw the basket among the reeds and sent her female slave to get it. She opened it and saw the baby. He was crying, and she felt sorry for him. "This is one of the Hebrew babies," she said.

Then his sister asked Pharaoh's daughter, "Shall I go and get one of the Hebrew women to nurse the baby for you?"

"Yes, go," she answered. So the girl went and got the baby's mother. Pharaoh's daughter said to her, "Take this baby and nurse him for me, and I will pay you." So the woman took the baby and nursed him. When the child grew older, she took him to Pharaoh's daughter and he became her son. She named him Moses, saying, "I drew him out of the water."

Consider This

Previously, on "plan B" we "stood at a distance" with big sister on the shoreline of the Nile, fighting back tears as we watched the tiny baby, tucked into the ark of God, float into the reeds of the river of faith.

Meanwhile—watch, no *behold*, what happened!

In case you missed it, Pharaoh's daughter came to the Nile to bathe and spotted the tiny ark of faith. She sent her slave over to investigate, and—just like that—this infant slave, condemned to death by her Pharaoh father, was in her arms.

It gets better. Remember big sister? She lets go of our hand and saunters up to Pharaoh's daughter with a strategic solution:

> "Shall I go and get one of the Hebrew women to nurse the baby for you?"

"Yes, go," she answered. So the girl went and got the baby's mother.

The plot keeps turning and eases into the category of "truth is stranger than fiction." In other words, you can't make this up.

> Pharaoh's daughter said to her, "Take this baby and nurse him for me, and I will pay you." So the woman took the baby and nursed him.

This, my friends, is how plan A works! The woman was the baby's mother, and Pharaoh's daughter agreed to pay her—the baby's mother—to nurse her own baby, the same baby she surrendered to God and pushed out into the Nile in the tiny ark of faith just hours before.

> When the child grew older, she took him to Pharaoh's daughter and he became her son. She named him Moses, saying, "I drew him out of the water."

This is how we get from plan B back to plan A: *surrender.* We renounce resignation to plan B, and we surrender to the God of plan A. We don't know how or when or where or even *if* much of the time (if we are honest), but we know God. We surrender and we do the next good, right, God thing in front of us. Plan B, the apparent lesser-evil choice, dictated throwing the baby in the river to drown because plan C promised a much worse outcome if plan B was not observed. Plan A seemed impossible, implausible, and, yes, even downright absurd. Can we make one last double take here so we might imprint on our hearts and minds what plan A often looks like? "But when she could hide him no longer, she got a papyrus basket for him and coated it with tar and pitch. Then she placed the child in it and put it among the reeds along the bank of the Nile" (Exodus 2:3).

Picture it. As she weaves the reeds together through her tears into the basket—the living God of heaven and earth weaves plan A right into the devastation and destruction of plan B. As she coats the basket with tar and pitch, the hand of God applies it like Holy Spirit mortar, salving the faith of this broken mother and sealing the fate of the wicked

Pharaoh decades in advance. That's how plan A works—quietly under the surface, hidden in the reeds, until suddenly, one day years later, at the appointed time, he rises up and splits the sea.

What Pharaoh intended for evil, God turned into good. Through these two exceedingly obscure and unimportant people at this very obscure moment in the history of the world, we get one of the most significant people who ever lived: Moses, the one drawn up out of the water.

Remember that the next time you think your choice or your voice or your courageous action doesn't matter.

Remember that in the present struggle in your own life, the one that has you tired beyond tired and ready to quit. Don't give up or give in to weak resignation. Surrender to Jesus. Let him start preparing the basket through your hands.

The Prayer for Deliverance

Lord Jesus, you are my Deliverer. I hear you decree a season of exodus over me, over my family, and over my church. I receive it. And as you decree it, I declare it. I receive your deliverance from the spirit of weak resignation and into the boldness of deep surrender to the will of our Father God. Prepare my heart, mind, soul, and strength for the deliverance that comes with exodus. Now let it be as you decree—for my good, for others' gain, and for your glory.

Glory be to the Father and to the Son and to the Holy Ghost.
As it was in the beginning, is now and ever shall be.
World without end. Amen! Amen!

The Questions

How are you inspired to renounce the spirit of weak resignation to your circumstances and to surrender to God in bold faith? How might you be standing from a distance and watching with curiosity at plan A in the works? How might you start walking toward the river and up to Pharaoh's daughter in the situation?

4

Exodus 2:11–15

How to Get from Wasteland Wandering to Wilderness Walking

One day, after Moses had grown up, he went out to where his own people were and watched them at their hard labor. He saw an Egyptian beating a Hebrew, one of his own people. Looking this way and that and seeing no one, he killed the Egyptian and hid him in the sand. The next day he went out and saw two Hebrews fighting. He asked the one in the wrong, "Why are you hitting your fellow Hebrew?"

The man said, "Who made you ruler and judge over us? Are you thinking of killing me as you killed the Egyptian?" Then Moses was afraid and thought, "What I did must have become known."

When Pharaoh heard of this, he tried to kill Moses, but Moses fled from Pharaoh and went to live in Midian, where he sat down by a well.

Consider This

There is the will of God, and then there are the ways of God. When the will of God is not executed in the ways of God, it leads to the wilderness of God. Today's text is a case in point.

The will of God opposes the cruel and unjust treatment of slaves. Backing up a step, the will of God opposes slavery altogether. Moses intervened against an Egyptian slave master who was abusing an Israelite slave. So far so good, right? He took it a step further and killed the Egyptian. That's where the road forked on the will of God. There is a God way of dealing with cruelty, injustice, and even abuse. However, when one does evil to defeat evil, it still leaves us with evil. The right thing done in the wrong way is the wrong thing. When the will of God is not carried out according to the ways of God, it leads to the wilderness of God.

The prophet Isaiah put it this way centuries later:

"For my thoughts are not your thoughts,
neither are your ways my ways,"
declares the LORD.
"As the heavens are higher than the earth,
so are my ways higher than your ways
and my thoughts than your thoughts." (55:8–9)

What happens when a person does the right thing in the wrong way? They lose credibility. Their authority is diminished. Their witness is destroyed. Isn't that what happened with Moses here?

> The next day he went out and saw two Hebrews fighting. He asked the one in the wrong, "Why are you hitting your fellow Hebrew?"

> The man said, "Who made you ruler and judge over us? Are you thinking of killing me as you killed the Egyptian?"

The end does not justify the means. It proved costly for Moses, sending him from his palace of extreme privilege into what would be a long and challenging season of wilderness. During these years, Moses would become trained in the ways of God and profoundly prepared to pursue the will of God in the deliverance of the people of God. When Moses killed the Egyptian slave master, he stepped out of plan A and into plan B.

> When Pharaoh heard of this, he tried to kill Moses, but Moses fled from Pharaoh and went to live in Midian, where he sat down by a well.

I am drawn to this phrase and image.

> He sat down by a well.

The Bible is full of well stories. See if you can remember some of them today. Very significant things happen at wells. I recently connected the notion of a well with the idea of wellness. It's a playful connection, admittedly, but I wonder if there might be more to it. A well is a place of refreshment and restoration. A well is a place of community and encounter. Ponder these connections today in your own life—a well and the wellness that comes with refreshment and restoration, with community and encounter. Wells, in the Bible, are turning points. They are places where the Spirit of God graciously narrates us back into plan A.

At these wells of God—strategically placed in the wilderness seasons of our lives—our painful wandering transforms into purposeful walking. In the interest of getting from plan B back to plan A, what we need most is a deeper well.

The Prayer for Deliverance

Lord Jesus, you are my Deliverer. I hear you decree a season of exodus over me, over my family, and over my church. I receive it. And as you decree it, I declare it. I receive your deliverance from my broken ways into the higher and better ways of God. I receive your deliverance from a wasteland of lostness into the wilderness of new life. Jesus, lead me to the deeper well of the Holy Spirit today. I thirst for living water.

Glory be to the Father and to the Son and to the Holy Ghost.
As it was in the beginning, is now and ever shall be.
World without end. Amen! Amen!

The Questions

Have you ever done what you understood to be the will of God yet not in the ways of God? What happened? How did that go? Are you experiencing a wasteland of lostness becoming a wilderness of purpose? Ask Jesus to meet you at a God well today.

5

Exodus 2:16–25

On the Journey from Wasteland to Graceland

Now a priest of Midian had seven daughters, and they came to draw water and fill the troughs to water their father's flock. Some shepherds came along and drove them away, but Moses got up and came to their rescue and watered their flock.

When the girls returned to Reuel their father, he asked them, "Why have you returned so early today?"

They answered, "An Egyptian rescued us from the shepherds. He even drew water for us and watered the flock."

"And where is he?" Reuel asked his daughters. "Why did you leave him? Invite him to have something to eat."

Moses agreed to stay with the man, who gave his daughter Zipporah to Moses in marriage. Zipporah gave birth to a son, and Moses named him Gershom, saying, "I have become a foreigner in a foreign land."

During that long period, the king of Egypt died. The Israelites groaned in their slavery and cried out, and their cry for help because of their slavery went up to God. God heard their groaning and he remembered his covenant with Abraham, with Isaac and with Jacob. So God looked on the Israelites and was concerned about them.

Consider This

Life is what happens when you are making other plans.

Moses's life seemed to have taken a detour. The text describes this season of Moses's life as a "long period."

He thought he did the right thing back in Egypt in coming to the defense of an Israelite slave. No sooner than he left Egypt, he found himself in another confrontation with a group of rogue shepherds trying to attack a band of seven defenseless sisters.

Moses was a good egg, but he was lost, and life went on. Though good things happened to him, including finding a wife and having a son, he still found himself somewhere between wasteland and wilderness. The name he gave his son tells the story.

> Zipporah gave birth to a son, and Moses named him Gershom, saying, "I have become a foreigner in a foreign land."

Moses must have wondered to himself, *Why this? Am I being punished? What did I do wrong?* He had been exiled twice, first as a baby—forced from his own people, the Israelites—and then from his adopted people, the Egyptians. He had gone from the privilege of the palace to herding sheep in Midian. The name Gershom says it all: "I have become a foreigner in a foreign land."

Have you ever felt exiled from your life, stuck in a moment you can't get out of? Things are not turning out as you planned. Something or someone intervenes in your best-laid plans and a promising path turns toward what seems to be an endless exile. "Where did I go wrong?" you ask. You find yourself saying things like, "I have become a foreigner in a foreign land."

Here's the good news. When you are doing your best to follow Jesus and it feels like you are exiled from your life, you are not being punished. You are being prepared.

At the same time, Moses was wondering aloud about what happened to his best life, another conversational drama was playing out a hundred miles away—as in, "Meanwhile, back at the ranch . . ."

> During that long period, the king of Egypt died. The Israelites groaned in their slavery and cried out, and their cry for help because of their slavery went up to God. God heard their groaning and he remembered his covenant with Abraham, with Isaac and with Jacob. So God looked on the Israelites and was concerned about them.

It can feel like life is an endless losing game of checkers until we discover it was not a game of checkers after all. God was playing chess. And he never loses.

In times like these, we must exchange the "Why me?" question for the "Why this?" inquiry. We must turn out the lights on our pity party and open our hearts to the curriculum of circumstances through which God is preparing us for a future season we cannot yet see, much less imagine.

I have become a foreigner in a foreign land.

The future may be a lot closer to home than we realize.

The Prayer for Deliverance

Lord Jesus, you are my Deliverer. I hear you decree a season of exodus over me, over my family, and over my church. I receive it. And as you decree it, I declare it. Thank you for all the ways you take hardships and difficult circumstances and weave them into your plan for my good. Because of this, I can thank you for even the hardest of times. I offer up my circumstances, turning away from my victimhood and my bitterness, and even letting go of my own dreams and best-laid plans. I trust you, and because I trust you, I trust your path. You are the God who delivers me from lost to found, from exile to home, even from wasteland to graceland.

Prepare my heart, mind, soul, and strength for the deliverance that comes with exodus.

Now let it be as you decree—for my good, for others' gain, and for your glory.

Glory be to the Father and to the Son and to the Holy Ghost.
As it was in the beginning, is now and ever shall be.
World without end. Amen! Amen!

The Questions

How about it? Have you ever felt exiled from your life, like "a foreigner in a foreign land"? Maybe even now? How might you make the turn toward trusting God to do something new in the midst of it? What might that look like? How about heading back to yesterday's well again today?

6

Exodus 3:1

The Altar Calls Between the Far Side of the Wilderness and the Mountain of God

Now Moses was tending the flock of Jethro his father-in-law, the priest of Midian, and he led the flock to the far side of the wilderness and came to Horeb, the mountain of God.

Consider This

The mountain of God is at the far side of the wilderness.

Did you catch that? The mountain of God is at the far side of the wilderness. It rings true, doesn't it? This is where physical geography and spiritual geography meet.

From a condemned infant slave to the palace of Pharaoh, Moses enjoyed extreme privilege in the first season of his life. From the peak of power to the wilderness of Midian, he experienced great obscurity in the second season of his life. The text is careful to tell he herded not his own sheep but those of his father-in-law, Jethro (referred to as Reuel in previous verses). These incredible shifts of fortune pale in comparison to what happened next.

After decades of punching the clock, Moses found himself in the midst of another long day, perhaps daydreaming about retirement, if there was such a thing in those days. He was probably somewhere between seventy and eighty, somewhere between death and dying, somewhere between cynicism and nothing to look forward to.

> Now Moses was tending the flock of Jethro his father-in-law, the priest of Midian, and he led the flock to the far side of the wilderness and came to Horeb, the mountain of God.

It's the far side of the wilderness. And it is the mountain of God. He had lived some forty years in this valley of vision, preparing for this next moment, which would open the door into a pilgrimage to another mountain of God, Mount Sinai, and yet another forty years of wilderness wandering.

It is easy to look back from the vantage point of the whole story and marvel at the greatness of Moses and his singular importance to the will of God; yet the only reason we even know about his life is because of a late-life encounter with the greatness of God at a bush on fire yet not burning up.

Biographies aren't typically written until the end of one's story. I wonder how many other shepherds passed by the same burning bush and didn't even notice. We could just as well be reading about them instead.

There was something special about Moses. He was different. We remember his extraordinary life, yet we tend to brush over the extraordinary difficulties of his life. By my math, he wandered in the wilderness for a solid eighty of his one-hundred-twenty years.

Sometimes it takes a long season in the wilderness to learn the difference between one's importance and one's worth.

Sometimes it takes being sidelined by failure (moral or otherwise) or exiled by circumstances or the meaninglessness of a menial job to remind us that our worth doesn't come from what we can do for God but from who we are in Jesus.

I'm writing to a college student who needs to know Jesus doesn't need your skills and résumé to change the world. He wants your heart.

I'm writing to a young-ish mother who feels as though she has lost herself in diapers and dishes. Jesus is not interested in the former dreams of your earlier life. He wants your heart right now.

I'm writing to a middle-aged pastor who is angry at the mediocrity of the church and determined to do something about it. Jesus is not interested in your tireless ambition to make his church better. He wants your heart—just as it is.

I'm writing to a retired person who has mistaken their dreams for a relatively comfortable life. Jesus is not interested in fortunes and facelifts. He wants your heart as his treasure.

I'm writing to myself with all my self-important notions of grandeur to sow for a great awakening. Jesus is not interested in my noble ambitions. He wants my heart.

If these words feel crushing, as they do for me, it's probably because they need to be. Do you know what we call the thin place between the far side of the wilderness and the mountain of God? We call it the altar. The altar is where our earthbound dreams come to die so that the vision of heaven might be birthed in our hearts—anew, afresh, or maybe for the very first time.

This thin place between resignation and resurrection—let's call it the altar of relinquishment—is the place of letting go of everything but God.

The Prayer for Deliverance

Lord Jesus, you are my Deliverer. I hear you decree a season of exodus over me, over my family, and over my church. I receive it. And as you decree it, I declare it. I receive your deliverance from my own best ideas and plans. I receive your deliverance into the full-throated, full-throttled will of God for all my days—starting with this one. I receive your deliverance from the apathy of resignation. I receive your deliverance into the abiding life of resurrection. Thank you for this place between the far side of the wilderness and the mountain of God, this altar of relinquishment. Train my soul to relinquish everything but you, for this will be the place where my life catches fire with your glory like the bush that will not be consumed. Come, Holy Spirit, prepare my heart, mind, soul, and strength for the deliverance that comes with exodus. Now let it be as you decree—for my good, for others' gain, and for your glory.

Glory be to the Father and to the Son and to the Holy Ghost.
As it was in the beginning, is now and ever shall be.
World without end. Amen! Amen!

The Questions

How have you come to a deepened understanding of the difference between your importance and your worth?

How do you relate to this word ***relinquishment***? How might you make this altar of relinquishment?

What is the nature of the deliverance Jesus is bringing now? From what to what?

Week 1: Discussion Questions

Hearing the Text

Read Exodus 1:15–3:1.

Responding to the Text

- What did you hear?
- What did you see?
- What did you otherwise sense from the Lord?

Sharing Insights and Implications for Discipleship

Drawing from the Scripture text and daily readings, what did you find challenging, encouraging, provocative, comforting, invasive, inspiring, corrective, affirming, guiding, or warning?

Shaping Intentions for Prayer

Write your discipleship intention for the week ahead.

2
WEEK

Exodus 3:2–15

8

Exodus 3:2–3

The Bush Was on Fire . . . It Did Not Burn Up

There the angel of the Lord *appeared to him in flames of fire from within a bush. Moses saw that though the bush was on fire it did not burn up. So Moses thought, "I will go over and see this strange sight—why the bush does not burn up."*

Consider This

Ten words from today's text have rocked my world for the better part of ten years:

> The bush was on fire it did not burn up.

The burning bush. The more famous the story, the more we think we've got it and the less we return for closer examination. The mystery is not in the burning part; it is in the *not* burning up part.

The burning caught Moses's eye. The not burning up captured his soul.

> So Moses thought, "I will go over and see this strange sight—why the bush does not burn up."

Burning bushes are a phenomenon of nature, but burning bushes not burning up—clearly supernatural. Ordinary bush. Extraordinary fire.

I see this text as a profound sign of the calling of every Christian—to be burning but not burning up—on fire but not consumed.

> John answered them all, "I baptize you with water. But one who is more powerful than I will come, the straps of whose sandals I am not worthy to untie. He will baptize you with the Holy Spirit and fire." (Luke 3:16)

> When the day of Pentecost came, they were all together in one place. Suddenly a sound like the blowing of a violent wind came from heaven and filled the whole house where they were sitting. They saw what seemed to be tongues of fire that separated and came to rest on each of them. (Acts 2:1–3)

> But we have this treasure in jars of clay to show that this all-surpassing power is from God and not from us. (2 Corinthians 4:7)

I see in this burning bush the great mystery of holiness: ordinary human beings filled with the supernatural fire of the Holy Spirit.

This burning-bush reality in your life will run as deep as your desire for it. Be aware, though. The fiery trial of plan B in your life just now—it's trying to burn you down. Plan A comes in the form of ten words from God:

> The bush was on fire it did not burn up.

Flash-forward centuries into the future. God's people again found themselves living as foreigners in a foreign land; yet another wilderness season brought on by their hardness of heart. Here's their burning bush story:

> Then Nebuchadnezzar was furious with Shadrach, Meshach and Abednego, and his attitude toward them changed. He ordered the furnace heated seven times hotter than usual and commanded some of the strongest soldiers in his army to tie up Shadrach, Meshach and Abednego and throw them into the blazing furnace. So these men, wearing their robes, trousers, turbans and other clothes, were bound and thrown into the blazing furnace. The king's command was so urgent and the furnace so hot that the flames of the fire killed the soldiers who took up Shadrach, Meshach and Abednego, and these three men, firmly tied, fell into the blazing furnace.
>
> Then King Nebuchadnezzar leaped to his feet in amazement and

asked his advisers, "Weren't there three men that we tied up and threw into the fire?"

They replied, "Certainly, Your Majesty."

He said, "Look! I see four men walking around in the fire, unbound and unharmed, and the fourth looks like a son of the gods." (Daniel 3:19–25)

Be it in the wilderness of Midian or the wasteland of Babylon or the chaos that is your city, whenever that happens, this happens:

> So Moses thought, "I will go over and see this strange sight—why the bush does not burn up."

People are already being drawn to this peculiar and inexplicable reality in you. You carry the fire of God. He says even now, "Beloved, I am the fire. You are the burning."

The Prayer for Deliverance

Lord Jesus, you are my Deliverer. I hear you decree a season of exodus over me, over my family, and over my church. I receive it. And as you decree it, I declare it. Here is what I am hearing: "Beloved, I am the fire. You are the burning." Let your fire refine me until it defines me. Deliver me from trying to manage the fire and into the mystery of these ten words: The bush was on fire. It did not burn up.

Glory be to the Father and to the Son and to the Holy Ghost.
As it was in the beginning, is now and ever shall be.
World without end. Amen! Amen!

The Question

How deep is your desire for this burning-bush reality in your life?

9

Exodus 3:4–6

Take Off Your Shoes . . .

When the LORD saw that he had gone over to look, God called to him from within the bush, "Moses! Moses!"

And Moses said, "Here I am."

"Do not come any closer," God said. "Take off your sandals, for the place where you are standing is holy ground." Then he said, "I am the God of your father, the God of Abraham, the God of Isaac and the God of Jacob." At this, Moses hid his face, because he was afraid to look at God.

Consider This

On the far side of the wilderness, we come to the mountain of God, and God does not disappoint.

Moses's attention, riveted by the strange phenomenon captured in the ten words we explored yesterday—*the bush was on fire it did not burn up*—walked toward the bush to investigate.

> When the LORD saw that he had gone over to look, God called to him from within the bush, "Moses! Moses!"

What does a person do when they hear their name called twice by an unburning bush? They respond in good biblical form:

> "Here I am."

I wonder how the shape of my days would change if the first words from my mouth were "Here I am." Do you know what God would say next?

> "Do not come any closer. . . . Take off your sandals, for the place where you are standing is holy ground."

This whole affair with the unburning bush was exceptional and extraordinary, a onetime deal. After all, there is only one burning bush in the whole Bible, right? It's easy to marvel at these kinds of stories and then dismiss them as having little bearing on our own lives and experiences.

It is true these stories are unique in the history of the world. They are in many ways unrepeatable. The Bible does not attempt to normalize the voice of God coming from a bush on fire but not burning up. God did extraordinary things at particular times with special people back then, but not so much anymore, right?

Wrong!

Friends, we live in the age of the Holy Spirit, who is being poured out all over the world, on all flesh, women and men, giving vision to the young and dreams to the old. We live in an age way more prolific with burning bushes. An oft-quoted verse of poetry from Elizabeth Barrett Browning (1806–61) fits here:

> Earth's crammed with heaven,
> And every common bush afire with God,
> But only he who sees takes off his shoes;
> The rest sit round and pluck blackberries.[1]

Our problem is that we are sleepwalking. We have lost our expectancy of hearing from God in the early morning, of standing on holy ground in the low valley of high noon, and of walking with him in the cool of the evening. The active prevenient working of the Holy Spirit in every person we encounter so easily slips out of our awareness. We forget that *we* are the burning bush—ordinary human beings illuminated with the fiery love of God. The Spirit of God is renewing the face of the earth right here, right now. All ground is holy ground.

"Only he who sees takes off his shoes."

> Then he said, "I am the God of your father, the God of Abraham,

---

1. Elizabeth Barrett Browning, "Earth's Crammed with Heaven," in *Aurora Leigh*, Book VII (London, 1864).

> the God of Isaac and the God of Jacob." At this, Moses hid his face, because he was afraid to look at God.

Are your shoes off yet?

The Prayer for Deliverance

Lord Jesus, you are my Deliverer. I hear the word exodus. You decree it over me. Over my family, my church, my whole town. I receive it. And as you decree it, I declare it. Exodus! I confess how easily I slip into slumber. I wake up only to hit the snooze bar in my spirit. My vision of your plan A gets obstructed by the circumstances of plan B all around me. Wake me up. Give me ears to hear and eyes to see. In this moment, I speak aloud in faith, "Here am I." And now I step forward onto the holy ground of your presence—for my good, for others' gain, and for your glory.

Glory be to the Father and to the Son and to the Holy Ghost.
As it was in the beginning, is now and ever shall be.
World without end. Amen! Amen!

The Questions

Do you think it could be possible that you are sleepwalking in this season of your life? Would you be open to the possibility that this could be true? Only those who are open to the possibility of being asleep dare to ask God to wake them up. Don't wait for plan B to get louder and more painful.

10

Exodus 3:7–10

So Now, Go. Welcome to the Elder Awakening

The Lord *said, "I have indeed seen the misery of my people in Egypt. I have heard them crying out because of their slave drivers, and I am concerned about their suffering. So I have come down to rescue them from the hand of the Egyptians and to bring them up out of that land into a good and spacious land, a land flowing with milk and honey— the home of the Canaanites, Hittites, Amorites, Perizzites, Hivites and Jebusites. And now the cry of the Israelites has reached me, and I have seen the way the Egyptians are oppressing them. So now, go. I am sending you to Pharaoh to bring my people the Israelites out of Egypt."*

Consider This

I love what God doesn't say to Moses. He doesn't say, "Moses, I love you and have a wonderful plan for your life." Rather, he says, "I want your life for my plan."

Notice the verbiage in today's text:

> I have seen . . . I have heard . . . I am concerned . . . I have come down.

Moses was likely excited to hear the details of how God was going to solve this vexing problem of the enslavement of the Israelites. Finally, he must have been thinking to himself, God is going to intervene in this abominable mess and save our people. After all this demonstrative reporting, we get this sudden, dramatic shift:

> So now, go. I am sending you.

Moses must have thought, *You must have the wrong Moses, here. That ship has sailed in my life.* At this point in his life, he was out to pasture in every sense of the term. Why would God come to an assisted living community to find a candidate to deliver a nation from the oppressive rule of a cruel dictator?

The better question may be this one: Why wouldn't God do this? Isn't it just like God to do just this kind of thing?

There are still places in the world where to be old is to be revered and set apart as "the elders." The idea of putting the elderly out to pasture would be anathema. The elders are the most experienced, wisest, most spiritually mature members of any community. Moreover, they have the most discretionary time and, in many cases, the most wealth.

Still, in most of our culture (i.e., America), the elderly are increasingly sidelined, rotated off of boards, and encouraged to vacate positions of leadership so younger people can have a turn. At the same time they are asked to step aside, we expect them to write checks. It's wrong. I am beginning to think of these years between sixty and heaven as one's kingdom prime—comprising what could be the most fruitful season of one's life.

Youth and young adulthood are filled with idealism. The tests of midlife lead to an overabundance of realism and often cynicism. But what of old age? That is the question. There is a higher way—the antithesis of cynicism. Dreams.

On the day of Pentecost, Peter proclaimed the prophecy of Joel fulfilled, which declared that the old will dream dreams (see Acts 2:17; Joel 2:28).

We need the dreams of the elders to converge and commingle with the visions of the young. The sociological principles of our time have formed our churches more than the theology of the Bible. The homogeneous unit principle is a good example. It explains why most people in most of our churches look just like most of us. Segmenting groups in the church according to age is another. The nature of the church, however, is intergenerational. We have to get the old and the young into the same rooms again. What the elders need more of in their lives is the young, and what the young need more of in their lives are the elders. So many of our young are struggling and suffering in the full panoply of the Egyptian enslavements of our time.

All this is to say, old age (whatever *old* means) is not a season to retire. Okay, sure, quit your job if you want and can. You just can't retire. Your kingdom prime is ahead of you. This is a season to become wildly open to the dreams of God. This is a season to sow your life into the young. This is a season to enter into new assignments of prayer. This is a season to "Wake up, sleeper! Rise from the dead, and Christ will shine on you" (Ephesians 5:14).

> So now, go. I am sending you to Pharaoh to bring my people the Israelites out of Egypt.

It starts with the preferred biblical response to God: "Here I am!"

The Prayer for Deliverance

Lord Jesus, you are my Deliverer. I hear you decree a season of exodus over me, over my family, and over my church. I receive it. And as you decree it, I declare it. Deliver me from the conventional thinking of you having a plan for my life—and into the bigger picture of me offering my life for your plan. Deliver us from our conventional and predictable thinking about our elders. Forgive us for believing that with age comes diminished capacity in the kingdom of God. Deliver us from our ways of church that separate the old from the young. Restore the intergenerational genius of your church. Recover for us the gift of spiritual parenting. Come, Holy Spirit. Fill our elders with dreams. Fill our young with visions. And bring these two realms of the church into collaborative convergence. Now let it be as you decree—for our good, for others' gain, and for your glory.

Glory be to the Father and to the Son and to the Holy Ghost.
As it was in the beginning, is now and ever shall be.
World without end. Amen! Amen!

The Questions

Are you in the category of people I speak to today? How does what I am saying impact you? If you are not in the elder category, does this positively (and at least biblically) impact how you see our elders and their potential in the kingdom?

11

Exodus 3:11

Who Am I?: From Here I Am to Who Am I?

But Moses said to God, "Who am I that I should go to Pharaoh and bring the Israelites out of Egypt?"

Consider This

Just one verse today? I know. I know. It's like we've come to a complete stop right here at the unburning bush, haven't we?

But isn't that the point?

The Bible wants what happened on its pages to keep on happening as its pages are turned. The aspiration of the inspired text is to combust into fire, right? I gather this is happening to many of you.

Our shoes are off. We are low to the ground. We just said, "Here I am" (Exodus 3:4), and God is speaking.

> So now, go. I am sending you to Pharaoh to bring my people the Israelites out of Egypt. (v. 10)

Ready for our response?

> But Moses said to God, "Who am I that I should go to Pharaoh and bring the Israelites out of Egypt?"

That's what I would have said. You too?

Who am I? It's three questions really.

Who am I? This one is filled with absurd incredulity, as in, *There's no way you would be calling me to such a thing at such a time as this. I am no one. Unqualified. Not (fill in the blank) enough. Wrong number. Call someone else. I am out. It's a hard pass.*

Who am I? This one is filled with implausible possibility, as in, God must see something in me. I don't see it, but I am willing to look deeper.

Is there a superhero suit in my closet I don't yet know about? Maybe there's more to me than anyone, including me, knows. I am leaning in. It's a definite maybe.

Who am I? This one is filled with humble consideration, as in, I'm clearly not qualified, but I did hear my name called . . . twice. The challenge is stratospherically beyond me, and yet I am not being asked for initiative but response. God, for whom nothing is impossible, is calling. This is not about me but him. I am willing. It's a "where do I sign?" yes.

Real faith most often moves from *no* to *maybe* to *yes*. It's why God never stops sowing into people and also why we must never stop. To God *no* means not now—tell me more; *maybe* means definitely later—check back tomorrow; and *yes* means I've already ordered my uniform.

The truth? As we will see in the coming days, God is not so much asking us to do something as he is calling us to become someone—someone who is deeply surrendered to him and someone who trusts in the Lord with all their heart and leans not on their own understanding, who acknowledges him in all their ways so he can direct their path (see Proverbs 3:5–6). That someone is who you most truly are in your deepest self, and so often it's the someone (aka your false self) you've settled for that's in the way. Truth be told, the real reason for our reluctance is that we fundamentally lack confidence in God—more specifically, God in us. It's why we need deliverance.

> But Moses said to God, "Who am I that I should go to Pharaoh and bring the Israelites out of Egypt?"

So which version of "Who am I?" is it for you? Hard pass? Definite maybe? Where do I sign?

The Prayer for Deliverance

Lord Jesus, you are my Deliverer. I hear you saying it: exodus—over me, my family, my church, even my city. I receive it. And as you decree it, I declare it. I receive your deliverance from my incredulity that you would call me, from my reluctance and resistance, from my recalcitrance. I receive your deliverance from my false self with its fake humility. I receive your deliverance into my true self and my real authority in you. I receive your deliverance into ever-deepening confidence in you and you in me. Now let it be as you decree—for my good, for others' gain, and for your glory.

Glory be to the Father and to the Son and to the Holy Ghost.
As it was in the beginning, is now and ever shall be.
World without end. Amen! Amen!

The Questions

Which version of "Who am I?" is it for you? And in what ways have you settled for a lesser version of who you know God has called you to become?

12

Exodus 3:12

I Will Be with You—the Word of All Words of God

> *And God said, "I will be with you. And this will be the sign to you that it is I who have sent you: When you have brought the people out of Egypt, you will worship God on this mountain."*

Consider This

Previously, at the unburning bush, God said to Moses, "So now, go. I am sending you to Pharaoh to bring my people the Israelites out of Egypt" (Exodus 3:10). To which Moses replied, "Who am I that I should go to Pharaoh and bring the Israelites out of Egypt?" (v. 11).

Here may be the most beautiful and powerful part of the whole encounter. Behold God's answer to Moses's question: "I will be with you."

God did not tell Moses why he was selected for the mission. He didn't say a single word about Moses's qualifications or lack thereof. God did not attempt to build up Moses's sense of self-worth or credibility or give him a pep talk or say, "You can do this, Moses!" The answer to "Who am I?" was "I will be with you."

In the face of impossible things and insurmountable challenges, God doesn't ask us to develop a strategic plan and then raise a gazillion dollars to make it happen. The truth? If it can be done with a strategic plan and a gazillion dollars, it's not big enough for God.

Get back in touch with the moment. The God of the cosmos appeared through an unburning bush on the far side of the wilderness to an octogenarian sheepherder and said he was sending him to rescue and deliver a nation of a million or more slaves from their oppressor—a man who happened to be the most powerful person in the world leading the most powerful nation on the planet.

And to all of our quandaries about impossible things and our quizzical inquiries about improbable outcomes, God responds with "I will be with you."

It's fascinating to jump another fifteen hundred or so years to another unburning-bush moment on the mountain of God. This time it's the Son of God, our risen Lord, Jesus Christ, with eleven disciples in tow:

> All authority in heaven and on earth has been given to me. Therefore go and make disciples of all nations, baptizing them in the name of the Father and of the Son and of the Holy Spirit, and teaching them to obey everything I have commanded you. And surely I am with you always, to the very end of the age. (Matthew 28:18–20)

It's like déjà vu, right? Jesus said, "Go, I am sending you." The disciples probably thought, *Who are we?* And Jesus closed with, "I am with you."

There's one more bit here. God gave Moses the sign of how he would know that the God of heaven and earth was sending him to do these impossible things (as if it were some other "god"!).

> And this will be the sign to you that it is I who have sent you: When you have brought the people out of Egypt, you will worship God on this mountain.

"I will be with you," though a rock-solid promise, can seem a little touchy-feely at times. "You will worship God on this mountain" is a quite tangible, measurable, KPI (key performance indicator) kind of outcome.

Still, here's the kicker: You receive the confirmation as a consequence of obedience to the vision. The sign comes after, not before. That's why we call it the obedience of faith.

Remember, though, it starts with a good old-fashioned, "Here I am!"

The Prayer for Deliverance

Lord Jesus, you are my Deliverer. I hear you say "exodus" over me, over my family, over my friends in need, and over my church, my city, and my country. I receive your deliverance from "Who am I?" and into your eternal word "I will be with you." Here I am! Fill me with the fullness of Jesus. Here I am! Give me the audacity of Moses to have the guts to continue such a conversation with the Almighty. I claim the faith to trust a confirmation that comes after obedience rather than insisting on a sign as a precondition. Now let it be as you decree—for my good, for others' gain, and for your glory.

Glory be to the Father and to the Son and to the Holy Ghost.
As it was in the beginning, is now and ever shall be.
World without end. Amen! Amen!

The Questions

How are you stirred by today's text and reflection? Do you sense the Spirit calling forth your audacity? Your obedience? Your faith? Are you declaring, "Here I am"?

13

Exodus 3:13–15

I Am Who I Am—Welcome to Ontology 101

Moses said to God, "Suppose I go to the Israelites and say to them, 'The God of your fathers has sent me to you,' and they ask me, 'What is his name?' Then what shall I tell them?"

God said to Moses, "I AM WHO I AM. This is what you are to say to the Israelites: 'I AM has sent me to you.'"

God also said to Moses, "Say to the Israelites, 'The LORD, the God of your fathers—the God of Abraham, the God of Isaac and the God of Jacob—has sent me to you.'

"This is my name forever,
the name you shall call me
from generation to generation."

Consider This

I am going to introduce a word today that may put me in hot water with my dad (and some of you). The word is *ontology*. Know what it means?

To show that it is not an overly complicated word, I can change the *t* to a *c*, and you will know exactly what that word—*oncology*—means. Oncology, of course, is the study of cancer; something far too many of us know far too much about. It has become painfully practical in our lives.

Ontology is a term from the field of metaphysics. More precisely, according to the *Oxford English Dictionary*, ontology is "the philosophical study of the nature of being, becoming, existence, or reality." It's all the stuff we assume but never think about because our lives are moving too fast to even consider it. Metaphysics is for a rainy day, but then it rains and we have a leak in the roof that must be fixed. If we had to name a subject for which the Bible is a textbook, it wouldn't be world religions. It would be ontology.

So why does this word matter today in the middle of what is now a weeklong encounter at a bush on fire but not burning up? Moses asked God an ontological question:

> Suppose I go to the Israelites and say to them, "The God of your fathers has sent me to you," and they ask me, "What is his name?" Then what shall I tell them?

Don't you love how Moses warms up to the idea of obeying God with "Suppose I go . . . ?"

Moses wanted to know with whom he was dealing here. Was this the desert god or the sun god or the moon god or the slave-delivering God—which divine being was Moses engaging at this unburning bush? And God dropped the ontological boom sauce:

> I AM WHO I AM. This is what you are to say to the Israelites: "I AM has sent me to you."

The ontological trump card is:

> I AM WHO I AM.

It means something like, "I am God, and there is no other. I am the ground of all being. There is no one like me. There is no equal to the being who precedes all beings."

> God also said to Moses, "Say to the Israelites, 'The LORD, the God of your fathers—the God of Abraham, the God of Isaac and the God of Jacob—has sent me to you.'"

For whatever reason, this God of all gods—aka "I AM WHO I AM"—chose to make a covenant with this obscure family-become-nation and favored them above all other peoples so that they might live as God's sign of majestic and merciful glory for the sake of all other peoples.

Now I AM was about to rescue them with a mighty hand and an outstretched arm.

So why does ontology matter? Here's how I see it. There are two modes of life: our existence and our being. There is how we exist in the world and who we are at the core. To the extent the core of our being is grounded in the ontological being of almighty God, who is I AM, we will flourish in peace and prosperity irrespective of our circumstances.

To the extent our core being is not grounded in the ontological being of almighty God, we will slavishly strive to maintain our existence, whether we be rich or poor, by any and all means available to us, turning to any and every god we can conjure up who might help us, including I AM as part of the pantheon.

God desires and delights to be with us in a comprehensive fashion, not as a peripheral help. He is looking for people who will pray, "Have me!" rather than just plead, "Help me!" He wants us to build our house on the rock rather than the sand because the storms are coming. Is our core being flourishing in a grounded relationship with the one, true, and living God, or are we just scraping out an existence the best we can?

So let me practically serve you as an ontologist today by asking you these questions:

1. Is the God and Father of our Lord Jesus Christ the core and central reality of your being and reality, or do you turn to God only when you need help?
2. Are you increasingly abiding all the time in relationship with Jesus Christ, or is he someone you once trusted for eternal salvation?
3. Do you depend on the fullness of the Holy Spirit to flourish in your daily life, or are you hardly conscious of the Holy Spirit's presence and activity?

Why do I ask you such probing questions?
I AM sent me.

The Prayer for Deliverance

Lord Jesus, you are my Deliverer. I hear you saying "exodus" over me, over my family, over so many people I love who are struggling right now, and over my church, my city, my country, even the whole world.

I receive your deliverance from myself as the center of my universe and my need to have you revolve around me. I receive your deliverance into a universe where you are the center of gravity and I revolve around you. I have so often and for so long turned to you as a transactional God for functional help. I need you when I need you and I don't when I don't. I am coming to the place where the center of gravity in my life must shift from me to you. You will be the ground of my being. Your life will become my life. Your love will become my love. Your power will become my power. Thank you, Jesus, for making me a disciple of yours rather than me constantly calling on you to run my errands. I receive it. And as you decree it, I declare it. Now let it be as you decree—for my good, for others' gain, and for your glory.

Glory be to the Father and to the Son and to the Holy Ghost.
As it was in the beginning, is now and ever shall be.
World without end. Amen! Amen!

The Questions

Is the God and Father of our Lord Jesus Christ the core and central reality of your being and reality, or do you turn to God only when you need help?

Are you increasingly abiding all the time in relationship with Jesus Christ, or is he someone you once trusted for eternal salvation?

Do you depend on the fullness of the Holy Spirit to flourish in your daily life, or are you hardly conscious of the Holy Spirit's presence and activity?

Week 2: Discussion Questions

Hearing the Text

Read Exodus 3:2–15.

Responding to the Text

- What did you hear?
- What did you see?
- What did you otherwise sense from the Lord?

Sharing Insights and Implications for Discipleship

Drawing from the Scripture text and daily readings, what did you find challenging, encouraging, provocative, comforting, invasive, inspiring, corrective, affirming, guiding, or warning?

Shaping Intentions for Prayer

Write your discipleship intention for the week ahead.

3
WEEK

Exodus 4:10–8:15

15

Exodus 4:10–17

Now Go and I Will Help You

Moses said to the Lord, "Pardon your servant, Lord. I have never been eloquent, neither in the past nor since you have spoken to your servant. I am slow of speech and tongue."

The Lord said to him, "Who gave human beings their mouths? Who makes them deaf or mute? Who gives them sight or makes them blind? Is it not I, the Lord? Now go; I will help you speak and will teach you what to say."

But Moses said, "Pardon your servant, Lord. Please send someone else."

Then the Lord's anger burned against Moses and he said, "What about your brother, Aaron the Levite? I know he can speak well. He is already on his way to meet you, and he will be glad to see you. You shall speak to him and put words in his mouth; I will help both of you speak and will teach you what to do. He will speak to the people for you, and it will be as if he were your mouth and as if you were God to him. But take this staff in your hand so you can perform the signs with it."

Consider This

Meanwhile, back at the unburning bush, as the details unfolded, Moses brought up more reasons why doing what God asked might not be a good idea.

> Moses said to the Lord, "Pardon your servant, Lord. I have never been eloquent, neither in the past nor since you have spoken to your servant. I am slow of speech and tongue."

What gave Moses the idea that God needed a silver-tongued preacher? Why is it that we tend to make the calling of God about our own qualifications or lack thereof? Do we think God is somehow not aware of our foibles, weaknesses, and incompetencies? What if God calls us into a particular assignment precisely because of our foibles, weaknesses, and incompetencies?

What if God is looking for people who have been broken enough by life and mended enough by mercy that they know they are hopeless without God, that they can do nothing apart from Jesus? Isn't this the whole point of 2 Corinthians 4:7? "But we have this treasure in jars of clay to show that this all-surpassing power is from God and not from us."

Did Moses really think the secret sauce of his success in delivering the Israelites from the most powerful person on the planet was his eloquence of speech? Seems like Paul had something to say about eloquence, now that I think about it:

> And so it was with me, brothers and sisters. When I came to you, I did not come with eloquence or human wisdom as I proclaimed to you the testimony about God. For I resolved to know nothing while I was with you except Jesus Christ and him crucified. I came to you in weakness with great fear and trembling. My message and my preaching were not with wise and persuasive words, but with a demonstration of the Spirit's power, so that your faith might not rest on human wisdom, but on God's power. (1 Corinthians 2:1–5)

God does not need our talent, skills, or abilities to accomplish his will in the world. He can use them, but he doesn't need them. The only thing God needs from us is our availability, faithfulness, and teachability. God is good even in the face of our worst moments. Look at how he responded to Moses:

> Now go; I will help you speak and will teach you what to say.

Indulge my translation in the form of an overused cliché: "God doesn't call the equipped. He equips the called." Feel this word from the Lord today. It is full of tender compassion and intimate care:

> Now go; I will help you speak and will teach you what to say.

I don't know about you, but I needed to hear that today. It speaks to me on a lot of fronts in my life. Let's focus on just this part:

> Now go; I will help you.

To hear "I will be with you" is good, but God is even better than that. He says, "I will help you." Flash-forward centuries later and hear what God says to his people through the prophet Isaiah: "For I am the LORD your God who takes hold of your right hand and says to you, Do not fear; I will help you" (Isaiah 41:13).

Christian, you have a God who takes hold of your right hand and says to you, "Do not fear; I will help you." Look at your right hand—right now—and fathom this truth. Speak it aloud so your ears can hear it: "For I am the LORD your God who takes hold of your right hand and says to you, Do not fear; I will help you" (Isaiah 41:13).

Still, after all God's patient coaxing, Moses (in what feels like his best British accent) said it was a hard pass:

> Pardon your servant, Lord. Please send someone else.

But, don't we see ourselves in good ol' Moe? When it comes to the weighty matter of God's calling on our lives (and he calls us all), our insufficiency is a given. Now hear this: God's calling is about God's sufficiency, not our insufficiency. Okay, once again, and this time with feeling: God's calling is about God's sufficiency, not our insufficiency. Maybe the most important two words in the whole exchange today are these two: "Now go." It is as though God is saying, "Just take the first step." That's always the hardest one, isn't it?

Feel God's hand take yours. And get up. No, you don't know where you are going. No, you don't know how to get there. No, you don't know what you will do when you get there. No, you don't really have a plan. You have God. Even better—God has you. You hear him say:

> Now go; I will help you.

The Prayer for Deliverance

Lord Jesus, my Deliverer. Exodus. I hear you saying it. It is a whisper today and yet it is a word—the word. I receive it. And as you decree it, I too will declare it, even as a whisper today: exodus. I receive your deliverance from focusing on my sufficiency or on my insufficiency. You are delivering me into focusing on your sufficiency. But even more, you are delivering me into the wakeful realization that you are holding my right hand—and that you are helping me. That I'm going to just go with you. Forgive me for making your calling about myself, for thinking you somehow need my gifts to accomplish your will or, worse, for thinking my lack of giftedness could somehow impede your work. Give me the grace to understand that when you call me you know what you are doing. Train my spirit to be available, faithful, and teachable.

Glory be to the Father and to the Son and to the Holy Ghost.
As it was in the beginning, is now and ever shall be.
World without end. Amen! Amen!

The Questions

Do you have a real, felt, and regular experience of God with you, holding your right hand and helping you? It's okay if you don't. What's important is to become honest about where you actually are and to move toward God from there. Let your hunger for God become honest before him. Now, on another front, how will you begin to make the transition in relating to God not according to your insufficiency but according to his sufficiency?

16

Exodus 4:18–23

The Movement from Penultimate to Ultimate

Then Moses went back to Jethro his father-in-law and said to him, "Let me return to my own people in Egypt to see if any of them are still alive."

Jethro said, "Go, and I wish you well."

Now the Lord *had said to Moses in Midian, "Go back to Egypt, for all those who wanted to kill you are dead." So Moses took his wife and sons, put them on a donkey and started back to Egypt. And he took the staff of God in his hand.*

The Lord *said to Moses, "When you return to Egypt, see that you perform before Pharaoh all the wonders I have given you the power to do. But I will harden his heart so that he will not let the people go. Then say to Pharaoh, 'This is what the* Lord *says: Israel is my firstborn son, and I told you, "Let my son go, so he may worship me." But you refused to let him go; so I will kill your firstborn son.'"*

Consider This

Penultimate—that's the word of the day. It means something like "secondary" or "second to the ultimate." And that's the problem. We get caught up in penultimate things to the point that we lose sight of the ultimate thing.

We need to remember the big picture, to see beyond the penultimate to the ultimate. A critical word got lost in all of the back-and-forth conversation between Moses and God. We see it in verse 23 as God told Moses what to say to Pharaoh:

> Let my son go, so he may worship me.

It appeared earlier when God told Moses that the confirming sign of the whole affair would be the worship of God on Mount Horeb. Before it was all said and done, we would hear this refrain over and over and over again: "Let my people go, so that they may worship me."

Penultimate = "Let my people go"
Ultimate = "so that they may worship me"

The penultimate purpose of deliverance is for the good of the people. The ultimate purpose of deliverance is for the glory of God. This is why worship matters so much. We were created to worship God. You and I and every other person on the face of planet Earth were made for one thing and one thing only: to worship the one true and living God—Father, Son, and Holy Spirit. We aren't worshipers because we worship. We worship because we are worshipers.

Right up to the present moment, history shows us that human beings will worship anything and everything under the sun, including the sun! The very essence of salvation and deliverance is to be rescued from the slavish oppression of a false god and brought into the kingdom of the gracious true and living God.

When was the last time you worshiped God?

To worship God is to orient one's entire being and life around the presence, purpose, and power of the God of heaven and earth, whom to know is to love. It is to live with an openhearted, single-minded, undivided love for God, his creation, and especially people. When we worship God, he brings our entire existence into the peace-filled, joyful life of love-governed power we were made for.

God knows our hearts will not rest until they rest in him; therefore, his mission is to deliver us from our every unholy attachment, broken inclination, and involuntary bondage to worship false gods. We can think our mission is to do this good deed and give to that good cause and wrap it all up in religious garb and completely miss the point of the whole thing—more worshipers bringing more worship to God.

As John Piper famously says, "Missions exist because worship doesn't."[1] When we forget the ultimate thing, it's only a matter of time before penultimate things get our attention.

---

1. John Piper, *Let the Nations Be Glad! The Supremacy of God in Missions* (Baker, 2010), 35.

Worship is ultimate. God saves, delivers, redeems, and blesses us so we can be burning bushes—on fire but not consumed—in our homes, neighborhoods, workplaces, churches, grocery stores, city centers, and everywhere else under the sun.

Christian, you were meant for glory. You are made to be on fire with the God who made you. He made you to burn brightly for his glory and for your neighbor's gain and for your own good—indeed, for the deepest and most satisfying life you never imagined possible.

The Prayer for Deliverance

Lord Jesus, you are my Deliverer. I receive the exodus of your deliverance into a life of unfettered worship. I confess that I so easily get lost in the weeds of life, forgetting what it's all for and what it all means. I want to stop right now and open my heart to worship you, to stand in awe of you, even to kneel in humble reverence. Let my every waking minute take on that posture in everything I am doing. Let the fiery glory of your love burn in me until all that is left is you, for then I will truly be myself.

Glory be to the Father and to the Son and to the Holy Ghost.
As it was in the beginning, is now and ever shall be.
World without end. Amen! Amen!

The Questions

Do you find yourself caught up in penultimate matters? Do you need to be reset for ultimate matters? Will you find a quiet place, a closet, somewhere you can open up your adoration to the God and Father of our Lord Jesus Christ? Don't forget to say, "Here I am!"

17

Exodus 5:1–5

Things Get Worse Before They Get Better

> *Afterward Moses and Aaron went to Pharaoh and said, "This is what the Lord, the God of Israel, says: 'Let my people go, so that they may hold a festival to me in the wilderness.'"*
>
> *Pharaoh said, "Who is the Lord, that I should obey him and let Israel go? I do not know the Lord and I will not let Israel go."*
>
> *Then they said, "The God of the Hebrews has met with us. Now let us take a three-day journey into the wilderness to offer sacrifices to the Lord our God, or he may strike us with plagues or with the sword."*
>
> *But the king of Egypt said, "Moses and Aaron, why are you taking the people away from their labor? Get back to your work!" Then Pharaoh said, "Look, the people of the land are now numerous, and you are stopping them from working."*

Consider This

Moses and Aaron must have thought to themselves, *This will only take a couple of days.* They were obeying God—moving in his grant of authority. They had received the favor of the elders of Israel. A couple of conversations with Pharaoh should do the trick. After all, they were doing the will of God, right?

"If God is for us, who can be against us" (Romans 8:31), right?

Short answer: Pharaoh and all his armies can be against us. Though God has won, it doesn't mean there will not be a ton of opposition, struggle, hardship, and loss along the way. There is the war, and then there are the battles. And though the war is won, the battles must still be fought.

Notice the interpretive heading over chapter 5 in your Bible. My NIV has these three words: "Bricks Without Straw."

As Moses and Aaron delivered God's message to Pharaoh, Pharaoh gave this order to the slave drivers and overseers:

> You are no longer to supply the people with straw for making bricks; let them go and gather their own straw. But require them to make the same number of bricks as before; don't reduce the quota. They are lazy; that is why they are crying out, 'Let us go and sacrifice to our God.' Make the work harder for the people so that they keep working and pay no attention to lies. (Exodus 5:7–9)

In the matter of deliverance, the bricks-without-straw principle teaches us that things will often get worse before they get better. I hate to say it, but I think this is par for the course. The will of God diametrically opposes the will of Satan. The forces of evil, the powers, principalities, rulers, and authorities of this present darkness, will not release their hold without a fight. Pharaoh will not willingly give up his slave labor force. They are building his kingdom.

> Moses returned to the LORD and said, "Why, Lord, why have you brought trouble on this people? Is this why you sent me? Ever since I went to Pharaoh to speak in your name, he has brought trouble on this people, and you have not rescued your people at all." (Exodus 5:22–23)

The minute Moses spoke the command of God to Pharaoh, the Israelites were freed from slavery. "Let my people go." God decreed it. Moses declared it. It was done. This is the meaning of exodus. Freedom is a proclamation. Deliverance is a process. The rest of the story of exodus is the process of deliverance whereby the proclamation of freedom becomes a realized promise.

Let me explain how the battle between Moses and Pharaoh translates into our lives. We are now squarely in the battle of deliverance. Though human slavery remains a vexing problem in the world, there is a much larger problem—one that underlies human slavery and every other wicked problem in the world. The originating problem is sin. Sin is the willful choice to forgo God's will and ways (plan A) by choosing our own will and ways. Remember, sin created plan B (see Genesis 3–11).

Ever since Genesis 3, humanity has been hopelessly trapped in

Egypt, which is another name for slavery to sin. Anything and everything we attach ourselves to other than the living God in order to create sustenance, security, provision, protection, prosperity, or survival increases the slavehold of sin over our lives. It has the effect of creating what the Bible calls a sin debt. We were born into this debt. We added to it, and the interest constantly accrues. The problem is we can't pay it back. The Bible speaks of this condition as being "dead in our sins." Here's how I like to say it: He (Jesus) paid a debt he did not owe because we owed a debt we could not pay.

> But because of his great love for us, God, who is rich in mercy, made us alive with Christ even when we were dead in transgressions—it is by grace you have been saved. (Ephesians 2:4–5)

This is the decree. Now, here is the deliverance:

> But thanks be to God that, though you used to be slaves to sin, you have come to obey from your heart the pattern of teaching that has now claimed your allegiance. You have been set free from sin and have become slaves to righteousness. (Romans 6:17–18)

In like fashion, the minute a human soul receives the finished work of Jesus Christ in his death and resurrection, they are free from sin. The freedom is decreed. The war is won. Now the battles of deliverance must be fought.

Back to Exodus for a minute:

> The Israelite overseers realized they were in trouble when they were told, "You are not to reduce the number of bricks required of you for each day." When they left Pharaoh, they found Moses and Aaron waiting to meet them, and they said, "May the LORD look on you and judge you! You have made us obnoxious to Pharaoh and his officials and have put a sword in their hand to kill us." (Exodus 5:19–21)

The Prayer for Deliverance

Lord Jesus, you are my Deliverer. Exodus! I hear you saying, "Exodus!" I receive it for myself, my family, my friends and loved ones, my church, my town, and even beyond. I declare it now in Jesus's name: Exodus! Thank you for winning the war against sin, darkness, evil, death, and all that plan B can throw at us. Now, train me to win the battles and fully demonstrate the victory of plan A. Prepare my heart, mind, soul, and strength for the deliverance that comes with exodus—for my good, for others' gain, and for your glory.

> Glory be to the Father and to the Son and to the Holy Ghost.
> As it was in the beginning, is now and ever shall be.
> World without end. Amen! Amen!

The Questions

Are you grasping the difference between God winning the war against sin and decreeing our freedom and the process of deliverance and winning the battles to realize this freedom in our lives? Have you resigned yourself to staying stuck in the strongholds of plan B (a.k.a. sin) that remain in your life?

18

Exodus 6:1–8

Learning to Speak the Word of God

Then the Lord said to Moses, "Now you will see what I will do to Pharaoh: Because of my mighty hand he will let them go; because of my mighty hand he will drive them out of his country."

God also said to Moses, "I am the Lord. I appeared to Abraham, to Isaac and to Jacob as God Almighty, but by my name the Lord I did not make myself fully known to them. I also established my covenant with them to give them the land of Canaan, where they resided as foreigners. Moreover, I have heard the groaning of the Israelites, whom the Egyptians are enslaving, and I have remembered my covenant.

"Therefore, say to the Israelites: 'I am the Lord, *and I will bring you out from under the yoke of the Egyptians. I will free you from being slaves to them, and I will redeem you with an outstretched arm and with mighty acts of judgment. I will take you as my own people, and I will be your God. Then you will know that I am the* Lord *your God, who brought you out from under the yoke of the Egyptians. And I will bring you to the land I swore with uplifted hand to give to Abraham, to Isaac and to Jacob. I will give it to you as a possession. I am the* Lord.'"

Consider This

Will we trust the Word of God or defer to the experience of people?

The Word of God is powerful. We believe it. These eight verses from Exodus today are packed with powerful declarations from the mouth of God. Seventeen times he says some form of "I am" or "I will." Let's slow it down for the play-by-play:

I am the Lord, and

I will bring you out from under the yoke of the Egyptians.

I will free you from being slaves to them, and

I will redeem you with an outstretched arm and with mighty acts of judgment.

I will take you as my own people, and

I will be your God.

Then you will know that I am the Lord your God, who brought you out from under the yoke of the Egyptians.

And I will bring you to the land I swore with uplifted hand to give to Abraham, to Isaac and to Jacob.

I will give it to you as a possession.

I am the Lord.

People of God, do you know what that is? That's plan A! It is the unstoppable, unalterable, undefeated Word of God.

This is nothing short of incredible. It would be difficult to be more reassured by the Word of God than one would be in this instance.

So, how is it that we find ourselves feeling defeated and losing the race so much of the time? That's plan B. Plan B is our broken experience of a fallen world corrupted by sin and being desecrated by death. We hear the Word of God (if we actually "hear" it) through the framework of our own experiences—our experience of life, the world, sin, death, brokenness, betrayal, failure, success, trauma, pain, deception, disappointment, our strengths, our weaknesses, our Myers-Briggs personality type, our Enneagram number, and a thousand other things.

In light of their slavery and most recent episode of making bricks without straw, the Israelites, including Moses, allowed their experience of plan B to override their faith in plan A and the Word of God: "Moses reported this to the Israelites, but they did not listen to him because of their discouragement and harsh labor" (Exodus 6:9).

Though the power of the Word of God is to the power of our experience as the power of the sun is to that of the moon, somehow the gravity of our experience manages to tip the scale all too often. The Israelites' powerful experience of "discouragement and harsh labor," though clearly inferior to the power of God's Word, overcame their confidence in the Word of God: "Then the Lord said to Moses, 'Go, tell Pharaoh king of Egypt to let the Israelites go out of his country'" (vv. 10–11).

The experience of early failure in the mission also tipped the scale on Moses's confidence in God's Word. He regressed all the way back to his faltering speech excuse: "But Moses said to the Lord, 'If the Israelites will not listen to me, why would Pharaoh listen to me, since I speak with faltering lips?'" (v. 12).

The Word of God is just that: the Word of God. Our experience as humans is just that: our experience. The thing that tells the difference is the quality of our faith. Will we offer faith in the face of our faltering experience? Will we trust God's Word anyway?

The tumor is malignant, and the cancer has spread. The marriage is irreconcilable. Your son or daughter has forayed into a socially affirmed yet biblically forbidden lifestyle. Will you place your faith in the Word of God or defer to your experience and that of others?

When we allow our broken experiences, our disappointments, and our discouragements to speak louder than the Word of God in our lives, we slowly sink into the ruts of plan B and assume this is just how it's going to be. It is imperative in these moments to give voice to plan A, which is God's Word in our lives—out loud. Yes, give voice—your voice—to God's Word. Every word written in the Bible has been decreed by God. It is now ours to declare. This literally paves the path of deliverance. It's why God's Word declares about itself things like this:

> Your word is a lamp for my feet,
> a light on my path. (Psalm 119:105)

> [Your words] are more precious than gold,
> than much pure gold;
> they are sweeter than honey,
> than honey from the honeycomb. (Psalm 19:10)

> [My word] will accomplish what I desire
> and achieve the purpose for which I sent it. (Isaiah 55:11)

> For the word of God is alive and active. Sharper than any double-edged sword, it penetrates even to dividing soul and spirit, joints and marrow; it judges the thoughts and attitudes of the heart. (Hebrews 4:12)

And here's my favorite:

> The grass withers and the flowers fall,
> but the word of our God endures forever. (Isaiah 40:8)

Okay, do you have time for one more from Jesus?

> Heaven and earth will pass away, but my words will never pass away. (Matthew 24:35)

Faith in the Word of God leads to another kind of experience. Given time and patient trust, faith in the Word of God leads to the indelible, life-changing experience of the faithfulness of God to the promise of his Word. All of this would form the curriculum for the people of God for the next forty years.

The Prayer for Deliverance

Lord Jesus, you are my Deliverer. Exodus! I hear you now. It is now an audible word. And as I hear my voice say it, I sense your Spirit amplifying the reality. I receive deliverance from my quiet and mostly silent expression of your Word and into giving your Word volume and amplitude in my everyday life. I receive deliverance from a confidence that rises and falls based on my life's experiences. I receive deliverance into a Holy Spirit–fired confidence in the forever-enduring Word of God. As the angel decreed for the Lord, I now declare: "No word from God will ever fail" (Luke 1:37).

Glory be to the Father and to the Son and to the Holy Ghost.
As it was in the beginning, is now and ever shall be.
World without end. Amen! Amen!

The Questions

What is it that most convinces you that your experience or that of another should be trusted over and above the Word of God? How do you see this struggle in your own life? How are you doing with it? How will you begin to audibly declare the Word of God throughout your day? What if the Word of God became like the spoken GPS throughout your day? Sketch a map of such a thing.

19

Exodus 7:1–7

On Sovereignty, Freedom, and the Will of God

Then the Lord said to Moses, "See, I have made you like God to Pharaoh, and your brother Aaron will be your prophet. You are to say everything I command you, and your brother Aaron is to tell Pharaoh to let the Israelites go out of his country. But I will harden Pharaoh's heart, and though I multiply my signs and wonders in Egypt, he will not listen to you. Then I will lay my hand on Egypt and with mighty acts of judgment I will bring out my divisions, my people the Israelites. And the Egyptians will know that I am the Lord when I stretch out my hand against Egypt and bring the Israelites out of it."

Moses and Aaron did just as the Lord commanded them. Moses was eighty years old and Aaron eighty-three when they spoke to Pharaoh.

Consider This

We come today to what we might call a "sticky wicket," or a conundrum, or at the very least, a quandary. I can't explain it; thus, I want to avoid it, but it must be dealt with. It comes in verse 3:

> But I will harden Pharaoh's heart.

How is it fair if God punishes Pharaoh for something God does to Pharaoh? In other words, how is Pharaoh responsible for a condition God brought upon him? I can't explain it. I will point out the following, though.

Ten times we see this reference to God hardening Pharaoh's heart (see Exodus 4:21; 7:3; 9:12; 10:1, 20, 27; 11:10; 14:4, 8, 17). Here's the interesting part. Ten times we see references to Pharaoh hardening his own heart (see Exodus 7:13, 14, 22; 8:15, 19, 32; 9:7, 34, 35; 13:15). Can we call it a tie?

Does God predestine every outcome to the nth detail, or does God allow human beings the free will and agency to make their own choices? Just like this tie, the debate between predestination and free will is utterly unresolvable. Depending on which side people take, they can marshal the evidence either way. Though I believe the predestinarians come up short—as a lawyer, I will grant they can make a straight-faced case before the judge.

I am not a predestinarian. I believe God gives people free will and holds them responsible for their choices. Having debated it exhaustively (and exhaustingly), I am also thoroughly uninterested in debating the unresolvable issue any further. I have had too many near-death experiences on that hill to do it again.

In the present case, I look to Pharaoh's very first response to the Word of God: "Pharaoh said, 'Who is the Lord, that I should obey him and let Israel go? I do not know the Lord and I will not let Israel go'" (Exodus 5:2).

Pharaoh's heart was a hard heart from the start. To say that God allows a person to harden their heart to the point of thwarting his word and will does not mean that God hardened their heart. It means God allows people to go their own way and, in the end, to suffer the consequences.

When hard-hearted people go their own way, it creates enormous hardship and suffering for many others. To agree that God willed Pharaoh's hardened heart seems necessarily to agree that God also willed all of the consequent destruction and losses to many people who were not themselves culpable. To attribute responsibility to Pharaoh for his own hardness of heart means he is also responsible for the far-reaching consequences his ill will wrought on the nation. It seems more just, doesn't it?

Bottom line: To say God hardened Pharaoh's heart, in my judgment, means God allowed Pharaoh to harden his own heart. Said another way, God gave Pharaoh over to the hardness of his own heart. Pharaoh was given at least ten chances to reverse course, to repent, and to relent from his rebellion.

I see the same general principle operative in Romans 1:24–25:

> Therefore God gave them over in the sinful desires of their hearts to sexual impurity for the degrading of their bodies with one another.

They exchanged the truth about God for a lie, and worshiped and served created things rather than the Creator—who is forever praised. Amen.

One final exhibit: after all the extraordinary deliverance and advantage he would give the Israelites, God would allow his own people to harden their hearts against him.

Psalm 95:7b–10 recounts the story for all the future generations to come—especially ours:

Today, if only you would hear his voice,
"Do not harden your hearts as you did at Meribah,
as you did that day at Massah in the wilderness,
where your ancestors tested me;
they tried me, though they had seen what I did.
For forty years I was angry with that generation;
I said, 'They are a people whose hearts go astray,
and they have not known my ways.'"

God wants our hearts, friends, our soft, pliable, clay-like hearts in his hands, where he can mold them, by the power of the Word and the Spirit, into vessels of his liking, for his purposes, for our good and his glory. Flash-forward to the now fulfilled prophecy of Ezekiel and marvel at the fusion of God's sovereignty and human freedom in their glorious interplay in fulfilling the will of God:

I will give you a new heart and put a new spirit in you; I will remove from you your heart of stone and give you a heart of flesh. And I will put my Spirit in you and move you to follow my decrees and be careful to keep my laws. (Ezekiel 36:26–27)

The Prayer for Deliverance

Lord Jesus, you are my Deliverer. Thank you for decreeing exodus over me, over my family, over this whole world. I receive it. And as you decree it, I declare it. I receive your deliverance from any hardness of heart in me. Break through the outer hardness and heal inner hardness, and restore the fullness of your image in me. I trust you, yet I want to trust you more. Teach me to hear your voice, even your whisper.

Glory be to the Father and to the Son and to the Holy Ghost.
As it was in the beginning, is now and ever shall be.
World without end. Amen! Amen!

The Questions

How do you relate to this reflection on the issue of God hardening Pharaoh's heart and Pharaoh hardening his own heart? But before you answer that question, what is the state of your heart?

20

Exodus 8:15

What Does Real Repentance Look Like?

> *But when Pharaoh saw that there was relief, he hardened his heart and would not listen to Moses and Aaron, just as the* Lord *had said.*

Consider This

We come now to the dreaded plagues.

As I ponder these ten plagues that occur between chapters 7 and 11, I would like to test an observation with you. I observe a behavioral phenomenon in Pharaoh's response to the plagues that illuminates a broken pattern in human nature in the midst of a crisis situation.

Here's the pattern: Plague comes. Pharaoh agrees to relent and release the Israelites. Plague stops. Pharaoh reverts to his former recalcitrance. Rinse and repeat.

Here is an example of what I reference:

> Then Pharaoh summoned Moses and Aaron. "This time I have sinned," he said to them. "The LORD is in the right, and I and my people are in the wrong. Pray to the LORD, for we have had enough thunder and hail. I will let you go; you don't have to stay any longer." (Exodus 9:27–28)

Watch what happens next:

> When Pharaoh saw that the rain and hail and thunder had stopped, he sinned again: He and his officials hardened their hearts. (Exodus 9:34)

It's tempting to characterize Pharaoh's response as a change of heart. It even appears to be confession and repentance. Once the plague relents, though, he reverts to his former posture. He has not changed at all. He merely responded to a crisis in what seemed to him as an expedient solution.

After each plague, we see the same pattern. What if this is the definition of hard-heartedness—the refusal to see repentance through to real change? A hard-hearted person will respond to disaster just like everyone else. They want relief. The difference is that a hard-hearted person will not ultimately change. They simply readjust.

When they go back to their old normal, it creates a new normal for everyone else. Because I refuse to change, other people are forced to adjust to the conditions created by my hard heart. Note how costly Pharaoh's hard-heartedness proves for the people of Egypt. It will result in enormous losses, the chief of which will be the death of the firstborn son in every single household.

As we struggled our way through COVID-19, we felt ourselves under a plague. It passed. The question is: Did we change temporarily and then seamlessly shift into the new normal, or did we attune our lives to the ways God was calling us to repent and realign with his kingdom going forward?

The question I'm asking has to do with awakening. Sometimes we confuse waking up with hitting the snooze bar. The alarm of crisis goes off, and it registers, yet we all too easily hit the snooze bar for another nine minutes of sleep. We sort of woke up but not really. I'm afraid that's how it is with these situations like we find ourselves in now. The alarm can be deafening, and yet we somehow find a way to hit snooze until the next one.

What if the matter of hard-heartedness is not as simple as comparing oneself to the obvious example of an ancient abusive pharaoh? What if the more subtle symptom of hard-heartedness is waking up just enough to push the snooze bar and then going back to the slumber of the old normal?

We've been through this enough now to know it is likely to happen again. How many new normals must we adjust to before saying, "enough"?

> But when Pharaoh saw that there was relief, he hardened his heart and would not listen to Moses and Aaron, just as the LORD had said.

It comes down to this: When the tough times of plan B arise, the thing we most want is relief. God is looking for people who want him. That's what plan A is all about. It's not a temporary relief strategy. It is the sustained presence of almighty God in our midst.

The Prayer for Deliverance

Lord Jesus, you are my Deliverer. I hear you decree a season of exodus over me, over my family, and over my church. I receive your deliverance from my deep-rooted tendency simply to want relief from symptoms or escape from problems. I receive your deliverance into a heart that wants you alone. At least I want to want you more. Teach my heart to understand that exodus is not relief from symptoms but a cure for the deep-seated disease in me of sin and death. Deliver me from symptom management, and lead me to the deep cure only your sustained presence brings.

Glory be to the Father and to the Son and to the Holy Ghost.
As it was in the beginning, is now and ever shall be.
World without end. Amen! Amen!

The Questions

How about you? I know you want relief from the problems and pains of plan B. Here's what I want to ask you: Do you really want God? How much? When was the last time you told him so?

Week 3: Discussion Questions

Hearing the Text

Read Exodus 4:10–8:15.

Responding to the Text

- What did you hear?
- What did you see?
- What did you otherwise sense from the Lord?

Sharing Insights and Implications for Discipleship

Drawing from the Scripture text and daily readings, what did you find challenging, encouraging, provocative, comforting, invasive, inspiring, corrective, affirming, guiding, or warning?

Shaping Intentions for Prayer

Write your discipleship intention for the week ahead.

4
WEEK

Exodus 11:6–14:4

22

Exodus 11:6–7

The Lord Makes a Distinction

> *"'There will be loud wailing throughout Egypt—worse than there has ever been or ever will be again. But among the Israelites not a dog will bark at any person or animal.' Then you will know that the* Lord *makes a distinction between Egypt and Israel."*

Consider This

The concept of judgment, unpopular as it may be with many, is a monumental reality in Scripture and the Christian faith. There is something within all of us that both wants to judge but does not want to be judged. And let's be honest, the effect of judgment is discrimination, which is the absolute anathema of our age.

In the matter at hand, God clearly discriminated between the Israelites and the Egyptians. He judged the Israelites favorably while condemning the Egyptians:

> Then Moses summoned all the elders of Israel and said to them, "Go at once and select the animals for your families and slaughter the Passover lamb. Take a bunch of hyssop, dip it into the blood in the basin and put some of the blood on the top and on both sides of the doorframe. None of you shall go out of the door of your house until morning. When the Lord goes through the land to strike down the Egyptians, he will see the blood on the top and sides of the doorframe and will pass over that doorway, and he will not permit the destroyer to enter your houses and strike you down." (Exodus 12:21–23)

What would have happened if an Egyptian had put the blood of a lamb over their own doorframe? My hunch: They would have been spared. Why? Because the judgment of God comes down to one thing—the blood of the Lamb. A person is covered by the blood of the Lamb, or they are not. It is that simple. "The Lord makes a distinction," but it is not according to the nature of the people but according to the presence of the blood.

It is astonishing to think about Jesus and his final Passover meal and his earthshaking claim regarding the bread and the cup, that it was his very body and his blood. He is our Passover, but this Passover is not restricted to the Jewish people. This Passover is for everyone. Judgment is coming upon the whole earth. Mercy is freely available in Jesus Christ. We are saved by his blood shed on the cross. He is the Lamb of God who takes away the sins of the world. This is the gospel of God.

I struggle to grasp how it is somehow unfair and discriminatory that eternal salvation and entrance into the kingdom of God is offered freely and inclusively to the entire human race, exclusively through the life, death, and resurrection of Jesus Christ. Though many refuse to believe, no one is excluded. It is all at once the most exclusive and inclusive offer imaginable.

Why is this unfair? The human race, for all our good qualities, is utterly wicked and totally depraved. No one is righteous, not even one (see Romans 3:10). No one deserves the grace and mercy of God. God owes salvation to no one. It is the free gift of grace to all who believe and receive. Like the ancient Israelites, when we trust in the blood of the Lamb, we are delivered from slavery and set free to live the life for which we were created.

In the end, it is judgment to be sure, but judgment crowned with mercy. Read these next words very deliberately and carefully. Everything, literally everything, we believe is anchored in these revealed words:

> All this is from God, who reconciled us to himself through Christ and gave us the ministry of reconciliation: that God was reconciling the world to himself in Christ, not counting people's sins against them. And he has committed to us the message of reconciliation. We are therefore Christ's ambassadors, as though God were making his appeal through us. We implore you on Christ's behalf: Be reconciled to God. God made him who had no sin to be sin for us, so that in him we might become the righteousness of God. (2 Corinthians 5:18–21)

The Prayer for Deliverance

Lord Jesus, you are my Deliverer. Thank you that exodus means judgment and mercy—that it is not your judgment but your mercy that is over all your works. I confess my own depravity of soul. I receive your deliverance from every ounce of self-righteousness in me. I am a broken sinner. You are my whole Savior. Jesus, I receive your mercy, which has come in the form of you taking my judgment on yourself. Amazing love, how can it be that you, my God, would die for me?

Glory be to the Father and to the Son and to the Holy Ghost.
As it was in the beginning, is now and ever shall be.
World without end. Amen! Amen!

The Questions

Do you struggle with the exclusive message of the gospel? If so, why does it seem unfair to you? If you had terminal cancer and there was only one cure—and you had access to the cure—would you be offended by that? What is the difference? How much do you grasp the mercy of God in Jesus Christ? Do you still think you aren't really that in need of mercy?

23

Exodus 12:37–42

It Was a Night of Watching by the Lord

The Israelites journeyed from Rameses to Sukkoth. There were about six hundred thousand men on foot, besides women and children. Many other people went up with them, and also large droves of livestock, both flocks and herds. With the dough the Israelites had brought from Egypt, they baked loaves of unleavened bread. The dough was without yeast because they had been driven out of Egypt and did not have time to prepare food for themselves.

> *Now the length of time the Israelite people lived in Egypt was 430 years. At the end of the 430 years, to the very day, all the Lord's divisions left Egypt. Because the Lord kept vigil that night to bring them out of Egypt, on this night all the Israelites are to keep vigil to honor the Lord for the generations to come.*

Consider This

Four hundred thirty years. Wrap your mind around that. For those of us who live in the United States, we have only been a country for 248 years. I don't have a calculation for how many of those 430 years the Israelites spent enslaved, but it was likely most of them. In other words, no one's great-great-great-grandfather, who was already long dead, likely remembered a time when slavery was not the norm. Just as freedom rings in the deepest sense of our identity as Americans.

Other than some prevenient whisper of freedom resident in their deepest DNA as human beings, they had utterly no concept of anything else but slavery. There were no Ten Commandments yet, no tabernacle, no sacrificial system to speak of, no priests, Levites, or anything of the sort. There was the aging memory of Abraham, Isaac, and Jacob. They did have one thing going for them: I Am was with them. The God of Abraham, Isaac, and Jacob was for them.

Six hundred thousand men plus women and children and livestock—conservatively, two million people. Wrap your mind around that. As a point of reference, that is roughly the population of Houston, Texas. They had just been through ten successive plagues of absolute cataclysmic proportion. They were on foot, walking out of the country en route to the promised land. It would take forty years to get there. They would then get out of Egypt overnight. It would take another forty years to get Egypt out of them.

Here's a marvel. Despite centuries of captivity, from generation to generation to generation, the Israelites never stopped crying out to God. They kept their watch. They never gave up: "The Lord said, 'I have indeed seen the misery of my people in Egypt. I have heard them crying out because of their slave drivers, and I am concerned about their suffering'" (Exodus 3:7).

While I don't believe God is waiting for a threshold count of numbers of people or years of duration praying before he responds, there is something about a slow-growing wave of prayer over time that, historically speaking, precedes awakenings. There is no formula, just deep, sustained yearning that can come only from a real, deep place of travail.

I love how the ESV renders verse 42 of today's text. Referencing the night of the exodus from Egypt, we read,

> It was a night of watching by the LORD, to bring them out of the land of Egypt.

A night of watching by the Lord.

Wrap your mind around that. It is one thing to have our eyes on the Lord but quite another for his eyes to be on us. What if that's at least a part of the holy secret of deliverance—that the Lord's watchfulness patiently waits for the watchfulness of his people? When the watchfulness of the people meets up with the watchfulness of the Lord, the miracle begins to happen.

Then comes this final word from the ESV text:

> So this same night is a night of watching kept to the LORD by all the people of Israel throughout their generations.

There are so many stories I could share. Only one seems necessary. Twenty-five years ago, I received a calling within my calling. It is one I have both succeeded and failed to fulfill. This calling came to me with clarity during a winter sunrise. It emerged from this Scripture: "Devote yourselves to prayer, being watchful and thankful" (Colossians 4:2).

The Lord impressed upon me these words: "Create space for prayer." From that day forward, I have stumbled and fallen and stumbled again, and yet I keep getting back up.

I believe I am hearing those words from the Lord again. "Create space for prayer." I sense the Lord is creating a new house of prayer in my midst again. As I look at the words I wrote, it feels both overwhelming and right.

Devote yourselves to prayer, being watchful and thankful.

The Prayer for Deliverance

Lord Jesus, you are my Deliverer. Thank you for the exodus, and thank you for the exodus you are bringing forth around me and my family and friends and within my church and for this land. I receive it. And as you decree it, I declare it. I receive your deliverance from my passive good intentions and into your very watchfulness. Let the watchful care of the Holy Spirit rise up within me to create new space for prayer.

Glory be to the Father and to the Son and to the Holy Ghost.
As it was in the beginning, is now and ever shall be.
World without end. Amen! Amen!

The Questions

Are you growing in your sense of the Lord's watchful care over your life? Are you sensing his Spirit rising up in you to enact this very watchfulness in and through you? What holds you back from an undivided heart of watchfulness and prayer? What do you have to lose? What might there be to gain?

24

Exodus 13:3–10

Jesus Is My Passover

Then Moses said to the people, "Commemorate this day, the day you came out of Egypt, out of the land of slavery, because the Lord brought you out of it with a mighty hand. Eat nothing containing yeast. Today, in the month of Aviv, you are leaving. When the Lord brings you into the land of the Canaanites, Hittites, Amorites, Hivites and Jebusites—the land he swore to your ancestors to give you, a land flowing with milk and honey—you are to observe this ceremony in this month: For seven days eat bread made without yeast and on the seventh day hold a festival to the Lord. Eat unleavened bread during those seven days;

nothing with yeast in it is to be seen among you, nor shall any yeast be seen anywhere within your borders. On that day tell your son, 'I do this because of what the Lord *did for me when I came out of Egypt.' This observance will be for you like a sign on your hand and a reminder on your forehead that this law of the* Lord *is to be on your lips. For the* Lord *brought you out of Egypt with his mighty hand. You must keep this ordinance at the appointed time year after year."*

Consider This

If I asked you to tell me your story, chances are you wouldn't include the Passover and exodus story. I probably wouldn't either. Why is this?

If you asked me to tell you my story, I couldn't tell it without talking about Jesus and the resurrection. Same for you, right?

The question, though, is how does the story of Jesus make sense without the story of the Passover? He is, after all, our Passover Lamb. We are saved from damnation and death by his blood.

So what gives? Why don't we consider the Passover as core to our story as we do the cross? To this day, Passover is the central celebration of the Jewish people. But it is a bit of a novelty for most Christians. Many have observed it a time or two, but it is not a regular event in our year. Why not? Because this is Jesus's story, it is our story.

Today's text makes it explicitly clear. God expects his people to remember and celebrate the Passover.

> Commemorate this day, the day you came out of Egypt, out of the land of slavery, because the Lord brought you out of it with a mighty hand.

The reason we don't do this is because we don't think of them (the Israelites) as us. Permit me to be emphatic. We are them. Those ancient Israelites are us. This is our story as much as it was their story. It doesn't matter that most of us are Gentiles.

Perhaps the most unfortunate words in our Christian Bibles are *Old Testament* and *New Testament*. The Bible, from Genesis to Revelation, is one story, and it is our story—the story of Father, Son, and Holy

Spirit. Consider how Luke described Jesus helping a couple of depressed disciples on the road to Emmaus, "And beginning with Moses and all the Prophets, he explained to them what was said in all the Scriptures concerning himself" (Luke 24:27). In other words, the whole Bible is the story of Jesus.

This brings me back to my favorite verse from today's text:

> On that day tell your son, "I do this because of what the LORD did for me when I came out of Egypt."

Year after year, as they gathered for the Passover meal, Joseph would tell his young son, Jesus, "I do this because of what the Lord did for me when I came out of Egypt." Hang on. Joseph didn't come out of Egypt, did he? Oh yes, he did. And I did too—even me. Even you. This is more than remembering a story from history. It is commemoration. To commemorate something is to remember it in a way that narrates you into the story itself.

> This observance will be for you like a sign on your hand and a reminder on your forehead that this law of the LORD is to be on your lips. For the LORD brought you out of Egypt with his mighty hand. You must keep this ordinance at the appointed time year after year.

The Prayer for Deliverance

Lord Jesus, you are my Deliverer. I hear you saying exodus. I hear you decree a season of exodus over me, over my family, and over my church. Jesus, you are my exodus, which is another way of saying you are my Passover. Your sacrifice on the cross is my deliverance. You split the sea so I could walk right through it on dry ground. You delivered me from darkness to light and from death to life and now from chaos to new creation. You delivered me up out of Egypt, and now you are delivering me from Egypt within me. I receive it. And as you decree it, I declare it. Show me the way to demonstrate it in reality, to commemorate it and celebrate it, and, in doing so, to coronate you as my Deliverer King. Prepare my heart, mind, soul, and strength for the deliverance that comes with exodus. Now let it be as you decree—for my good, for others' gain, and for your glory.

Glory be to the Father and to the Son and to the Holy Ghost.
As it was in the beginning, is now and ever shall be.
World without end. Amen! Amen!

The Questions

Are you a student of the whole Bible, or have you tended to focus on the New Testament? Why do you think that is? How can you tangibly make these connections between the exodus of the Passover and the Passover of Jesus? How can it become more than a history lesson and actually part of your real story?

25

Exodus 13:17–18

When God Takes the Long Road

> *When Pharaoh let the people go, God did not lead them on the road through the Philistine country, though that was shorter. For God said, "If they face war, they might change their minds and return to Egypt." So God led the people around by the desert road toward the Red Sea. The Israelites went up out of Egypt ready for battle.*

Consider This

We've all heard the cliché bandied about that God doesn't give us anything he knows we can't handle. I've never given it much credence and filed it in the folder that holds other so-called biblical sayings like "God helps those who help themselves." I've never seen this phrase in the Bible about God not giving us more than we can handle—until today.

> When Pharaoh let the people go, God did not lead them on the road through the Philistine country, though that was shorter. For God said, "If they face war, they might change their minds and return to Egypt."

I bet they were furious. After all, they had been through the bricks-without-straw program and the ten plagues ordeal and the bloody lambs and the sudden departure—at night—with all the kids and the sheep and cows and everything else. Why on earth would they take the long way around the bend at a time like this? Did Moses just not know the shortcut? Did he think they couldn't defeat the Philistines? After all, the text tells us they left Egypt "ready for battle." To the average Israelite, the whole thing must have felt questionable. Truth be told, the plan would soon go from questionable to certifiably insane.

God knew. He knew what they could and could not handle. God knew the mileage differential between the two routes. He knew the soldier count in the Philistine armies, and he knew what the Israelite body count would be on the other side of a battle. He knew they would be ready to turn around and go back to Egypt, settle back into their slavish existence, and count it all as a bad dream. God chose not to give them more than he knew they could handle.

Instead, he took them by a longer route that felt like lost wandering, only to arrive at a dead end and their impending doom. God knew they could handle this, perhaps because it would put them in the kind of impossible situation from which only God could save them. Isn't that how it goes?

We can trust God. He engineers our circumstances beyond our knowing. Often it will not make sense to us at the time. It will seem like the worst possible thing has happened, that we have gone from bad to worse, from lost to hopeless. Our prayers will seem to bounce off the ceiling. God has a higher plan, a better plan, with endless contingencies, and everything can ultimately be worked together for our good and God's glory. Keep on trusting. Cloud by day. Fire by night. Never give up. Death on Friday. Resurrection on Sunday.

So God led the people around by the desert road toward the Red Sea.

Though I feel lost and in the valley of the shadow of death, yet I will trust him.

The Prayer for Deliverance

Lord Jesus, you are my Deliverer. I receive the deliverance of your exodus. You are my Passover—the Lamb of God who takes away the sins of the world—the Lamb of God who conquered death. Even still, I confess that I wonder at your ways, and I second-guess your plans. The better way seems so clear to me, yet I know your ways are higher and better than mine. You see the end from the beginning. You see the things that are not as though they were. I am tempted by the shorter route and the easier way. Teach me to trust the long road and to know you will not give me more than I can bear. Prepare my heart, mind, soul, and strength for the deliverance that comes with exodus. Now let it be as you decree—for my good, for others' gain, and for your glory.

Glory be to the Father and to the Son and to the Holy Ghost.
As it was in the beginning, is now and ever shall be.
World without end. Amen! Amen!

The Questions

Have you witnessed or experienced a situation that didn't make sense at all but that later worked itself into unforeseeable redemptive outcomes? Are you in such a situation now that has yet to resolve into any form of redemption? How might God be engineering your circumstances to effect maximum deliverance instead of taking the shortcut?

26

Exodus 13:19–22

Nine Rules of the Road with God

Moses took the bones of Joseph with him because Joseph had made the Israelites swear an oath. He had said, "God will surely come to your aid, and then you must carry my bones up with you from this place."

After leaving Sukkoth they camped at Etham on the edge of the desert. By day the Lord *went ahead of them in a pillar of cloud to guide them on their way and by night in a pillar of fire to give them light, so that they could travel by day or night. Neither the pillar of cloud by day nor the pillar of fire by night left its place in front of the people.*

Consider This

Cloud by day. Fire by night.

Overnight the Israelites moved from the complete and total predictability of slavery to the complete and total unpredictability of freedom. They were not following a strategic plan. They had no initiatives, objectives, or goals. They could only follow God. Every single aspect of their predictable lives was gone. What would they do? They would follow God. Where would they go? They would follow God.

> By day the Lord went ahead of them in a pillar of cloud to guide them on their way and by night in a pillar of fire to give them light, so that they could travel by day or night.

We all crave the rhythms, routines, and schedules of a predictable life. It is not a bad thing, but it can lead to the slow onset of spiritual sleep. Our spirits were made for the movement of faith. We were made to hear and be responsive to the voice of God. Something in us wants to domesticate our faith and turn it into a predictable set of routines, to keep it in a comfortable comfort zone, something that enhances our lives but doesn't actually control us. It can be a long way from . . .

Cloud by day. Fire by night.

I know I'm stepping on toes here. So what gives? How do we live in an everyday world and follow a pillar of cloud by day and a pillar of fire by night? Here are nine rules, if you will, for walking the road of faith.

1. Faith makes life better, not easier. Stop expecting the life of faith to make life easier.
2. Faith calls for life-support dependence on Word and Spirit.
3. Faith is not an individual competition. It is a team sport. It requires a few others in close fellowship.
4. Faith means loosening your grip on yourself and your agenda and your aspirations and dreams so you might tighten your hold on Jesus and his kingdom.
5. Faith means abandoning yourself to Jesus Christ. Jesus is not a part of your life. He's the whole of your life. The problem is often not unbelief but double-mindedness.
6. Faith means struggling mightily at times (see Hebrews 11).
7. Faith is not a weeks and months sprint but a years and decades marathon.
8. Faith means the fulfillment of all your deepest hopes and longings—only differently than you ever imagined.
9. Faith means hand to the plow and not looking back. "Forget the former things. Do not dwell on the past. Behold, I am doing a new thing . . ." Now finish the sentence.

Cloud by day. Fire by night.

Jesus showed us what this looks like. "Very truly I tell you, the Son can do nothing by himself; he can do only what he sees his Father doing, because whatever the Father does the Son also does" (John 5:19).

We are talking about the abiding life, which means less "Help me, Jesus!" and more "Have me, Jesus!" We are talking about the narrow way that few find. My hero and mentor, Maxie Dunnam, says it this way, "Most people prefer the hell of a predictable situation rather than risk the joy of an unpredictable one," and then he says it again.

Cloud by day. Fire by night.

The Prayer for Deliverance

Lord Jesus, you are my Deliverer. As I hear you decree exodus over me, I want to be honest. I prefer a comfortable life. I prefer predictability. I like to be in control of things. No, I need to be in control. I really don't want to be dependent on anyone or anything. I wonder if the life I have built and want is really compatible with the faith you are looking for. I invite you to meet me here, in this real place with my real life. I sense you want this kind of honesty from me. I want to walk by faith and the nine rules of the road, but if I'm honest, I'm often running from the bully of fear in a state of anxiety and frustration. I've been saying I receive your deliverance, but in reality, it's more like I am more open to it than I used to be. I'm not sure I am ready to receive it. Will you work with me right here and right now in this honest place?

Glory be to the Father and to the Son and to the Holy Ghost.
As it was in the beginning, is now and ever shall be.
World without end. Amen! Amen!

The Questions

Cloud by day. Fire by night. How does that strike you today? It's one thing to try and follow a set of directions; it's quite another to follow someone who clearly knows where they are going.

27

Exodus 14:1–4

We Need the Mind of Christ to Think the Thoughts of God

Then the LORD said to Moses, "Tell the Israelites to turn back and encamp near Pi Hahiroth, between Migdol and the sea. They are to encamp by the sea, directly opposite Baal Zephon. Pharaoh will think, 'The Israelites are wandering around the land in confusion,

> *hemmed in by the desert.' And I will harden Pharaoh's heart, and he will pursue them. But I will gain glory for myself through Pharaoh and all his army, and the Egyptians will know that I am the Lord." So the Israelites did this.*

Consider This

I'm going to coin a saying as we begin today: We need the mind of Christ to think the thoughts of God.

Try saying that with a bit of iambic pentameter (heartbeat rhythm). We-need-the-mind-of-Christ-to think-the thoughts-of God.

Why? Because the thoughts of God are confounding to the minds of people. Look at today's text.

> Tell the Israelites to turn back.

God wanted Pharaoh to pursue his people. Why would God want this? So he could defeat Pharaoh and his army. God's strategy? Make it appear to Pharaoh that the Israelites were lost and confused.

> Pharaoh will think, "The Israelites are wandering around the land in confusion, hemmed in by the desert."

You know what that felt like for the Israelites? It felt like they were "wandering around the land in confusion, hemmed in by the desert." They felt lost and confused. Doomed. Meanwhile, Pharaoh could taste the victory. It was literally a worst-case scenario for the Israelites. Everything must have seemed so wrong to them at the time. Why would God put them through so much and bring them so far only to let them perish like this?

Short answer: he wouldn't.

Maybe you've heard the saying, "Not all who wander are lost." Israel proved the point. You may be in the midst of the lowest moment of your life. You may feel lost and confused and in despair. It may even feel like it's all your fault. Renounce despair, forsake self-pity, and look to God. He has a plan.

Remember, the thoughts of God are confounding to the minds of people. How do we know this? First witness—Isaiah:

> "For my thoughts are not your thoughts,
> neither are your ways my ways,"
> declares the LORD.
> "As the heavens are higher than the earth,
> so are my ways higher than your ways
> and my thoughts than your thoughts." (Isaiah 55:8–9)

Second witness—Paul:

> For the foolishness of God is wiser than human wisdom, and the weakness of God is stronger than human strength. (1 Corinthians 1:25)

So, back to our text of the day. Did you pick up on the confounding absurdity of the instructions?

> Tell the Israelites to turn back and encamp near Pi Hahiroth, between Migdol and the sea.

Translation: "Not only does it appear that you are lost and doomed to certain destruction, but I want you to make camp there."

In the life of following Jesus in pursuit of God's will, it can feel like a holy-ground burning-bush encounter last week and a holy-hell house fire the next. Don't forget—God has a plan. God can work his best magic in our worst messes. The new creation often emerges from chaotic circumstances. It takes growing up in our faith to grasp this. It's why we must "have the mind of Christ" (1 Corinthians 2:16).

We need the mind of Christ to think the thoughts of God.

The mind of Christ is a cultivated faith that trusts God with all one's heart and leans not on our own understanding (see Proverbs 3:5)—even in the most desperate situations; no, especially in the most desperate situations. To gain the mind of Christ, we must fix our eyes on Jesus: "For the message of the cross is foolishness to those who are perishing, but to us who are being saved it is the power of God" (1 Corinthians 1:18).

Following Jesus can feel like making camp in the middle of chaos. Isn't that what the cross actually is—the Son of God making camp in the worst chaos of the fallen creation? And look what happened. Light destroyed darkness. Life desecrated death. New creation sprung forth from chaos.

We need the mind of Christ to think the thoughts of God.

The Prayer for Deliverance

Lord Jesus, you are my Deliverer. I hear you decree a season of exodus over me, over my family, and over my church. I confess that my perception is limited by my experience. I want my perception to be enlarged by your Word and Spirit. I receive your deliverance from my flawed and limited ways of thinking about you and your ways. I receive the mind of Christ that I might think the thoughts of God. Eye has not seen, nor ear heard, nor human mind conceived the things God has prepared for those who love him. Yes, Lord, I receive the mind of Christ that I might think the thoughts of God. Stretch my comprehension to the possibilities of your capacities.

Glory be to the Father and to the Son and to the Holy Ghost.
As it was in the beginning, is now and ever shall be.
World without end. Amen! Amen!

The Questions

Have you experienced or witnessed one of these situations where the thoughts and ways of God were confounding to conventional wisdom? Are you in one of those situations now? How are you growing in your reception and appropriation of the mind of Christ?

Week 4: Discussion Questions

Hearing the Text

Read Exodus 11:6–14:4.

Responding to the Text

- What did you hear?
- What did you see?
- What did you otherwise sense from the Lord?

Sharing Insights and Implications for Discipleship

Drawing from the Scripture text and daily readings, what did you find challenging, encouraging, provocative, comforting, invasive, inspiring, corrective, affirming, guiding, or warning?

Shaping Intentions for Prayer

Write your discipleship intention for the week ahead.

5 WEEK

Exodus 14:5–28

29

Exodus 14:5–9

The (Often) Protracted Battle of Divine Deliverance

When the king of Egypt was told that the people had fled, Pharaoh and his officials changed their minds about them and said, "What have we done? We have let the Israelites go and have lost their services!" So he had his chariot made ready and took his army with him. He took six hundred of the best chariots, along with all the other chariots of Egypt, with officers over all of them. The L*ORD hardened the heart of Pharaoh king of Egypt, so that he pursued the Israelites, who were marching out boldly. The Egyptians—all Pharaoh's horses and chariots, horsemen and troops—pursued the Israelites and overtook them as they camped by the sea near Pi Hahiroth, opposite Baal Zephon.*

Consider This

Pharaoh had one priority: building his kingdom.

The God of Israel also had one priority: building his kingdom.

Pharaoh was looking for slaves.

God wanted sons and daughters.

This is the perennial battle. Every soul hangs in the balance: slave or son/daughter. Will we succumb to the slavery of building the kingdoms of this world, or will we become sons and daughters and inherit the now-and-still-coming kingdom of God?

Pharaoh represents the powers of darkness, and darkness will not release its slaves without a fierce battle. The text is careful to tell us Pharaoh sent six hundred of the best chariots along with all the other chariots of Egypt. He sent the entire army with many officers, troops, horses, and riders. Finally, Pharaoh rode into battle himself in his own chariot, an extraordinary response. This is the power of darkness.

A larger principle is at work here, the principle of the principalities of darkness: the kingdom and principalities of darkness will not readily or willingly or easily release their prisoners. Human effort is of no avail. It requires the delivering power of God Almighty. The power of darkness is extremely powerful, far more powerful than mere mortals. However, compared to the power of God, the power of darkness is no power at all.

Divine deliverance is a complex process, and it can take a protracted period of time. The main reason for this is the preference of God to deploy human agents in the process of divine deliverance. Notice the long-game strategy of deliverance. It began with a period of intense darkness in Egypt—the lawful murder of all the Israelite baby boys in the country. God began with a pair of courageous parents who made a way for their baby boy to escape death. God used the household of Pharaoh to save this child who would grow up to become Pharaoh's nemesis. This son would grow up witnessing the cruelty of Pharaoh as an oppressor of God's people. Moses would grow up under the power paradigm of Pharaoh, leading him to commit murder to defeat a murderer. Moses needed deliverance. When Moses was forty years old, God took him out of Egypt, and over the next forty years, God took Egypt out of Moses. Are you watching the timeline here? It took eighty years to launch this plan.

After launch and the unforeseen bricks-without-straw program, Moses had a near mutiny on his hands. It took many meetings with repeated requests, and ten catastrophic plagues to bring Pharaoh to his knees. This whole matter of divine deliverance was extremely complex, profoundly chaotic, and maddeningly unpredictable at every juncture. Despite all of this, God was in complete control every step of the way.

As we observed, after all this protracted preparation, God delivered the Israelites from Egypt in one night, and yet the deliverance was hardly over. Though Pharaoh was brought to his knees, he quickly got back up. It must have seemed to everyone on the field he would have things back in hand overnight. God had other plans.

I labor to make this point for two reasons. First, we need to read far more deeply into these ancient stories of our faith because they hold deep wisdom and insight. Second, we need to understand the sophisticated complexities of the kingdom of darkness in our own time in our own lives, families, churches, and communities. We must come to grips with our utter inability and incompetence to combat it on our own with our own resources. Chiefly, we must come to a far deeper awareness and acuity with the incredible, unstoppable power of God over darkness for us who believe. Today we desperately need divine deliverance from the deep infestation of compounded darkness in every aspect of the world around us. Our young are especially vulnerable and victimized. We need a great awakening. Hence, we sow—even as we anticipate the culmination of all deliverance—signaled by a trumpet blast and the resounding voices coming from the heavens. They are shouting:

> "The kingdom of the world has become
> the kingdom of our Lord and of his Messiah,
> and he will reign for ever and ever." (Revelation 11:15)

The Prayer for Deliverance

Lord Jesus, you are my Deliverer. We receive your deliverance as well as your patience and fortitude, which may be required of us to appropriate your work in us. We pray today the prayer you gave Paul to pray for us:

> I pray that the eyes of my heart may be enlightened in order that I may know the hope to which you have called me, the riches of your glorious inheritance in your holy people and your incomparably great power for us who believe. That power is the same as the mighty strength you exerted when you raised Christ from the dead and seated him at your right hand in the heavenly realms, far above all rule and authority, power and dominion, and every name that is invoked, not only in the present age but also in the one to come. (adapted from Ephesians 1:18–21)

Teach us and train us in your ways of deliverance. We confess our relative ignorance, and we repent from our apathy. And ever remind us that you, the one who is in us, are greater than our enemy who is in the world.

Glory be to the Father and to the Son and to the Holy Ghost.

As it was in the beginning, is now and ever shall be.
World without end. Amen! Amen!

The Questions

On a scale of 1 to 10, with 10 being the highest, where do you rate your knowledge, understanding, and experience of the ministry of divine deliverance? Do you grasp that we are up against forces (aka principalities and powers) that cannot be combated by mere education or even more money? Are you open and willing to learn more about the ministry of deliverance?

30

Exodus 14:10–14

The Zero-Sum Game of Fear and Faith

> *As Pharaoh approached, the Israelites looked up, and there were the Egyptians, marching after them. They were terrified and cried out to the Lord. They said to Moses, "Was it because there were no graves in Egypt that you brought us to the desert to die? What have you done to us by bringing us out of Egypt? Didn't we say to you in Egypt, 'Leave us alone; let us serve the Egyptians'? It would have been better for us to serve the Egyptians than to die in the desert!"*
>
> *Moses answered the people, "Do not be afraid. Stand firm and you will see the deliverance the Lord will bring you today. The Egyptians you see today you will never see again. The Lord will fight for you; you need only to be still."*

Consider This

Today's text unfolds the worst-case-possible doomsday scenario. The newly freed Israelites stared down the barrel of the most powerful army in the world on one side of them. On the other side was the Red Sea. Moments like these expose our deepest dispositions. Will we find fear or faith?

I want us to examine the conversation between Moses and the Israelites and the story it tells. The Israelites asked three questions and made a declaration. Moses offered three responses and made a proclamation. Note how they intertwine and correspond:

Question 1: Was it because there were no graves in Egypt that you brought us to the desert to die?
Response 1: Do not be afraid.
Question 2: What have you done to us by bringing us out of Egypt?
Response 2: Stand firm and you will see the deliverance the LORD will bring you today.
Question 3: Didn't we say to you in Egypt, "Leave us alone; let us serve the Egyptians"?
Response 3: The Egyptians you see today you will never see again.
Declaration of fear: It would have been better for us to serve the Egyptians than to die in the desert!
Declaration of faith: The Lord will fight for you; you need only to be still.

Fear is a given. The question is faith. Here's the interesting calculus of faith—think of a spectrum of 0 to 100 percent. What part of the spectrum will be taken up by fear? In this case, the Israelites were at 100 percent fear on the spectrum. There was no room for faith in their response. Fear and faith are a zero-sum game.

Moses, however, spoke to them of the power of God. Moses knew all he needed was a movement of 1 percent to win the day. If he could push their fear back from 100 to 99 percent, it would leave room for a 1 percent faith response. Just as Moses knew 1 percent was all that was needed, so did Jesus:

> Truly I tell you, if you have faith as small as a mustard seed, you can say to this mountain, "Move from here to there," and it will move. Nothing will be impossible for you. (Matthew 17:20)

The issue is not the size of one's faith but the strength of their God.

It's why when we want to see faith rise up, we don't try to talk people into having more faith. Nor are we likely to be successful in trying to talk them out of their fear. We win when we witness to them about the nature, character, and power of God. One percent is all it takes.

Moses was the 1 percent:

> Moses answered the people, "Do not be afraid. Stand firm and you will see the deliverance the LORD will bring you today. The Egyptians you see today you will never see again. The LORD will fight for you; you need only to be still."

The Prayer for Deliverance

Lord Jesus, you are my Deliverer. Thank you for the way you are showing me exodus is tied to my vision of you. I confess how I can put the emphasis on fear and what I am afraid of. Then I try to shift my focus to my faith or lack thereof and miss the point of who my faith is in. I receive your deliverance from fear and even from faith in faith. I receive my sight to behold you in all your love and might and delivering power. Now, let faith arise from the vision of you.

Glory be to the Father and to the Son and to the Holy Ghost.
As it was in the beginning, is now and ever shall be.
World without end. Amen! Amen!

The Questions

Do you think you don't have enough faith? How does this 1 percent principle impact you? Think of a challenging set of circumstances you are facing just now. On a scale of 1–10 (10 is highest), what is the level of your fear? Now subtract the level of your fear from 10, and that is the level of your faith. How might you move your level of faith by one degree upward? (Hint: Sharpen your focus on the words, deeds, stories, and signs of God.)

31

Exodus 14:15–18

A Wake-Up Call for Our Times

Then the Lord said to Moses, "Why are you crying out to me? Tell the Israelites to move on. Raise your staff and stretch out your hand over the sea to divide the water so that the Israelites can go through the sea on dry ground. I will harden the hearts of the Egyptians so that they will go in after them. And I will gain glory through Pharaoh and all his army, through his chariots and his horsemen. The Egyptians will know that I am the Lord when I gain glory through Pharaoh, his chariots and his horsemen."

Consider This

Moses had just had his best *Braveheart* speech:

> Do not be afraid. Stand firm and you will see the deliverance the Lord will bring you today. The Egyptians you see today you will never see again. The Lord will fight for you; you need only to be still. (Exodus 14:13–14)

Then, in an apparent contradiction of Moses's uber cinematically spiritual message to the Israelites, God said,

> Why are you crying out to me? Tell the Israelites to move on.

It appears that Moses expected God was going to hurl bolts of lightning and destroy the Egyptian army. He expected God would slay the Egyptians as the Israelites stood by and watched. Clearly, the notion of parting the waters of the sea would not have entered even their wildest imaginings. There was no category for such a thing.

> Raise your staff and stretch out your hand over the sea to divide

> the water so that the Israelites can go through the sea on dry ground.

God called Moses to part the sea. God would give the power, but he wanted Moses to exercise it:

> Raise your staff and stretch out your hand.

So why didn't God just do it by himself? Why Moses and his staff and his outstretched hand? God desires to work through human agency. God did not need Moses's staff and hand in order to part the Red Sea. No one thinks Moses parted the Red Sea. We all know God did it. But what if we only know God did it (and not some phenomenology of nature) because Moses raised his staff and stretched out his hand?

> Raise your staff and stretch out your hand over the sea to divide the water so that the Israelites can go through the sea on dry ground.

We see God working through human agents and agency throughout Scripture—from prophets, priests, and kings to shepherds, fishermen, and expectant mothers—anyone willing to raise their staff and stretch out their hand in God's stead and on his behalf.

So often in our praying, we plead with God to act on our behalf. I often wonder if God is looking for a mode of prayer whereby we are acting on God's behalf and at his behest. I think, in fact, this is the whole point of sending his ultimate agent—his Son—to redeem the whole creation and to reconcile the lost. As he stretched out his hands on the cross, it became the divine staff of heaven lifted up over all the earth—parting the seas of sin and death—paving the pathway from Eden to eschaton, from exile to eternity, from wasteland to graceland, from slaves to beloved sons and daughters.

As we look upon God's Son, God intends for us to behold the image in whom we are made and like whom we are meant to become—stretching out our hands and raising the staff of the cross over the swirling seas of chaos surging all around us.

> Raise your staff and stretch out your hand over the sea to divide the water so that the Israelites can go through the sea on dry ground.

One more bit. We hear this sentimental sap about God having no hands but our hands to do his will on earth. Malarky! God has his own hands. He does not need my hands or yours. He chooses to put his staff of authority in our hands. He awaits a generation who will again raise the staff of the cross and stretch out our hands in the face of impossible things, who will declare what he decrees and demonstrate what he desires, who will raid the gates of hell and raise the dead.

The Prayer for Deliverance

Lord Jesus, you are my Deliverer. And yet I hear you calling me to raise my staff and stretch out my hand over the sea to divide the waters so that your people can go through the sea on dry ground. In the face of sickness and sorrow, of depression and death, to raise the staff of the cross and stretch out my hand as your agent to do your will, even on earth as it is in heaven. Would you lead me beyond the metaphor here and into the literal active truth of it? You said we would do even greater things than these because you go to the Father. Show me how to raise the staff of the cross and stretch out my hand over my life, my home and family, my church, my neighborhood and town, and over the sick, the poor, and the downtrodden.

Glory be to the Father and to the Son and to the Holy Ghost.
As it was in the beginning, is now and ever shall be.
World without end. Amen! Amen!

The Questions

Are you stirred by this passage? Will you begin to experiment with raising the staff of the cross and stretching out your hand—literally doing it—and declaring what God is decreeing? Start in the secret place. Go from there. Report back what happens.

32

Exodus 14:19–20

The Call to Holy Imagination

Then the angel of God, who had been traveling in front of Israel's army, withdrew and went behind them. The pillar of cloud also moved from in front and stood behind them, coming between the armies of Egypt and Israel. Throughout the night the cloud brought darkness to the one side and light to the other side; so neither went near the other all night long.

Consider This

Maybe you've heard the story of the seven-year-old boy who learned the story of the Israelites and the Red Sea in Sunday school. His mother asked what he learned in class. Here's the exchange:

> "Well, Mom, our teacher told us how God sent Moses behind enemy lines on a rescue mission to lead the Israelite people out of Egypt. When he got to the Red Sea, he had his army build a pontoon bridge, and all the people walked across safely. Then he radioed headquarters for reinforcements. They scrambled a squadron of F-16 Falcon fighter jets to blow up the bridge, and all the Israelites were saved."
>
> "Now, Billy, is that really what your teacher taught you?" his mother asked.
>
> "Well, no, Mom, but if I told you what the teacher said, you'd never believe it in a million years!"

Today's text gives us the incredible true story of what happened that night at the Red Sea. It merits a second reading to take it all in:

> Then the angel of God, who had been traveling in front of Israel's army, withdrew and went behind them. The pillar of cloud also moved from in front and stood behind them, coming between the armies of Egypt and Israel. Throughout the night

> the cloud brought darkness to the one side and light to the other side; so neither went near the other all night long.

Imagine trying to explain your iPhone or the internet to your great-great-grandmother. Where would you start? You would say things like, "Grandma, I can talk to a person in London, England, right now while seeing their face on the screen and sending them a photograph of my children via a text message at the same time."

What would she do with that? She wouldn't believe it even if you demonstrated it before her very eyes. All you could do would be to give her the outlandish, incredible, unbelievable yet true facts.

That is all Moses did here. He gave us the outlandish, incredible, unbelievable yet true facts. It is one thing to try to explain something from today to an earlier time. Moses was telling the story of something way back then to people thousands of years later—believe it or not.

Angels and armies, pillars of cloud and fire, as a group of millions of refugees walked toward an impenetrable wall of water (aka the Red Sea) while being pursued by the most formidable army on earth. And then we get this:

> Then Moses stretched out his hand over the sea, and all that night the LORD drove the sea back with a strong east wind and turned it into dry land. The waters were divided, and the Israelites went through the sea on dry ground, with a wall of water on their right and on their left. (Exodus 14:21–22)

Rather than say much else, let's practice the exercise of holy imagination. As divine image-bearers, we possess the gift of imagination. When the Holy Spirit touches our imagination, we are given the capacity to enter into a kind of sacred seeing. The word is *beholding*.

Now, behold the scene. Reread Exodus 14:19–22 out loud. Your ears need to hear it. The information enters through our eyes and goes straight to our brains. Remember, we live by faith, not by sight (see 2 Corinthians 5:7). Faith does not come through sight but by hearing. Faith, through hearing (see Romans 10:17), gives something beyond mere eyesight. Faith gives our hearts and souls the vision of God.

After hearing the text read aloud, ask the Holy Spirit to open the eyes of your heart to behold this vision—and open your heart to visualize it happening in as much detail as your Spirit-empowered imagination can muster: Moses stretched out his hand over the sea, and all that night the Lord drove the sea back with a strong east wind and turned it into dry land.

The Prayer for Deliverance

Lord Jesus, you are my Deliverer. I marvel at this word:
"The cloud brought darkness to the one side and light to the other side." There is none like you, Lord. I marvel at this word: "The waters were divided, and we went through the sea on dry ground, with a wall of water on our right and on our left." There is none like you, Lord. Glory be to the Father and to the Son and to the Holy Ghost.
As it was in the beginning, is now and ever shall be.
World without end. Amen! Amen!

The Questions

Did you do it—the exercise of holy imagination? What did you see?

33

Exodus 14:23–25

On Staying Awake in the Last Days

The Egyptians pursued them, and all Pharaoh's horses and chariots and horsemen followed them into the sea. During the last watch of the night the Lord *looked down from the pillar of fire and cloud at the Egyptian army and threw it into confusion. He jammed the wheels of their chariots so that they had difficulty driving. And the Egyptians said, "Let's get away from the Israelites! The* Lord *is fighting for them against Egypt."*

Consider This

As you might imagine, I get a fair amount of reader mail. Most of it is encouragement, for which I am grateful. Sometimes a reader takes issue with something I wrote, which I appreciate and try to respond to. I often get questions like this: "Why did the Egyptian army enter the water trap when its occurrence obviously defied all laws of physics?"

Here is my initial response: "Bloodlust, greed, and the maintenance of their own kingdom and way of life. The slaves were their Dow Jones Industrial Average."

It's a good question. In the best of times, people make irrational decisions. Amid unrelenting chaos, people make horribly irrational decisions. The Israelites walked into the sea, pursuing the kingdom of God. Pharaoh and his armies charged into the sea, chasing the kingdom of Egypt, protecting their way of life.

Life comes down to such a simple choice. Sometimes life can take a plague, or ten, to bring such clarity. Other times all the shiny things whirring around our heads and filling up our phones keep the chaos churning.

For so many, every day starts with coffee in the morning and ends with wine at night, with a long day's labor between to get to the next income bracket with better schools, nicer vacations, and richer retirement accounts. We live from deer season to turkey season, from the Super Bowl to the World Series, from Augusta National to the Final Four.

And, to be clear, none of these things is bad in itself. Yet these things can keep us in a state of constant distraction so that we miss the real point and purpose of our lives. Coffee and wine, lunch and supper, Saturday and Sunday—and where on earth is God in all of that?

Blaise Pascal (1623–62) said it thus: "We run heedlessly into the abyss after putting something in front of us to stop us from seeing it."[1] Most don't realize it until they are miles into the Red Sea, chasing after a mirage surrounded by water walls threatening to become waterfalls.

Jesus said so decisively and clearly, "But seek first his kingdom and

---

1. Blaise Pascal, *Christianity for Modern Pagans: Pascal's* Pensees, ed. Peter Kreeft (Ignatius, 1993), 145.

his righteousness, and all these things will be given to you as well" (Matthew 6:33). For so many churchgoing (or at least church-saluting) Christians, it can be more like, "Seek all these things, ask for God's help to get them, and consider yourself blessed by God when they come. And the kingdom of God and his righteousness will be added unto you."

This is the peak of deception. God and the things of God occupy such a small compartment in far too many lives. Church fills such a stale, stifling, and predictable category. When will we finally wake up? My prayer is that in these days of chaos, you crave the gift of clarity. Notice this moment of deep soul clarity.

> During the last watch of the night the LORD looked down from the pillar of fire and cloud at the Egyptian army and threw it into confusion.

As it comes to world history and the story of God, we are in the last watch of the night. This text comes to mind: "In the past God spoke to our ancestors through the prophets at many times and in various ways, but in these last days he has spoken to us by his Son, whom he appointed heir of all things, and through whom also he made the universe" (Hebrews 1:1–2).

Everything noted in the Apostles' Creed has happened save this one thing: "From thence he shall come to judge the quick and the dead."

I am not one given to stirring apocalyptic anxiety, and clearly, no one knows the times or dates. All this said, we are living in the last days—even the last watch of the night. How long these last days will last is unknowable. Concerning such things, Jesus put it this way:

> But about that day or hour no one knows, not even the angels in heaven, nor the Son, but only the Father. As it was in the days of Noah, so it will be at the coming of the Son of Man. For in the days before the flood, people were eating and drinking, marrying and giving in marriage, up to the day Noah entered the ark; and they knew nothing about what would happen until the flood came and took them all away. That is how it will be at the coming of the Son of Man. (Matthew 24:36–39)

This is why every single day I encourage you to say the words to one another: "Wake up, sleeper, rise from the dead, and Christ will shine on you" (Ephesians 5:14). It won't mean giving up everything you enjoy—not for a minute. It will mean something infinitely greater to live for. That is awakening. And it's never too late. Jesus—not stale religion, not a caricature of church, not self-righteous, pompous religion, just Jesus—is better than the best.

And one more pro tip from the lips of the Lord Jesus: "Heaven and earth will pass away, but my words will never pass away" (Matthew 24:35).

The Prayer for Deliverance

Lord Jesus, you are my Deliverer. Exodus! You keep decreeing it. I keep declaring it—over my heart, my home, my church, my city, my friends, and even over those who consider me their enemy. And I am beginning to lift up the staff of the cross and stretch out my hand over people and situations around me—at least I'm beginning to visualize myself doing such a thing in my mind's eye. At the same time, I find myself busy all the time and often with distraction and mindless activity. I receive your deliverance from distraction and the subtle deception to which it leads. I receive your deliverance into the gentle attentiveness inspired by the Holy Spirit in me. I receive the Holy Spirit, the breath of God, and also the unhurried pace at which you breathe. I want to live my life at the pace of Jesus in me, in step with the Holy Spirit—awake but not anxious, alert without preoccupation. Together we are not afraid, nor are we anxious. We are joyful in hope as we walk each other home.

Glory be to the Father and to the Son and to the Holy Ghost.
As it was in the beginning, is now and ever shall be.
World without end. Amen! Amen!

The Questions

If I've offended you today, will you forgive me? Now, will you ask yourself why you were offended?

34

Exodus 14:26–28

How the Wrath of God Is the Love of God and Vice Versa

> *Then the* Lord *said to Moses, "Stretch out your hand over the sea so that the waters may flow back over the Egyptians and their chariots and horsemen." Moses stretched out his hand over the sea, and at daybreak the sea went back to its place. The Egyptians were fleeing toward it, and the* Lord *swept them into the sea. The water flowed back and covered the chariots and horsemen—the entire army of Pharaoh that had followed the Israelites into the sea. Not one of them survived.*

Consider This

With so much to deal with, it is easy to get lost in the details—to become preoccupied with the faith of Moses, the fear of the Israelites, the hard-heartedness of Pharaoh, and so on. We can draw lessons about fear, faith, obedience, and rebellion until the cows come home. We can walk around the burning bush a thousand times, get a different life application each time, and still miss the point of the whole thing.

This is not a story about Moses or Pharaoh or the Israelites or the Egyptians. It is not a story about you or me. This is the story of God.

All of these biblical stories are meant to do one thing: to reveal the God of heaven and earth. I am convicted by just how easy it can be to deal with everything else in the text but God. It can all be so interesting and helpful and meaningful and yet stultifyingly trifling (great word, by the way—*stultifyingly*!).

Today let's focus on the awe-inspiring sovereignty of almighty God. I see both the unity and integrity of God's character in two very different expressions. I see the love of God on full display, delivering the Israelites through the Red Sea. And at the same time, I see the wrath of God bringing the Egyptians to utter ruin and desolation.

For my money, the most powerful words in today's text are "Not one of them survived." The same waters through which Israel was delivered proved to be the death of the Egyptians. The same God brings deliverance and doom through the same act at the same time. The love of God is the wrath of God. They cannot be separated or divided, as they are seamless dimensions of the same whole.

Here I must correct a common misconception. People don't like to deal with the idea of the wrath of God, largely because they associate the concept of wrath with some angry man in their past. The wrath of God must not be equated with the anger of God as though wrath were some kind of divine emotional response. The wrath of God is simply the effect of his nature on all who are unprepared for his unmitigated presence. The wrath of God is what happens when the holy love of God encounters sin. They simply cannot coexist.

Consider the image of fire. Fire either burns or refines; it destroys or purifies. The outcome depends not on the nature of the fire but on the properties of the substance entering the flames. Straw will fare quite differently than steel. Interestingly, the writer of Hebrews reminded us: "our 'God is a consuming fire'" (12:29). That is why earlier the same writer warned, "It is a dreadful thing to fall into the hands of the living God" (10:31).

The wrath of God is the effect of the holy love of God on sin.

It is why the Gospels feature John the Baptist preaching a baptism of repentance from sin, with the stark warning, "You brood of vipers! Who warned you to flee from the coming wrath?" (Luke 3:7).

In his letter to the Roman Christians, Paul made profoundly clear the truth that God's wrath is the effect of his holy love on sin: "The wrath of God is being revealed from heaven against all the godlessness and wickedness of people, who suppress the truth by their wickedness" (Romans 1:18).

Paul went on to make clear that "all have sinned and fall short of the glory of God" (Romans 3:23), setting the stage for the merciful miracle of the gospel of Jesus Christ: "But God demonstrates his own love for us in this: While we were still sinners, Christ died for us. Since we have now been justified by his blood, how much more shall we be saved from God's wrath through him!" (5:8–9).

And to the Corinthians, Paul said it even more clearly: "We are therefore Christ's ambassadors, as though God were making his appeal through us. We implore you on Christ's behalf: Be reconciled to God. God made him who had no sin to be sin for us so that in him we might become the righteousness of God" (2 Corinthians 5:20–21).

At the cross, we simultaneously behold the great mystery of Christ—the wrath of God against sin and the love of God for sinners—and we are saved.

From the parting of the sea to a hill far away, our God reigns. His wrath is real, but his love endures forever.

The Prayer for Deliverance

Lord Jesus, you are my Deliverer. Thank you that "the wrath of God is being revealed from heaven against all the godlessness and wickedness of people, who suppress the truth by their wickedness" (Romans 1:18). This is the mercy of deliverance. You reveal your wrath before you exercise it, holding back to give us opportunity to turn away from it and to turn to you. Thank you. And thank you that it is your love—the staff of the cross—that delivers us from your Red Sea wrath by the blood of Jesus, who took our place and accepted our just punishment and in exchange gives us his righteousness. This is the mercy of deliverance. "God made him who had no sin to be sin for us, so that in him we might become the righteousness of God" (2 Corinthians 5:21). As sinners deserving wrath, you robbed us of our sin, and in its place you invested the eternal treasure of your amazing grace. Thank you. Awaken our awareness of this miracle of divine deliverance and redemption.

Today, in case it was not clear before, I put my full trust and the eternal weight of my everlasting soul on the redemption of Jesus Christ, by which I have been delivered from the wrath of God and into the love of God.

Glory be to the Father and to the Son and to the Holy Ghost.
As it was in the beginning, is now and ever shall be.
World without end. Amen! Amen!

The Questions

Do you struggle with the idea of the wrath of God? Why or why not? Are you still struggling in the slavery of trying to be good enough or thinking you really aren't that bad of a sinner? Are you grasping yet that you are not a sinner because you sin, but that you sin because you are a sinner, and that divine salvation cuts to the core of dealing with your sin problem and only then begins to deal with the problem of your sins?

Week 5: Discussion Questions

Hearing the Text

Read Exodus 14:5–28.

Responding to the Text

- What did you hear?
- What did you see?
- What did you otherwise sense from the Lord?

Sharing Insights and Implications for Discipleship

Drawing from the Scripture text and daily readings, what did you find challenging, encouraging, provocative, comforting, invasive, inspiring, corrective, affirming, guiding, or warning?

Shaping Intentions for Prayer

Write your discipleship intention for the week ahead.

6

WEEK

Exodus 14:29–15:27

36

Exodus 14:29–31

When the Red Sea Parts and When It Doesn't

But the Israelites went through the sea on dry ground, with a wall of water on their right and on their left. That day the Lord *saved Israel from the hands of the Egyptians, and Israel saw the Egyptians lying dead on the shore. And when the Israelites saw the mighty hand of the* Lord *displayed against the Egyptians, the people feared the* Lord *and put their trust in him and in Moses his servant.*

Consider This

This must be one of the most astonishing sentences in all of the Bible:

> But the Israelites *went* through the sea on dry ground, with a wall of water on their right and on their left. (emphasis added)

The NIV translates the Hebrew word *halak* as "went" (in italic above). A better translation, in my opinion, is "walk," which many English translations use as well.

> The Israelites *walked* through the sea.

Many of us need some kind of essential deliverance, and yet our experience feels like an unparted sea. The mountain will not move. The cancer is too metastasized to leave. The memory loss is not coming back. The depression won't lift. The marriage won't mend this time. The grief of a lost loved one is too much to bear. And so many are facing the Red Sea of the end of life, and though you are prepared to pass through, you aren't ready to let go.

Recently I visited an aging man coming to the end of his days. He was hopeful yet deeply discouraged. I asked him, "Do you want faith to live or courage to die?" He whispered a shout back, "I want both!" We all do, don't we? We want Eden. Meanwhile, we live in exile. We want a better city. Meanwhile, we live in tents. We want a triumphant victory, but whether we win or lose the present battle we are facing, what we must come to grips with is this fact: We have a triumphant God who won the war.

> The angel said to the women, "Do not be afraid, for I know that you are looking for Jesus, who was crucified. He is not here; he has risen, just as he said. Come and see the place where he lay. Then go quickly and tell his disciples: 'He has risen from the dead and is going ahead of you into Galilee. There you will see him.' Now I have told you." (Matthew 28:5–7)

When it comes to troubles, what we want is the deliverance of a Red Sea success story. What we get is the struggle of the cross and the story of the empty tomb—a God who struggles as one of us and dies from the cruelty of injustice, then rises from the dead. We are looking for a triumphant victory from our broken circumstances. What we get is a triumphant God in the midst of them.

What if that's the real story of Exodus? It wouldn't take long until the Israelites were grumbling at Moses and pining for Egyptian slavery again. What could have been a fourteen-day journey into the promised land turned into a forty-year ordeal of feckless, faithless wandering in the wilderness.

And what if that's the real story of life? We want everything to work out just like we want it to, and it just doesn't. But we have a triumphant God. No matter how many battles we may lose, he has won the war.

It's not the law of averages, but it is the rule of baseball. We are going to win some. We are going to lose some. And some will get rained out. But we keep playing. No matter how many strikeouts, we keep stepping up to the plate and cheering one another on.

I'll be honest. I can get really discouraged and even depressed when my Red Sea doesn't part. I need to grow in this area. I go inward and isolate myself. Something I've noticed about my parents' generation—when they get down and out and discouraged about their circumstances and situations, they go help somebody else who is struggling. Though the waters might not be parting in their situation, they always manage to be part of someone else's deliverance.

> But the Israelites *walked* through the sea on dry ground, with a wall of water on their right and on their left.

It's what I love about this Hebrew word *halak*. At the end of the day, that's what we are doing, isn't it? We are walking one another home. Every single one of us has the opportunity every single day to help walk somebody home.

The Prayer for Deliverance

Lord Jesus, you are my Deliverer. As you gave up the brutal struggle that was your life, with your final breath from the cross you spoke the words "It is finished!" As the curtain in the temple tore from top to bottom, rending the veil between heaven and earth, the Red Sea of all eternity was parted, opening the way through the wall of water of sin on the one side and the wall of water that was death on the other. Deliver me from my feckless, faithless mentality as I face what feels like Red Sea challenges in my life, and deliver me into the resilience of the Holy Spirit who trains my spirit to stand on the ultimate victory in the face of my struggles, hardships, losses, and disappointments. And lead me to someone whom I can help walk a few miles on the journey home today.

Glory be to the Father and to the Son and to the Holy Ghost.
As it was in the beginning, is now and ever shall be.
World without end. Amen! Amen!

The Questions

So, are you more like me in the face of a sea that isn't parting (allowing discouragement or despair to take over)? Or are you more like my parents (getting up and going to help someone else in their struggle)? How can we encourage one another to grow? How can we do better at walking one another home?

37

Exodus 15:1–18

The Way Is Made by Worship

Then Moses and the Israelites sang this song to the LORD:

"I will sing to the LORD,
for he is highly exalted.
Both horse and driver
he has hurled into the sea.
"The LORD is my strength and my defense;
he has become my salvation.
He is my God, and I will praise him,
my father's God, and I will exalt him.
The LORD is a warrior;
the LORD is his name.
Pharaoh's chariots and his army
he has hurled into the sea.
The best of Pharaoh's officers
are drowned in the Red Sea.
The deep waters have covered them;
they sank to the depths like a stone.
Your right hand, LORD,
was majestic in power.
Your right hand, LORD,
shattered the enemy.
"In the greatness of your majesty
you threw down those who opposed you.
You unleashed your burning anger;
it consumed them like stubble.
By the blast of your nostrils
the waters piled up.
The surging waters stood up like a wall;
the deep waters congealed in the heart of the sea.

The enemy boasted,
'I will pursue, I will overtake them.
I will divide the spoils;
I will gorge myself on them.
I will draw my sword
and my hand will destroy them.'
But you blew with your breath,
and the sea covered them.
They sank like lead
in the mighty waters.
Who among the gods
is like you, LORD?
Who is like you—
majestic in holiness,
awesome in glory,
working wonders?
"You stretch out your right hand,
and the earth swallows your enemies.
In your unfailing love you will lead
the people you have redeemed.
In your strength you will guide them
to your holy dwelling.
The nations will hear and tremble;
anguish will grip the people of Philistia.
The chiefs of Edom will be terrified,
the leaders of Moab will be seized with trembling,
the people of Canaan will melt away;
terror and dread will fall on them.
By the power of your arm
they will be as still as a stone—
until your people pass by, LORD,
until the people you bought pass by.
You will bring them in and plant them
on the mountain of your inheritance—
the place, LORD, you made for your dwelling,

> *the sanctuary, Lord, your hands established.*
> *"The* Lord *reigns*
> *for ever and ever."*

Consider This

This short Latin phrase attributed to Saint Augustine captured my attention from the moment I read it: *Solvitur ambulando.*

Translation: "The way is made by walking."

This truth was on full display as the Israelites walked out of Egypt and through the Red Sea and now walk the way through the wilderness. The way is being made by walking. In today's devotional, they take it a step further. (See what I just did there?) Notice my amendment: The way is made by worship.

No fewer than six times we get some form of this decree from God to Pharaoh through Moses: "Then say to him, 'The Lord, the God of the Hebrews, has sent me to say to you: Let my people go, so that they may worship me in the wilderness'" (Exodus 7:16; 8:1, 20; 9:1, 13; 10:3).

Here's what strikes me about this word: God wants our worship in the wilderness.

He wants our worship in the midst of the difficulty of deliverance. Notice how the song in today's text begins with the nature of God and how it moves to the story of deliverance:

> I will sing to the Lord,
> for he is highly exalted.
> Both horse and driver
> he has hurled into the sea.

I sat across the table from a young man recently who is part of a powerful recovery ministry I have gotten involved with near where I live in southeast Arkansas. It's called ARM180. There was hardly a space on this man's arms without ink from tattoos. He told me the story of how Jesus delivered him from enslavement to drug addiction. Now he lives in the glorious freedom of the goodness of God. He was a worshiper in the wilderness. He knew in his bones that he had been set free from slavery so he might worship God in the wilderness en route to the promised land. I noticed what looked to be the centerpiece of the tattoo on one of his arms, which said, "Though he slay me, yet will I praise him" (inspired by Job 13:15).

Those are the words of a man who knows the cruelty of slavery in Egypt, who knows the difficult deliverance from Pharaoh, who knows the impossible crossing of the Red Sea, and who knows the challenge of walking the way of God in the wilderness. The way is made by worship. It reminded me of an insight Jesus had given me a few days earlier. The opposite of addiction is abiding.

The way is made by worship.

The Prayer for Deliverance

Lord Jesus, you are my Deliverer. I am learning that I am a worshiper. I am not a worshiper because I worship, but I worship because I am a worshiper. I confess that my soul is looking for someone or something to worship, whether I realize it or not. Deliver me from the worship of idols, which is whatever I think will make my life work and to which I become dependent on and even addicted to. Deliver me into the worship of the one true and living God, and teach me this way of worship in the wilderness like I have not yet known. Yes, Lord, the way is made by worship.

Glory be to the Father and to the Son and to the Holy Ghost.
As it was in the beginning, is now and ever shall be.
World without end. Amen! Amen!

The Questions

How are you discovering a way of worship in the wilderness? How are you pressing through acts and even songs of worship and into a heart of worship (i.e., "I will sing to the LORD, for he is highly exalted")? How are you celebrating the story of your deliverance in your worship of God (i.e., "Both horse and driver he has hurled into the sea")?

38

Exodus 15:22

From the Win to the Wilderness

> *Then Moses led Israel from the Red Sea and they went into the Desert of Shur. For three days they traveled in the desert without finding water.*

Consider This

And just like that, the Israelites descended from the Red Sea win into the waterless wilderness. Say it isn't so!

Let's be honest. We want a trouble-free life. We want our lives to be easier, not harder. We want to struggle less, not more. We expect that after a lifetime of cruel slavery and a cataclysmic deliverance like the Red Sea, we might be in for a nice, extended vacation at the beach. Instead of getting the beach, the Israelites got the desert.

> For three days they traveled in the desert without finding water.

But what if God's purpose is not to make our lives easier but to make our souls stronger?

This is the meaning of the wilderness.

We want to get out of the wilderness and into the promised land, but what if the wilderness is God's plan—not forever, but for a season? What if, in fact, the longer we resist the wilderness, the longer it will last? What if the sooner we submit to the Spirit's wilderness work in our lives, the sooner we enter into the destiny of God's promise for our lives?

And this kind of thinking, my friends, is our problem. As I wrote the last paragraph, I wanted it to be true, but the Spirit chided me. I have chosen to leave it in order to demonstrate just how seductive this kind of thinking can be. We think the wilderness is the exception, a short break from an otherwise prospering life. What if the wilderness is actually the rule? What if the will of God in the wilderness is to teach us the true meaning of prosperity—that it does not rise and fall with the tides of the stock market or our health or any other set of myriad circumstances constantly befalling us? The real prosperity gospel is the Father blessing us through Jesus with us and the Holy Spirit filling us—all the time, no matter what, come what may. It is through the fire that Jesus forges our souls with all his goodness and glory.

The apostle Paul showed us the outcome of a wilderness-tested soul:

> I am not saying this because I am in need, for I have learned to be content whatever the circumstances. I know what it is to be in need, and I know what it is to have plenty. I have learned the secret of being content in any and every situation, whether well fed or hungry, whether living in plenty or in want. I can do all this through him who gives me strength. (Philippians 4:11–13)

I will re-ask the question: What if the sooner we submit to the Spirit's wilderness work in our lives, the sooner we enter the destiny of God's promise for our lives? See the flaw in this thinking? It's like I'm saying the sooner we get the lesson of the wilderness, the sooner we get out of it. Here's the real question: What if the destiny of God's promise for our lives is different than we thought? Though the prosperity gospel intends well, it misses the point. In the kingdom of God, prosperity is not tied to our temporal circumstances.

Here's the lesson: God's promises and prosperity transcend our circumstances—need or plenty, hungry or full. The secret is *Christ in me*. This is why the wilderness is the proving ground of the Holy Spirit, who takes our circumstances and translates them into the deep formation of Jesus Christ in us. And this is the meaning of the wilderness—the strengthening of our souls in the midst of struggle through the power of the Holy Spirit. I'm going to say what we all know in our bones but don't want to be true: The wilderness is the rule of life, not the exception. The sooner we can accept this truth is not the sooner we can escape the wilderness but instead is the sooner we can embrace our destiny of true prosperity in Jesus in the wilderness.

The old hymn says it best: "When peace like a river attendeth my way, when sorrows like sea billows roll; whatever my lot, Thou has taught me to say, 'It is well, it is well with my soul.'"[1]

The Prayer for Deliverance

Lord Jesus, you are my Deliverer. Indeed, the horse and the rider you have thrown into the sea. And yet I sense a deeper exodus rising up in me. I receive your deliverance from the way my soul is tossed to and fro by my circumstances. If my life is smooth sailing, my soul is good, but if I run into stormy seas, my soul plunges into the depths. Deliver me from this thinness of soul and into the depths of the wellness of the presence of Jesus in me through the Holy Spirit—come what may—no matter what. Anyone can be happy when things are going well. Only Jesus can rejoice when conditions are collapsing. I desire the prosperity of Jesus in my deepest soul, who brings the land of promise smack dab in the middle of the wilderness. Yes, Lord, that! Please! I know this will require some unlearning in me and some new training. I am here for it. It will be for my good, for others' gain, and for your glory.

Glory be to the Father and to the Son and to the Holy Ghost.
As it was in the beginning, is now and ever shall be.
World without end. Amen! Amen!

The Questions

How difficult will it be to shift your mindset from trying to escape the discomfort of the wilderness to embracing God's purpose and prosperity in the wilderness? Why is this? What must you unlearn? What is the new learning?

---

1. "It Is Well with My Soul," Horatio Spafford, public domain.

39

Exodus 15:22–25

The Journey from Grumbling to Prayer

Then Moses led Israel from the Red Sea and they went into the Desert of Shur. For three days they traveled in the desert without finding water. When they came to Marah, they could not drink its water because it was bitter. (That is why the place is called Marah.) So the people grumbled against Moses, saying, "What are we to drink?"

Then Moses cried out to the Lord, and the Lord showed him a piece of wood. He threw it into the water, and the water became fit to drink.

There the Lord issued a ruling and instruction for them and put them to the test.

Consider This

We've all heard and said things like, "It's always something!" or "If it's not one thing, it's another." While one thing is happening, the next problem or challenge catches us by surprise. Things break. Tires go flat. Bones get broken. The wine runs out. Marriages collapse. Cancer strikes. Someone has a heart attack. Jobs are lost. Hard drives crash.

I remember, as a kid, riding out to the farm with my dad after a big rain. A rain in the midst of a drought is Christmas in July for a farmer. But Dad had to know exactly how much it rained—in every rain gauge! Per usual, after about the third rain gauge check, we would get the truck stuck in the thick, black, buckshot mud. Dad and I would walk a mile through the mud to get a tractor to pull the truck out, and what do you know—we would get the tractor stuck and walk another mile back to get yet another tractor. But it had rained, which was good news! And you see where this is going. I would learn lots of choice new vocabulary words on those outings. This is life.

This is wilderness.

> For three days they traveled in the desert without finding water.

A week earlier, the problem was Pharaoh. Three days earlier, the Red Sea was the obstacle. Now they couldn't find water to drink. Then the miracle happened and they found water, but there was a problem with the water—it was bitter and undrinkable.

It's always something! If it's not one thing, it's another.

> So the people grumbled against Moses, saying, "What are we to drink?"

Here's my question. These people knew how to cry out to the Lord. That's how they got out of Egypt. So why were they now grumbling at Moses? This brings us to Wilderness Lesson #1: While it's always easier to grumble at our leaders in the wilderness, the secret to success is crying out to God.

Watch Moses.

> Then Moses cried out to the LORD, and the LORD showed him a piece of wood. He threw it into the water, and the water became fit to drink.

Moses was starting to look more than a little Eagle Scout-ish here. Something tells me Moses knew a thing or two because he'd seen a thing or two. Here's what I love, though: Moses was not confident in himself but in God. Even better, I have a sense that Moses had learned to become confident in himself in God. This is my early hypothesis on Moses that I would like to test with you as we move along on this journey.

There is a progressive journey of maturity in the ways and means of God. We begin with a lack of self-confidence. We grow to master something and become self-confident. Still, the world has a way of beating the confidence out of us. Through the grace of our brokenness, we meet God and gain a whole new kind of confidence anchored in him.

People try to affirm us, and we deflect. We say things like, "That was not me. It was all God." At this stage, it is a zero-sum game. Either God gets the glory or I do, so I give it to God. We know it is not a "me and God thing," as though we were somehow partners. A lot of people want to believe this (I call it braunschweiger theology—think really nasty sausage in a paste form)—that God actually needs people to accomplish his will and is bereft without them. It's the sentiment behind those cute little poems that say things like, "God has no hands but our hands."

The next phase of maturity is the God-in-me phase, where I know it's not me but God in me doing the stuff. Here is where confidence in God flourishes. At this point, a willingness to descend into hiddenness will lead to the me-in-God phase, a sanctified confidence in ourselves, anchored not in ourselves but in our union with God. This is rarified air, and we see far too little of it. This is the place where God teaches us to stretch out our hand only to find it is his hand stretching out beyond us.

Finally, we come to the we-in-God phase, where we begin to find a kind of union with other people wholly anchored in union with God: Father, Son, and Holy Spirit. This is what the terribly misunderstood word *church* actually means. It is the deep and abiding trinitarian mystery of friendship. This is where the magic happens, where we participate in the answer to Jesus's prayer, "That all of them may be one, Father, just as you are in me and I am in you. May they also be in us so that the world may believe that you have sent me" (John 17:21).

Where can we learn such things but in the wilderness, where the Holy Spirit transforms our grumbling and complaining into outcries of prayer—where God shows us a piece of wood and gives us the sense to throw it in the bitter water, where he makes it fit to drink? And then we get this ponderous word:

> There the LORD issued a ruling and instruction for them and put them to the test.

Now, what could this be about? Keep walking.

The Prayer for Deliverance

Lord Jesus, you are my Deliverer. Thank you for the classroom of the wilderness. You are delivering me from seeing the wilderness as a place to escape to seeing it as the place where I am learning to embrace you and depend on you, as the place where desperation for relief transforms into delight in your nearness. For starters, today I receive your deliverance from grumbling to prayer. Thank you that you and your ways are the curriculum, and all I need to do is behold you, for as I behold you—I am being transformed from one degree of glory to the next (see 2 Corinthians 3:18). Keep moving me further on and deeper in until my confidence is unshakable in you in me and me in you. This is true holiness—when I am wholly yours, and you are wholly mine. Here I am, Lord. All of this for my good, for others' gain, for your glory.

> Glory be to the Father and to the Son and to the Holy Ghost.
> As it was in the beginning, is now and ever shall be.
> World without end. Amen! Amen!

The Questions

What do you think of this progression of mature faith: from God-with-me to God-in-me to me-in-God to we-in-God? Where else do you see it leading and moving? God through me and God through us? How do you understand yourself on this continuum? What might the next step of transformation look like?

40

Exodus 15:25–26

On Health, the Human Body, and the Glory of God

> *Then Moses cried out to the Lord, and the Lord showed him a piece of wood. He threw it into the water, and the water became fit to drink.*
>
> *There the Lord issued a ruling and instruction for them and put them to the test. He said, "If you listen carefully to the Lord your God and do what is right in his eyes, if you pay attention to his commands and keep all his decrees, I will not bring on you any of the diseases I brought on the Egyptians, for I am the Lord, who heals you."*

Consider This

Something tells me the Egyptians were not the healthiest people on the planet. After all, the Israelites were doing all their heavy lifting. There is a reference coming in chapter 16 to the fleshpots of Egypt and eating their fill of bread. It seems reasonable to infer that the Egyptians ate pretty high on the hog and steered clear of the gym. I mean, if their slaves were enjoying all-you-can-eat "fleshpots" buffets, imagine what the average Egyptian ate on a daily basis.

Later in Exodus, we will see God give the Israelites all sorts of dietary restrictions as part of the Mosaic law. These dietary laws had to do with ritual purity, and yet they also had to do with good health. Some of you see where this is headed—straight to the refrigerator!

Today we get a bit of a foreshadowing. God puts the Israelites on notice that health and healthy living matter. He doesn't want them to live like the Egyptians, who were presumably overweight, with dangerously high cholesterol, suffering from hypertension and prediabetes, and consuming massive quantities of high fructose corn syrup. I'm kidding—sort of. It seems clear to me that this is what was going on here:

> If you listen carefully to the Lord your God and do what is right in his eyes, if you pay attention to his commands and keep all his decrees, I will not bring on you any of the diseases I brought on the Egyptians, for I am the Lord, who heals you.

God cares about our bodies and our health. So many Christians live with the illusion of a hard separation between spiritual and physical things, with the former being superior to the latter. At this point in history, we are settled into the deep ruts of a dualistic worldview, which at times borders on gnosticism, pitting the soul or spirit against the physical body. This worldview dominates our culture, as evidenced by the insanity we are witnessing around matters of gender, sexuality, and the human body.

Our bodies matter. They carry enormous weight (in my case, too much weight). Hear Paul in his letter to the Corinthian Christians: "Do you not know that your bodies are temples of the Holy Spirit, who is in you, whom you have received from God? You are not your own; you were bought at a price. Therefore honor God with your bodies" (1 Corinthians 6:19–20). Though he referenced sexual ethics here, which also figure prominently in the Mosaic law, there are much broader implications for the point he made.

Paul's intention is that we honor God with our bodies. God did not bring the Israelites into the wilderness to put them on a diet. He aimed to comprehensively change their entire way of life. He was crafting a people who would live for the praise of his glory at every level of life.

Let's revisit the question Paul asked the Corinthians: "Do you not know that your bodies are temples of the Holy Spirit, who is in you, whom you have received from God?"

It's a question. Until recently, I think I knew that more in theory than in fact.

Some readers may remember when I shared with God and the whole Wake-Up Call community the confession that I was obese. I noted I had been overweight by as much as sixty pounds. I confessed that I had tried every diet and exercise plan under the sun and failed at them all, and that I sensed the Lord was calling me to something altogether different than I had tried before. He was inviting me to transfer the title of my physical body to its Creator and true owner. He let me know he wanted me to take his Word both literally and seriously and to offer my body as a living sacrifice, holy and pleasing to God as my spiritual act of worship (see Romans 12:1). I remember getting down on the floor that day and making an altar. I didn't ask God to help me. I invited God to have me—my physical body—as a living sacrifice; that I no longer claimed ownership. On that day, I became a steward of his property.

I am not sure how to describe what happened other than to say God received my offering, and things began to change. He began a deliverance on that day, which continues to the present one. It has been well over a year since that day. My entire relationship with my body has changed. My entire relationship with food has changed. And while I don't want to make this about weight loss, I will testify that I have lost a lot of weight. Let's just say I am getting back down to my fighting weight.

I think my overall witness concerning this would be "For I am the LORD, who heals you."

The Prayer for Deliverance

Lord Jesus, you are my Deliverer. I want to bring you my physical body. I want to say that I don't have a body but that I am a body. And I want to say that my body is actually your property. My body is your temple. I confess that I have either indulged my appetites or battled against them. I have tried to do so much in my own strength when what I have needed is your power. I am ready for a new and better way. You are the Lord, my Healer. I receive your deliverance from the brokenness of my body and my ways of seeing my body. Today I give you my body. I renounce my self-will to make it a showplace for my vanity. I offer it to you as a living sacrifice for your glory—I receive your deliverance of my body into a temple for the demonstration of your kingdom on earth as it is in heaven. I renounce the idolatry of weight loss. I seek your kingdom and your righteousness and trust you will bring the increase I need (or decrease, as the case may be). Let it be now for my good, for others' gain, and for your glory.

Glory be to the Father and to the Son and to the Holy Ghost.
As it was in the beginning, is now and ever shall be.
World without end. Amen! Amen!

The Questions

I know the offering of our bodies as living sacrifices is a hard subject for many, if not most. I'm concerned about you. I don't want you to self-shame or, worse, to rev up your striving to do better. I want you to be healed. Let's sit with this word from God today: My body is a temple of the Holy Spirit. I am not my own. I was bought with a price. I will honor God with my body—the Lord as my Healer. So how does your temple, aka your body, need healing?

41

Exodus 15:27

How to Take a Real Rest

Then they came to Elim, where there were twelve springs and seventy palm trees, and they camped there near the water.

Consider This

Elim looks a lot like Psalm 23 before there was Psalm 23.

> twelve springs and seventy palm trees

Doesn't that sound great? After all the trauma of Passover, the turmoil of the Red Sea, and three days of walking without water, Elim looks like the ancient equivalent of the Four Seasons or the Ritz-Carlton. What a relief and respite this must have been for those beleaguered Israelites. Twelve springs and seventy palm trees and making camp near the water.

God knows what we need, and he knows we regularly need retreat and refreshment. We tend to think of this as optional or indulgent, but it is a requirement for a well-formed soul. Jesus often took his disciples away for a retreat of rest and refreshment, though as time wore on, it became very difficult for them to escape the constant needs pressing in on them.

For the ten-plus years my family lived in Kentucky, I was blessed to live within a ninety-minute drive of a celebrated Trappist monastery, the Abbey of Gethsemane. About once every six weeks or so, I would drive over and spend a day walking the historic grounds, following the serpentine trail through the woods to the famed statues, chanting psalms with the monks, and otherwise pretending to be a good Catholic. They were days of attuning my hearing and seeing, and of listening for fresh words from God. Without fail, as sure as I became still and quiet, I would sense the inner impression of God's voice. It led me to this realization: If I hear from God every time I get still and quiet, he must always be speaking.

You might be wondering why I decided to stop here at the end of Exodus 15 to devote an entire entry to this single verse denoting a rather unspectacular occasion. As I reflect, it occurs to me that this is the point. Imagine the storytelling and the note comparisons and the remarkable remembrances of what God had done in the Israelites' midst. This is what retreat is all about.

When was the last time you enjoyed such a time? For future reference, it is not some kind of indulgence, nor is it optional for a solid soul. Wilderness life demands real rest.

The Prayer for Deliverance

Lord Jesus, you are my Deliverer. Today I want to simply hear your words of invitation to rest, as translated by my late friend Eugene Peterson from Matthew 11:

> Are you tired? Worn out? Burned out on religion? Come to me. Get away with me and you'll recover your life. I'll show you how to take a real rest. Walk with me and work with me—watch how I do it. Learn the unforced rhythms of grace. I won't lay anything heavy or ill-fitting on you. Keep company with me and you'll learn to live freely and lightly. (vv. 28–30 MSG)

Yes, Lord, we hear your invitation to come to you. That's the deliverance we need today. We receive it and all it will lead to. It will be for our good, for others' gain, and for your glory.

> Glory be to the Father and to the Son and to the Holy Ghost.
> As it was in the beginning, is now and ever shall be.
> World without end. Amen! Amen!

The Questions

When was the last time you took a time away for a restorative and reflective retreat with the Lord? What happened? Confession: It's been way too long for me. You too?

Week 6: Discussion Questions

Hearing the Text

Read Exodus 14:29–15:27.

Responding to the Text

- What did you hear?
- What did you see?
- What did you otherwise sense from the Lord?

Sharing Insights and Implications for Discipleship

Drawing from the Scripture text and daily readings, what did you find challenging, encouraging, provocative, comforting, invasive, inspiring, corrective, affirming, guiding, or warning?

Shaping Intentions for Prayer

Write your discipleship intention for the week ahead.

7
WEEK

Exodus 16:1–30

43

Exodus 16:1–3

The Wilderness Pivot from Feelings to Longings

The whole Israelite community set out from Elim and came to the Desert of Sin, which is between Elim and Sinai, on the fifteenth day of the second month after they had come out of Egypt. In the desert the whole community grumbled against Moses and Aaron. The Israelites said to them, "If only we had died by the LORD's hand in Egypt! There we sat around pots of meat and ate all the food we wanted, but you have brought us out into this desert to starve this entire assembly to death."

Consider This

In case there was ever any doubt, the honeymoon was officially over. Forty-five days in and the wheels were falling off.

> In the desert the whole community grumbled against Moses and Aaron.

Grumbling. What a word. It's the place where griping and complaining meet mumbling. It implies speaking against someone rather than talking to or with someone. Worse, it really takes two to grumble. It's something two or more people do together against someone else who is usually not present. Children grumble together against their parents. Parents grumble together against their children (and their parents too). Management grumbles together against labor. Employees grumble together against the boss. Parishioners grumble together against the pastor. Pastors grumble together against their flocks. Citizens grumble together against the mayor or governor or president or any number of their other duly elected representatives.

There is simply no end to our grumbling. Why do we grumble? We gripe and complain because our expectations are not being met. We mumble because we don't really want the people we are complaining about to hear us—otherwise, we would be talking to them instead of one another. Why is it that it feels so much more satisfying to commiserate with fellow dissidents than to confront directly? Grumbling is a very contagious infection. In this situation, the text tells us the whole community grumbled against Moses and Aaron. Finally, someone ponied up the courage and obedience to actually talk to them.

> The Israelites said to them, "If only we had died by the LORD's hand in Egypt! There we sat around pots of meat and ate all the food we wanted, but you have brought us out into this desert to starve this entire assembly to death."

Read that bit again and note how grumbling is filled with criticism and blaming, and in full bloom, it becomes open contempt. Most of the time, grumblers play the victim card, and they tend toward passive-aggressive behavior patterns. And truth be told, we have all done it and are prone to do it again. Why are we grumblers?

Better question: Why do I grumble?

Here's my take. It's because I tend to live at the level of my needs-and-wants-driven expectations rather than the deep-seated, God-given longings of my soul. I must get beneath the shallows of my needs-and-wants-driven expectations and entitlements I so readily foist on other people. Our needs and wants will lead us like breadcrumbs to our deeper longings. Because our core longings are God-given, they can only be God-filled. Emotions are things like anger, fear, sadness, happiness, surprise, and disgust. Those can easily lead to grumbling and complaining against other people. Core longings are things like love, safety, understanding, belonging, purpose, and significance. These are the deeper realities under the felt emotions.

So the next time you are feeling angry or sad (which are common causes of grumbling against other people), ask yourself this question: What am I really mad or sad about? Even better, ask God to show you what you are mad or sad about. Most of the time, it will be completely different than the situation or person you are grumbling against. It will be something like, "I'm sad because I feel alone in life right now and feel like my own children couldn't care less about me," or "I'm angry because I feel almost constantly misunderstood by my wife (and before that, my mother), and I can't get that across to her." The Israelites weren't mad at Moses and Aaron. They were mad because everything in their lives had changed, and they moved from a predictable existence (secure but awful) to an unpredictable life (which felt free but very insecure).

We must learn to make the wilderness pivot, which is the shift from wants-and-needs-driven expectations to core God-given longings. This will mean the movement from grumbling against people to groaning with God. As the Scripture says,

> We know that the whole creation has been groaning as in the pains of childbirth right up to the present time. Not only so, but we ourselves, who have the firstfruits of the Spirit, groan inwardly as we wait eagerly for our adoption to sonship, the redemption of our bodies. . . . In the same way, the Spirit helps us in our weakness. We do not know what we ought to pray for, but the Spirit himself intercedes for us through wordless groans. (Romans 8:22–23, 26)

From grumbling against Moses and Aaron to groaning before God? Sounds simple. It is simple. And hard. It would take them years to get it. This is wilderness life, remember? We have a major league unfair advantage, though. The Spirit is on constant standby, ever ready to help us.

The Prayer for Deliverance

Lord Jesus, you are my Deliverer. I confess that I see myself in these Israelites. I am a grumbler and a complainer. I want to grow beyond this. I receive your deliverance from this condition of allowing my feelings to dictate my actions. I receive your deliverance into feeling something beyond my feelings. I receive your deliverance into access to my core longings—the ones you put in me and the ones only you can fulfill. Would you unveil the brokenness in my inmost self, those ways I have tried to get my core longings met by other means? And would you unravel the mess that I made by filling my longings with things that could never satisfy them? And would you forgive me for the ways I have hurt other people in that process, trying to selfishly make them more than they could ever become? You are the Lord, my Healer. I receive your healing. And would you train my innermost self to live and move and process at these new levels, not being driven by impulses but led by longings back to you? Teach me to groan with the Holy Spirit instead of grumbling at other people. All of this will be for my good, others' gain, and your glory.

Glory be to the Father and to the Son and to the Holy Ghost.
As it was in the beginning, is now and ever shall be.
World without end. Amen! Amen!

The Questions

What does today's text and reflection provoke in you? How are you identifying? What unmet core longings cause you the most struggle? Can you see patterns of broken behavior that have led to struggles in relationships as a result? Will you bring this before the Lord today? He can sort it out, but it may take time. Sharing such things with your study group is also a good path.

44

Exodus 16:4–5

The Wonder of the Wilderness

Then the LORD said to Moses, "I will rain down bread from heaven for you. The people are to go out each day and gather enough for that day. In this way I will test them and see whether they will follow my instructions. On the sixth day they are to prepare what they bring in, and that is to be twice as much as they gather on the other days."

Consider This

The Israelites pined for the good old days back in the land of slavery and those all-you-can-eat buffets. They sat around pots of meat and ate all the food they wanted (see Exodus 16:3).

Now is the appropriate moment to recite one of our favorite wilderness prayers: "Lord, you took me out of Egypt. Now take Egypt out of me."

Here's one of the biggest revelations in life: We long for God. We will settle for food.

I'll take it a step further. When we try to fill up our longing for God with food, we overeat. Further, when we try to fill up our longing for God with drink, we overdrink. Let's reverse the phrase: When we overeat or overdrink, we are trying to satisfy our longing for God.

We may overdo things like eat and drink without even knowing. Consider the oft-used phrases of "comfort food" or "soul food." Am I saying that eating and drinking are bad? No. I am saying that overeating and overdrinking are not good. We should pay attention to them in our lives for they are pointing to a much deeper dynamic at play. Further, overeating and overdrinking destroy the health of the body (aka the temple of God) and over time desecrate the body's internal infrastructure: the innermost being.

The core longing of the human being, created by God in God's own image, is for God alone. We were made to worship God—which is the totalizing orientation of our whole lives around the goodness and glory of God. This is where life comes from. When we orient our lives around other things, like food and drink (and money and thousands of other things), we think they will deliver life. They offer us brief boosts or escapes or highs, and in the process, they slowly steal our lives because they demand more value from us for the next round. Worship is not singing songs on a Sunday. No, worship is the everyday reality and relationship with the provider to whom we attribute value and worth, and the reception of provision, protection, and peace from this provider.

The issue is not whether we are worshiping. The issue is what god we are worshiping. Is it the one true and living God, or is it a false god—in which case our worship is idolatry? Idolatry is the process of giving worth to a false god in exchange for some manner of provision. It invariably leads to a cycle of dependence and often addiction, which promises life while delivering death. This is why we need deliverance. Egypt is that complex calculus of how we survived slavery and made our lives work without the intimate involvement and constant intervention of almighty God. The wilderness is the place where God takes Egypt out of us.

This brings me back to the big learning: We long for God. We will settle for food.

Now, with that setup, consider today's text:

> Then the LORD said to Moses, "I will rain down bread from heaven for you. The people are to go out each day and gather enough for that day. In this way I will test them and see whether they will follow my instructions. On the sixth day they are to prepare what they bring in, and that is to be twice as much as they gather on the other days."

I AM WHO I AM (aka God) established himself as the Israelites' protector in delivering them from Pharaoh. The problem is they had given themselves to Pharaoh, willingly or not, as slaves. In exchange, he gave them all-you-can-eat buffets. Now, I AM would begin the long deliverance process of taking Pharaoh out of them. I AM's next move would be to become their provider. He would supply them with food—not all-you-can-eat pots of meat—but daily bread from heaven. This is the wonder of the wilderness . . . bread from heaven . . . wonder bread.

Now, consider this:

> I am the living bread that came down from heaven. Whoever eats this bread will live forever. This bread is my flesh, which I will give for the life of the world. (John 6:51)

> Then Jesus declared, "I am the bread of life. Whoever comes to me will never go hungry, and whoever believes in me will never be thirsty." (John 6:35)

And he took bread, gave thanks and broke it, and gave it to them, saying, "This is my body given for you; do this in remembrance of me." (Luke 22:19)

The Prayer for Deliverance

Lord Jesus, you are my Deliverer. I'm not sure where to begin today, so I will begin with gratitude. Thank you for being my provider, my protector, and my peace. I confess my broken appetites, my unstable insecurity, and my anxious disposition. I confess to giving value and worth to so many other things to meet these core longings in my soul—which can only be oriented and integrated in you. I have believed lies and trusted liars. I was desperate. As much as my money and my possessions may try to convince otherwise, I am still desperate.

I am ready to detach from the false gods of food and drink. I am ready to know you as God, my provider. I am ready to orient my whole life around giving worth to you and receiving worth from you. Thank you for being my teacher in the wilderness. Thank you, Jesus, for teaching me to hunger and thirst for righteousness. I'm done with false religion. Jesus, you are life. Let's go!

Glory be to the Father and to the Son and to the Holy Ghost.
As it was in the beginning, is now and ever shall be.
World without end. Amen! Amen!

The Questions

What has been your experience with fasting? Struggle? Success? Some of both? Why do you think fasting is so hard for us? For you?

45

Exodus 16:6–12

On the Foible of Relational Triangulation

So Moses and Aaron said to all the Israelites, "In the evening you will know that it was the Lord *who brought you out of Egypt, and in the morning you will see the glory of the* Lord*, because he has heard your grumbling against him. Who are we, that you should grumble against us?" Moses also said, "You will know that it was the* Lord *when he gives you meat to eat in the evening and all the bread you want in the morning, because he has heard your grumbling against him. Who are we? You are not grumbling against us, but against the* Lord*."*

Then Moses told Aaron, "Say to the entire Israelite community, 'Come before the Lord*, for he has heard your grumbling.'"*

While Aaron was speaking to the whole Israelite community, they looked toward the desert, and there was the glory of the Lord *appearing in the cloud.*

The Lord *said to Moses, "I have heard the grumbling of the Israelites. Tell them, 'At twilight you will eat meat, and in the morning you will be filled with bread. Then you will know that I am the* Lord *your God.'"*

Consider This

Something in us does not want to deal with God. Truth be told, we don't want to deal with one another either. Could this be our greatest foible as a species—we do not want to deal directly with God or neighbor? Translation: We prefer to talk about people rather than to them. We would rather withdraw from God and grumble than groan with his Spirit. Deep within us we prefer to triangulate our relationships, diverting our case to a third party, rather than deal directly with the other person involved in the conflict.

Look carefully at the priestly work of Moses and Aaron.

"Who are we, that you should grumble against us?" Moses also said, "You will know that it was the LORD when he gives you meat to eat in the evening and all the bread you want in the morning, because he has heard your grumbling against him. Who are we? You are not grumbling against us, but against the LORD."

They were collapsing the triangle.

Then Moses told Aaron, "Say to the entire Israelite community, 'Come before the LORD, for he has heard your grumbling.'"

The work of a priest is to bring God and people together. We tend to think of a priest as someone who stands up at the front of a church and leads people in religious ceremonies. Priestly work is not ceremonial in nature. From beginning to end, priestly work is relational. Priests represent people to God, God to people, and people to people. God has always imagined his people as a kingdom of priests—people who help one another stay in direct, right relationship with God and with one another.

Living in a direct and right relationship with God paves the way to live in direct and right relationship with ourselves but also nurtures direct and right relationships with others. This is why the greatest commandment is so simple.

> "Love the Lord your God with all your heart and with all your soul and with all your mind." This is the first and greatest commandment. And the second is like it: "Love your neighbor as yourself." All the Law and the Prophets hang on these two commandments. (Matthew 22:37–40)

We must learn from the priestly work of Aaron and Moses to deal directly and primarily with God. As priests to one another, we have a sacred responsibility to collapse triangles, helping people relate rightly and directly with God and one another.

People tend to go in one of two broken directions in the face of conflict. They will under-own their fault and withdraw, or they will over-own their fault and pursue. What is your broken tendency with respect to interpersonal conflict?

Okay, I'll go first. I often under-own and withdraw. That is an aggressive way of being passive. So I ask myself the bigger question: What is it about me that makes me withdraw instead of trying to heal the broken relationship? I don't know. So I ask God, "Why do I do this?" And he whispers through the inner voice, "You are afraid of being rejected." And just like that, the deep fear of being alone and isolated is exposed, and the core longing of deep belonging is unveiled.

It makes sense, doesn't it? In the face of potential rejection, I withdraw, which is my way of rejecting the other person first. Next, I will discreetly and confidentially share this situation with a sympathizing friend who will support me in my position (aka triangulation). This is how cancer gets into a relationship or a family or a company. A lot more could be said here, but it's your turn.

The health and wellness of an organization—be it a family, a church, or a multinational corporation—will be the level with which people deal directly with God and with one another and resist triangulating their relationships. It's why grace and forgiveness and making amends are so critical. I hope I've made it clear that our capacity to live in right, direct relationships with one another comes from living in a right, direct relationship with God, which is only possible through the author of grace and pioneer and perfecter of our faith, Jesus Christ. It's why one of my mantras in life, in family, with church, and in work is "Our relationships are the mission."

The Prayer for Deliverance

Lord Jesus, you are my Deliverer. Would you reveal to me the deeper wisdom of your will and ways in the wilderness? Show me how I sin in my relationships, and then unveil to me the deeper reason behind my sin. Expose my fear and unveil my longings. I am tired of the lazy truces I settle for in life when what I need is healing. I look for sympathizers when what I need is a priest. Lead me to priestly friends and make me such a friend to others. And would you reveal to me the brokenness in my relationship with you and show me how all of this is bound up together? Finally, would you deliver me from this mess and into real peace and love in all my relationships?

Glory be to the Father and to the Son and to the Holy Ghost.
As it was in the beginning, is now and ever shall be.
World without end. Amen! Amen!

The Questions

Okay, your turn. What is your broken tendency in relational conflict? Are you an over-owner (peacekeeper) or an avoider-distancer? Do you have a tendency toward triangulation? What is it, in particular, about you that makes you this way? Try asking God.

46

Exodus 16:13–18

When Enough Is Truly Enough

That evening quail came and covered the camp, and in the morning there was a layer of dew around the camp. When the dew was gone, thin flakes like frost on the ground appeared on the desert floor. When the Israelites saw it, they said to each other, "What is it?" For they did not know what it was.

Moses said to them, "It is the bread the Lord has given you to eat. This is what the Lord has commanded: 'Everyone is to gather as much as they need. Take an omer for each person you have in your tent.'"

The Israelites did as they were told; some gathered much, some little. And when they measured it by the omer, the one who gathered much did not have too much, and the one who gathered little did not have too little. Everyone had gathered just as much as they needed.

Consider This

Give us this day our daily bread . . . and quail.

Cloud by day. Fire by night. Quail in the evening. Bread in the morning.

See if you can spot the word between the words in today's text. It is not written in English but is clearly present.

> The Israelites did as they were told; some gathered much, some little. And when they measured it by the omer, the one who gathered much did not have too much, and the one who gathered little did not have too little. Everyone had gathered just as much as they needed.

Enough.

No one had too much. No one had too little. Everyone had enough.

Over the centuries, people and societies have attempted to accomplish this outcome. From cults to communes and from communism to utopian visions of socialist nations, these idealistic fantasies always fail. Why? This kind of outcome cannot be legislated or governed into existence. Why? Because this is the kingdom of God we are talking about, not the kingdoms of this world.

So does this mean a community where everyone has enough is a pipe dream and not possible in a fallen world? No. Nothing is impossible with God.

It brings us to seven remarkable words in today's text. These words are the secret to the miracle of enough.

> The Israelites did as they were told.

The pathway toward enough is found through obedience to God alone. Obedience is perhaps the greatest lesson the wilderness can teach us. There's not really a word for "obey" in the Hebrew language. The concept of obedience is derived from the Hebrew word *shema*, which means "to hear." It's like when you don't do what your mom told you, and she says, "Do you hear me?" Obedience is not compliance with the rules; rather, it is a demonstration by faith. And where does the Bible say faith comes from?

Yes, hearing. "Faith comes from hearing, and hearing through the word of Christ" (Romans 10:17 ESV). Bringing it full circle, remember the Shema, "Hear O Israel: The Lord our God, the Lord is one" (Deuteronomy 6:4). Obedience is all about trusting the one you are listening to.

Sure, it is perhaps naive to believe that everyone will one day obey God. And, truth be told, it only takes a few to get the movement going. Obedience is contagious because once a few people start to obey, the Holy Spirit brings the momentum of movement. Others, who perhaps lacked the courage at first, will begin to lean in and join the movement. I think that's what Jesus had in mind when he said, "Therefore go and make disciples of all nations, baptizing them in the name of the Father and of the Son and of the Holy Spirit, and teaching them to *obey* everything I have commanded you. And surely I am with you always, to the very end of the age" (Matthew 28:19–20, emphasis added).

I have dedicated my life in recent years to this work with the Wake-Up Call—to help each other *hear* the Word of God, even to teach one another to obey everything Jesus commanded us.

We have enough to do this job. We have the Word of God and the Spirit of God and the Lord of the church on the job with us.

Completing the circle now: Obedience is enough. It is the enough that leads to *enoughness*—which is all we need to flourish.

The Prayer for Deliverance

Lord Jesus, you are my Deliverer. I confess that I am part hard of hearing and part hard-hearted, and I know those two things are somehow connected. Would you deliver me from both my deafness as it comes to hearing your Word and hard-heartedness as it comes to trusting what you say? Deliver me into a keenness of hearing, of having a heart that listens intently and trusts instinctively. I do love you with all my heart and with all my soul and with all my mind, and with all my strength.

Glory be to the Father and to the Son and to the Holy Ghost.
As it was in the beginning, is now and ever shall be.
World without end. Amen! Amen!

The Questions

Where are you on the journey of becoming an enough kind of person? Where might the Lord be asking for your obedience right now?

47

Exodus 16:19–20

Where Maggots Come From

> *Then Moses said to them, "No one is to keep any of it until morning."*
> *However, some of them paid no attention to Moses; they kept part of it until morning, but it was full of maggots and began to smell. So Moses was angry with them.*

Consider This

So, those seven significant words from yesterday's text: "The Israelites did as they were told" (Exodus 16:17)—maybe we spoke too soon.

Moses spoke clearly:

> "No one is to keep any of it until morning."

> However, some of them paid no attention to Moses; they kept part of it until morning.

What might it mean that the Israelites paid no attention? Here is a spectrum of possibilities.

1. They didn't hear what he said.
2. They didn't understand what he meant.
3. They heard the command and forgot.
4. They heard the command and considered it was unjust.
5. They heard the command and were afraid they would not have enough.

6. They heard the command and considered it didn't apply to them.
7. They heard the command and considered they deserved an exception.
8. They heard the command and paid it no regard.
9. They heard the command and willfully defied the authority.

We see in this spectrum ranging from ignorance to negligence to recklessness to willfulness the nuances of disobedience and sin.

There is another line of analysis here. Why would they keep the manna overnight? Maybe they took more than enough to begin with? Maybe they feared there would not be a fresh supply the next day. Is there any real harm here? What if it were toilet paper? What if the Lord put on our doorstep each morning just enough toilet paper for one day? And what if he instructed us to keep none until morning? Would we obey? Only if we really trusted God.

We want to trust God, but we also want a backup plan. We want to hedge the bet just in case our toilet paper—I mean manna—doesn't show up one day. What's so bad about that? Maybe it's not a matter of good versus bad or obedience versus disobedience. What if the real issue is fear versus faith? Will we trust in God's provision or our own? This is the lesson of the wilderness.

Jesus had something to say on this point:

> Therefore I tell you, do not worry about your life, what you will eat or drink; or about your body, what you will wear. Is not life more than food, and the body more than clothes? Look at the birds of the air; they do not sow or reap or store away in barns, and yet your heavenly Father feeds them. Are you not much more valuable than they? (Matthew 6:25–26)

This is so challenging. I'll admit, it even seems unreasonable. We can disagree with it. We can even choose to pay no attention to it. One thing we can't do is say he didn't mean it. At a very minimum, we must grapple with it. The kingdom of God is a very different place than the kingdom of the world, and the wilderness is the place where everything gets sorted out—the wheat from the chaff.

> However, some of them paid no attention to Moses; they kept part of it until morning, but it was full of maggots and began to smell. So Moses was angry with them.

When we don't pay attention to the instructions of God, we run the risk of seeing the happiness of manna turn into the horror of maggots. How can something so good turn into something so bad? I think we know the answer.

The Prayer for Deliverance

Lord Jesus, you are my Deliverer. Would you reveal to me the deeper wisdom of your will and ways in the wilderness? I'm not a hoarder, but I do like a backup plan. I want to believe I trust you, and yet something about this teaching challenges me to ask deeper questions of myself. I have absolutely no reason not to trust you, and yet I hedge. Deliver me from my fearfulness that there will not be enough. Deliver me into a state of trusting in you. In fact, I welcome you to deliver me into an unreasonable faith—a faith that stretches beyond reason. Something tells me that would please your heart.

Glory be to the Father and to the Son and to the Holy Ghost.
As it was in the beginning, is now and ever shall be.
World without end. Amen! Amen!

The Questions

So, back to the faith-fear scaling exercise. On a scale of 1–10, what is your level of fear that you do not or will not have enough to provide for your needs? Now subtract that from 10, and you will have your level of faith that God will supply all your needs. What about that? Does your fear of maggots exceed your fear of manna?

48

Exodus 16:21–30

Finding the Unforced Rhythms of Grace

Each morning everyone gathered as much as they needed, and when the sun grew hot, it melted away. On the sixth day, they gathered twice as much—two omers for each person—and the leaders of the community came and reported this to Moses. He said to them, "This is what the Lord commanded: 'Tomorrow is to be a day of sabbath rest, a holy sabbath to the Lord. So bake what you want to bake and boil what you want to boil. Save whatever is left and keep it until morning.'"

So they saved it until morning, as Moses commanded, and it did not stink or get maggots in it. "Eat it today," Moses said, "because today is a sabbath to the Lord. You will not find any of it on the ground today. Six days you are to gather it, but on the seventh day, the Sabbath, there will not be any."

Nevertheless, some of the people went out on the seventh day to gather it, but they found none. Then the Lord said to Moses, "How long will you refuse to keep my commands and my instructions? Bear in mind that the Lord has given you the Sabbath; that is why on the sixth day he gives you bread for two days. Everyone is to stay where they are on the seventh day; no one is to go out." So the people rested on the seventh day.

Consider This

A transformative movement was afoot here in the wilderness. It takes getting a little altitude over it to see, but it was taking shape.

The Israelites had lived the last long stretch of their history as slaves under the cruel oppression of Pharaoh. They had no control over their lives. Every day was the same. They probably had more in common with livestock than with the Egyptians around them. Their lives were not ordered; they were controlled.

All of a sudden, they were delivered from Egypt and the land of slavery—no longer slaves but free people. So, how do people live free when all they have ever known is slavery? Like accident or stroke victims who must relearn how to walk and eat and many other basic life functions, slaves must relearn how to live as free people. They must be discipled into a new way of life.

The wilderness season is all about discipleship.

Notice the gracious order emerging. What could have been an otherwise chaotic experience in the wilderness becomes structure, rhythm, and direction established by God. Cloud by day and fire by night. Quail in the evening and manna in the morning. Take only what is needed; no hoarding. Today we see a new feature of this gracious order: Sabbath. Six days of gathering, one day of rest. Slaves don't get Sabbath. Free people do.

If quail in the evening and manna every morning were not miraculous enough, notice the weekly miracle co-occurring with Sabbath. The same manna that would, if kept overnight, turn into maggots, miraculously maintained freshness one night every week prior to the Sabbath. Further, manna did not appear on the Sabbath day. This is exquisite, care-filled provision. This is our God. It's why he says things like this: "But seek first his kingdom and his righteousness, and all these things will be given to you as well" (Matthew 6:33).

I bet you can see the analogy and application. We are all born into slavery—the slavery of sin and death. Jesus will deliver anyone who follows him out of this cruel slavery and into a life of freedom and promise. We are saved by the blood of the Lamb. We are delivered by the decree and declaration of the Word of God. We experience freedom by the Spirit of God and then fullness to overflowing. There is deliverance, and then there is discipleship. Deliverance must be followed by discipleship. We witness the gracious order of the kingdom as we are discipled into the lifestyle of the King.

The transformative movement of salvation then and now is as follows: Egypt. Red Sea. Wilderness. Promised land. Deliverance + Discipleship = Transformational Glory

I want to issue a caution here. It is easy to shift from a life of everything being controlled by Pharaoh to a life of trying to control everything ourselves, including our faith and relationship with God. This usually looks like some form of designer religion, which people sometimes mistake for discipleship. It is not.

Discipleship to Jesus is life. It is not seven more principles, eight more practices, and ten more habits to add to your life. In recent years, I have begun to see all manner of what I would call "designer religion" springing up all over the place. It is an industry. Beware of complicating discipleship with lots of rules and feature sets and spiritual practices and rhythms. Jesus, who is life, will not be controlled by a program of rigorous religion. He brings the unforced rhythms of grace. I find that religion is often something people endlessly try to cobble together to make their lives work. Jesus is not religion. Jesus is life. He keeps things simple. We do need an ever-deepening understanding of the simplicity of Jesus. We don't need an endlessly complicated spirituality with lots of moving parts.

The Prayer for Deliverance

Lord Jesus, you are my Deliverer. You are unveiling and revealing the unforced rhythms of grace: Cloud by day and fire by night. Manna in the morning and quail in the evening. Six days of work and one day of rest. The way is made by worship. The path is walked by deliverance and discipleship. Your provision is both exquisite and extravagant. Thank you for the complexity of your care of us. And it is all a gift. All that is required is for us to receive it, and by faith we do. Grant us the grace to follow your gracious commands. You have delivered us from sin and into righteousness. Would you now disciple us into the fullness of life in your kingdom? It will be for our good, for others' gain, and for your glory.

Glory be to the Father and to the Son and to the Holy Ghost.
As it was in the beginning, is now and ever shall be.
World without end. Amen! Amen!

The Questions

How are you discovering and engaging with these unforced rhythms of grace? What about this pattern of Sabbath, of work and rest? (Or are you still caught in the weekend model, which is often just escaping into some form of entertainment (which isn't all bad) and/or trading one to-do list for another to-do list?)

Week 7: Discussion Questions

Hearing the Text

Read Exodus 16:1–30.

Responding to the Text

- What did you hear?
- What did you see?
- What did you otherwise sense from the Lord?

Sharing Insights and Implications for Discipleship

Drawing from the Scripture text and daily readings, what did you find challenging, encouraging, provocative, comforting, invasive, inspiring, corrective, affirming, guiding, or warning?

Shaping Intentions for Prayer

Write your discipleship intention for the week ahead.

8
WEEK

Exodus 16:31–18:12

50

Exodus 16:31–36

Take That, Science!

The people of Israel called the bread manna. It was white like coriander seed and tasted like wafers made with honey. Moses said, "This is what the Lord has commanded: 'Take an omer of manna and keep it for the generations to come, so they can see the bread I gave you to eat in the wilderness when I brought you out of Egypt.'"

So Moses said to Aaron, "Take a jar and put an omer of manna in it. Then place it before the Lord to be kept for the generations to come."

As the Lord commanded Moses, Aaron put the manna with the tablets of the covenant law, so that it might be preserved. The Israelites ate manna forty years, until they came to a land that was settled; they ate manna until they reached the border of Canaan.

(An omer is one-tenth of an ephah.)

Consider This

So, I have a question for Moses. How much is an ephah?

Seriously, that last parenthetical bit warms my heart.

> (An omer is one-tenth of an ephah.)

It tells me this. If Moses could have done it, he would have translated an ephah into pounds or fluid ounces or liters or whatever the measurement of the day might be. And suddenly, I remembered the internet, so I googled, "How much is an omer in today's measurements?" I got this: "An omer is a unit of measurement in the Bible that is equivalent to about 2.3 liters (0.61 US gallons) in today's measurements. It is also equivalent to the volume of 43.2 chicken eggs, or one-tenth of an ephah. In dry weight, an omer weighs between 1.56–1.77 kg (3.4–3.9 lb)."[1]

1. "How Much Is an Omer in Pounds?," Quora, accessed August 4, 2025, https://www.quora.com/How-much-is-an-omer-in-pounds.

Further, it told me the word *omer* is sometimes translated as "sheaf" and is the amount of grain large enough to be bundled together.

Why does all this detail matter? Because this is the stuff of history and not mythology. This is not a "once upon a time" story but, as Exodus 16:1 reports, an "on the fifteenth day of the second month after they had come out of Egypt" reality. Faith and religion readily get filed in the category of spirituality, and spirituality is inherently subjective and mystical and impossible to measure. And things mystical and unmeasurable, in time, become mythological. And centuries later they get cataloged in the "warm and fuzzy" fairy tale section of the bookstore. Moses was saying that this thing that was happening right then—this wonder bread that would miraculously appear on the desert floor every morning for the next forty years—was not that. It was as real as real gets. It could be measured and preserved and verified and seen with the eyes and touched with the hands.

> So Moses said to Aaron, "Take a jar and put an omer of manna in it. Then place it before the LORD to be kept for the generations to come."

Moses knew us. He knew we would never believe him if he just said manna mysteriously appeared on the desert floor every morning. He knew some of us would immediately spiritualize it and then turn it into some kind of metaphor, while others of us would mythologize it and explain that these ancient people were children of their age and hadn't yet arrived at the scientific revolution, which would explain how everything that couldn't be measured couldn't be proved. He knew us. Therefore he gave us this:

> (An omer is one-tenth of an ephah.)

Take that scientific method. It is 2.3 liters or .61 US gallons or just under 4 pounds dry.

Here's my big takeaway. The deliverance we need now is *from* religion and *into* reality. We must be delivered from our faith in God as religion and into our faith in God as everyday life. We must be delivered from our faith in God as subjective spirituality and into our faith in God as concrete reality.

It is not a matter of subjectivity and feeling but of something that can be measured and put in a jar and, as the text says so clearly, "kept for the generations to come."

It's in that same category that we will later see these words: "That which was from the beginning, which we have heard, which we have seen with our eyes, which we have looked at and our hands have touched—this we proclaim concerning the Word of life" (1 John 1:1).

The Prayer for Deliverance

Lord Jesus, you are my Deliverer. Thank you for revealing to us that an omer is one-tenth of an ephah and that it will almost fit into a half gallon mason jar. Thank you that the burning bush was a real bush burning with real fire and for the real miracle that it was not burning up. Thank you that you don't provide fuzzy feelings of spiritual support but of concrete bread that fills our empty stomachs and sustains our real lives. We receive your deliverance from a faith that feels like religion and into a faith that interacts and engages with real life. We receive your deliverance from religion as mythological stories and church as a sociological support group and into faith as an impenetrable shield and church as the only order on the face of the earth that the gates of hell cannot prevail against. Would you lead us into a way of discipleship and disciple-making that is of another order of magnitude from the thin and anemic version we have adopted? It will be for our good, for others' gain, and for your glory.

Glory be to the Father and to the Son and to the Holy Ghost.
As it was in the beginning, is now and ever shall be.
World without end. Amen! Amen!

The Questions

Have you tended to see faith in the category of subjective spirituality and even self-help philosophy? What will it take to bring faith out of these categories and back into the realm of hard data and concrete life? How might we help scientists understand that they stand on the shoulders of cosmologists and theologians?

51

Exodus 17:1–3

"I Thirst!"

> *The whole Israelite community set out from the Desert of Sin, traveling from place to place as the Lord commanded. They camped at Rephidim, but there was no water for the people to drink. So they quarreled with Moses and said, "Give us water to drink."*
>
> *Moses replied, "Why do you quarrel with me? Why do you put the Lord to the test?"*
>
> *But the people were thirsty for water there, and they grumbled against Moses. They said, "Why did you bring us up out of Egypt to make us and our children and livestock die of thirst?"*

Consider This

Is anyone thirsty?

The truth: Everyone is thirsty. Really, really thirsty.

It is fascinating how God provided quail in the evening and manna in the morning, yet he was willing to let the Israelites struggle and suffer with a lack of water. Why did he allow them to thirst? The average parent never tells their children to make sure they eat enough on a hot day, but you can bet they will tell them to drink lots of water. We can go quite a while without food, but we would never even consider fasting from water.

The Israelites added a new feature to their grumbling habit—quarreling. Look at Moses's terse response:

> Moses replied, "Why do you quarrel with me? Why do you put the Lord to the test?"

They only wanted a drink, Moses. How is that testing the Lord? They were thirsty.

Here's my take. Something about thirst creates desperation. Something about desperation focuses prayer. Something about prayers of desperation creates a context for divine breakthroughs. Something about divine breakthroughs transforms nominal religion into blazing faith. Something about blazing faith changes not just one life but transforms entire communities and traverses up and down generational lines.

Remember where we started—thirst creates desperation. Thirst is the setup for the miracle.

God allows them and us to thirst because he wants to give us the gift of desperation.

There is a profound connection between the thirst of our physical bodies and the much deeper thirst of our souls. Our souls thirst for the Spirit of God like people walking for days in the wilderness thirst for water. We try to quench our thirst in every conceivable way, yet our thirst only deepens.

I've always been fascinated by liquor stores often being called "spirit shops." There's something really ancient in this connection between drinking and spirits. In fact, Paul confirms the connection in his exhortation, "Do not get drunk on wine, which leads to debauchery. Instead, be filled with the Spirit" (Ephesians 5:18). It's why addiction has been called the sacred disease. Here is a great mystery, though. How is it that the people who drink the most alcohol become the greatest at living in denial of their thirst for it?

Here is a great truth: the deepest, most profound, and otherwise unquenchable thirst of every person on planet Earth is for God—namely, the Holy Spirit. Do we really believe this?

As we close today, let's remember this story from the Gospel of John.

Jesus once made a secret trip from Galilee to Jerusalem for the Feast of Tabernacles. This feast commemorated the Israelites' wilderness years. For the memory to lead them into the mystery and back into the movement, people would make little brush arbor huts and live in them throughout the feast.

By this time in John's gospel, Jesus was a wanted man, and he lay low for most of the week. He did some teaching in the temple courts. And then John shared this bit:

> On the last and greatest day of the festival, Jesus stood and said in a loud voice, "Let anyone who is thirsty come to me and drink. Whoever believes in me, as Scripture has said, rivers of living water will flow from within them." By this, he meant the Spirit, whom those who believed in him were later to receive. Up to that time, the Spirit had not been given, since Jesus had not yet been glorified. (John 7:37–39)

Here's the thing about thirst. As Jesus quenches our thirst with the gift of the Holy Spirit, we find ourselves both satisfied yet thirsting for more. This is the great challenge and inestimable gift of the wilderness. There is always more.

The Prayer for Deliverance

Lord Jesus, you are my Deliverer. We hear you from the cross speaking those words, "I thirst." You said them for yourself, and yet you said them for us—even for me. Yes, Lord, I thirst. Would you deliver me into the reality of my thirst, even let me walk around for days without water to unveil it? I receive your deliverance into real thirst and then from this kind of thirst into real drink. Put me in touch with the desperation of my soul to drink living water from the well of Jesus and disciple me into the experience of rivers of living water flowing from within me. It will be for my good, for others' gain, and for your glory.

> Glory be to the Father and to the Son and to the Holy Ghost.
> As it was in the beginning, is now and ever shall be.
> World without end. Amen! Amen!

The Questions

Are you in touch with your thirst? Do you know an experience of desperation for more of God? Are you willing to become more real with this than ever before—not religious, but real?

52

Exodus 17:4–7

From Ambivalence to Awakening

Then Moses cried out to the Lord, "What am I to do with these people? They are almost ready to stone me."

The Lord answered Moses, "Go out in front of the people. Take with you some of the elders of Israel and take in your hand the staff with which you struck the Nile, and go. I will stand there before you by the rock at Horeb. Strike the rock, and water will come out of it for the people to drink." So Moses did this in the sight of the elders of Israel. And he called the place Massah and Meribah because the Israelites quarreled and because they tested the Lord saying, "Is the Lord among us or not?"

Consider This

Is anyone thirsty?

The wilderness is a place where physical thirst points to the thirst of the soul. Things were not connecting for the Israelites. Despite extraordinary demonstrations of God's miraculous favor, not only did they have no faith, but they wanted to go back to their former lives.

This encounter at Meribah proved to be a tipping point in the wrong direction for the Israelites as far as God was concerned. Years later the psalmist penned his haunting epitaph as a warning for all souls in every successive generation:

> Today, if only you would hear his voice,
> "Do not harden your hearts as you did at Meribah,
> as you did that day at Massah in the wilderness,
> where your ancestors tested me;
> they tried me, though they had seen what I did.
> For forty years I was angry with that generation;
> I said, 'They are a people whose hearts go astray,
> and they have not known my ways.'" (Psalm 95:7b–10)

Despite the extraordinary miracle of water coming from the rock, the entire occasion is remembered quite differently.

> And he called the place Massah and Meribah because the Israelites quarreled and because they tested the LORD saying, "Is the LORD among us or not?"

We should be calling the place River Rock or Rock Water or Six Flags Over Moses. Instead, we call the place Massah and Meribah because of the quarreling unbelief of the people, even in the face of the unbelievable acts of God.

> Is the LORD among us or not?

This is not the sign of unbelief but rather of ambivalence. Ambivalence is the terminal cancer of the soul—hardness of heart. God can work with unbelief. Ambivalence is another story. Ambivalence is the willful disposition to be neither convinced nor unconvinced in the face of God's faithfulness.

> Is the LORD among us or not?

Ambivalence creeps in, especially into the hearts of men, through a subtle form of stoicism—a super reasonable, impenetrably invulnerable spirit of resignation.

Hardship in the wilderness will do one of two things in our lives. It will infuse character into our souls or wear calluses onto our hearts—holiness or hardness. The difference comes in our response. The psalmist shows us the way in the preceding verses.

> Come, let us sing for joy to the LORD;
> let us shout aloud to the Rock of our salvation.
> Let us come before him with thanksgiving
> and extol him with music and song.
> (Psalm 95:1–2)

The invitation is to sing. I find myself singing one of my favorite older new songs these days, "Blessed Be Your Name" by Matt Redman.

There's a great line in there: "When I'm found in the desert place, though I walk through the wilderness, blessed be your name."

I encourage you to take every opportunity you can, alone or with other people, to worship the Lord. Kneel in your home and sing and shout. Worship is the antidote to ambivalence. It is more than an invitation. It is a command. Do not harden your hearts.

> Come, let us bow down in worship,
>   let us kneel before the LORD our Maker;
> for he is our God
>   and we are the people of his pasture,
>   the flock under his care.
>
> Today, if only you would hear his voice,
> "Do not harden your hearts as you did at Meribah,
>   as you did that day at Massah in the wilderness."
>   (Psalm 95:6–8)

And the beautiful thing about singing is that you don't have to be a singer to do it. Just make a joyful noise. Our worship becomes a lightning rod for God's presence.

The Prayer for Deliverance

Lord Jesus, you are my Deliverer. I receive your deliverance from ambivalence into awakening. Here's a prayer for so many men in our midst—and some women. I confess that I believe some things about you, but I don't really believe you. I will lend you my strength if asked, but I do not give you my heart. I receive your deliverance from my beliefs into real and true believing. Thank you for this invitation to sing out our songs to you, to bow down in worship. Ferret out the creeping ambivalence that would harden my heart. Cut away the calluses and restore in me the Spirit of life that leads me to holiness. I want to live, not just exist.

All of this will be for my good, for others' gain, and for your glory.

Glory be to the Father and to the Son and to the Holy Ghost.
As it was in the beginning, is now and ever shall be.
World without end. Amen! Amen!

The Questions

Will you sing out to the Lord today? And men, am I right about the subtle form of stoicism—a super reasonable, impenetrably invulnerable spirit of ambivalence, even resignation? Could this be the reason you don't really sing anymore? Are you ready to sing that away?

53

Exodus 17:8–13

I'll See You on the Field

The Amalekites came and attacked the Israelites at Rephidim. Moses said to Joshua, "Choose some of our men and go out to fight the Amalekites. Tomorrow I will stand on top of the hill with the staff of God in my hands."

So Joshua fought the Amalekites as Moses had ordered, and Moses, Aaron and Hur went to the top of the hill. As long as Moses held up his hands, the Israelites were winning, but whenever he lowered his hands, the Amalekites were winning. When Moses' hands grew tired, they took a stone and put it under him and he sat on it. Aaron and Hur held his hands up—one on one side, one on the other—so that his hands remained steady till sunset. So Joshua overcame the Amalekite army with the sword.

Consider This

In today's devotional, the Israelites' wilderness struggle goes next level. They ran into a bona fide enemy: the dreaded Amalekites. Gandalf—I mean Moses, tapped his lay leader Joshua: "Choose some of our men and go out to fight the Amalekites." Now, watch what Moses did: "Tomorrow I will stand on top of the hill with the staff of God in my hands."

Joshua must have thought, *Hang on, Pastor. Isn't that your job? Shouldn't you be going to the battlefield to swing the staff of God while we go to the bleachers—I mean mountaintop, to pray for you?*

I know. I know. That's eisegesis (i.e., reading my own agenda into the text). I'm calling my own foul, and whether the text supports my point or not, we all know the point is on point.

While I am a deep appreciator of ordained clergy—I am one—I think the system of many of our churches has devolved into a culture that has become toxic for the whole people of God. It's why the proverbial Amalekites have been running up the score against our local churches, towns, and cities for the past too many years to count.

Can we be honest about something? The church doesn't have laypeople. The church is laypeople. If I hear one more person say something to the effect of, "I'm just a layperson," I'm going to swat them with the staff of God. And I know it's not your fault, laypeople. It's the system and church culture many of us find ourselves in. Too often when a layperson tries to get in the game (which effectively means starting a new game), they get the Heisman (stiff arm), not so much from the leadership but from the model. It's not the clergy's fault either. It's the broken model's fault.

To be clear, though, I'm not advocating for a new model, as though a model could somehow solve the problem. What we need is the army on the field, with everyone playing their distinctive part (lay and clergy) in the work of sowing for great awakening. To be clear, I'm not talking about church programs and activities here, but the movement of God's mission into all the places in a community (and the world) it takes the whole church to go. I'm talking about a genuine New Testament expression of church.

> As long as Moses held up his hands, the Israelites were winning, but whenever he lowered his hands, the Amalekites were winning.

This past Sunday, during the children's sermon, I asked the kids about the big football game on the prior Friday night. Then I asked them what the football team did every other day leading up to the game. They replied, "They practiced." Then I asked the children a ponderous question: "What do you think Sunday morning at church is; is it the big game, or is it practice?"

They mostly agreed that Sunday morning was the big game. I told them I saw it differently. I said Sunday morning is practice. The big game is Monday, Tuesday, Wednesday, Thursday, Friday, and Saturday, and the field was all the places their lives took them. On Sunday morning, we practice by getting our lives into the shape of worship, and we then live that out the rest of the week. If you want to win, you have to go to practice, but you don't win at practice. You win on the field of play.

> When Moses' hands grew tired, they took a stone and put it under him and he sat on it. Aaron and Hur held his hands up—one on one side, one on the other—so that his hands remained steady till sunset.

People of God, the action is not at the church. The game is on the field. Parents, we need you on the field, at home, praying with your children at bedtime and at breakfast, and talking together about the Word of God everywhere in between. Students, we need you at school, being salt and light, and making sure kids aren't excluded or left behind. Teachers, we need you at school, exuding the mercy of God and being sanctuary space for the Holy Spirit for your colleagues and your students. Doctors, we need you moving in the fullness of God's healing power at your clinics and hospitals, praying for divine intervention in your every decision and prescription, and exuding faith, hope, and love. Lawyers, we need you as beacons of justice and mercy, confounding the courts and judges with the wisdom of Heaven in your pleadings and the peace of God in your dispositions. Farmers, we need you in the fields with your laborers and caring for them as you care for your own families. Christians, we need you in the nursing homes and the recovery centers and the jails and the children's group homes, not occasionally but regularly, sowing the truth and love of God.

And pastors and church leaders, we need you up early every day for the big game, taking your place on prayer mountain—lifting your hands over the scattered army of God's people. We need you interceding, prophesying, praying, and groaning with the Spirit for the revelation of the sons and daughters of God all over the community—for the kingdom of heaven to come on earth in both ordinary and supernatural fashion. And we need to see you on the field, coming alongside and encouraging sowers, turning up at the hospital and the courtroom and the school pep rally and lunchroom. You are coaching, cheering, diagramming plays on the spot, encouraging, and always loving.

As for me, I'll be your Aaron on Monday and your Hur on Tuesday. And I'll see you on the field.

The Prayer for Deliverance

Lord Jesus, you are my Deliverer. Would you deliver me from being a spectator in the stands and put me in the big game of worshiping God in my everyday life? I want my life to count. It's the only one I have. Would you give me a share in a great awakening? It will be for my good, for others' gain, and for your glory.

Glory be to the Father and to the Son and to the Holy Ghost.
As it was in the beginning, is now and ever shall be.
World without end. Amen! Amen!

The Questions

What do you make of this shift in mindset—from Sunday as the big game to Sunday as the essential practice to play the big game of the other six days? What about the shift from the action being at the church to the action being on the field?

54

Exodus 17:14–16

Moses Built an Altar, and So Will I

Then the Lord *said to Moses, "Write this on a scroll as something to be remembered and make sure that Joshua hears it, because I will completely blot out the name of Amalek from under heaven."*

Moses built an altar and called it The Lord *is my Banner. He said, "Because hands were lifted up against the throne of the* Lord*, the* Lord *will be at war against the Amalekites from generation to generation."*

Consider This

Moses built an altar.

When was the last time you built an altar? Building an altar just may be the greatest act anyone could ever do. It says far more than words ever could.

What is an altar? We all think we know until we are asked. Here's the *Oxford English Dictionary* definition: "A table or flat-topped block used as the focus for a religious ritual, especially for making sacrifices or offerings to a deity."

Because of the offering of his own body as a sacrifice on the cross, the entire sacrificial system has been fulfilled once and for all by Jesus Christ. It is why the altars in our churches are tables or flat-topped blocks where the bread and the wine are offered as signs of the new covenant made by the body and blood of Christ.

So, does this obviate the need for us to make altars and sacrifices? I don't think so. The New Testament seems to envision otherwise. Consider Romans 12:1: "Therefore, I urge you, brothers and sisters, in view of God's mercy, to offer your bodies as a living sacrifice, holy and pleasing to God—this is your true and proper worship."

Our spirituality can be all too . . . well, spiritual. Altars have a way of landing our spirits in the earth. Altars ground us and make the whole concept of living sacrifice more than a nice sentiment. The deepest instinct in every human being ever born is the instinct to make an offering of oneself to God. The very essence of sin is anything that causes us to compromise or otherwise withhold the offering of ourselves to God. To make an offering of ourselves to God is what it means to love God with all our heart, mind, soul, and strength—to offer our bodies to him without reserve. There is only one reason we would not do this: We do not trust God.

This is why it is so important to build altars to God on occasions where God has acted or moved mightily in our midst. We need to make an immediate response. The combination of God's intervention and our responsiveness seals trust. Our general sense of gratitude is good but wholly inadequate.

God's significant work in our lives needs sufficient commemoration. This is the whole point of altars.

And those altars need to be named. Don't you love how Moses named the altar in today's text?

> Moses built an altar and called it The LORD is my Banner.

"The LORD is my Banner." The Hebrew words are *Yahweh Nissi*. Biblically speaking, altars are usually given a particular name of God that corresponds with the occasion.

When we look back over our lives, we want to see a trail of altars. Not only do they serve as the pillars of our autobiography, but they become signposts for those coming in our wake. When we build an altar, we leave it behind; yet because we took the time to build it, it gets built in our hearts and we carry it with us forever. Altars don't need to be elaborate structures; a pile of rocks will do. It's the deliberation that counts. In times past, I have planted a tree as an act of altar-making.

Allow me to ask myself the question I am asking you. *When was the last time I tangibly built or made an altar?* Honestly, I can't remember, and it bothers me. As I look back over my life, there are many occasions for which I wish I had built altars. I let myself feel grateful, maybe shared a testimony here and there, and quietly moved on. I didn't do the deeper work of reflecting significantly on how God revealed himself and how an altar might be named in the light of his name.

The Bible is filled with such naming opportunities ever in search of the altars of our lives and times. The Lord is my provider. The Lord is my Healer. The Lord is my peace. The Lord is my joy. The Lord is my light and my salvation. The Lord is my Shepherd. The Lord is my rock, my fortress, and my strong tower.

> Moses built an altar and called it The Lord is my Banner.

The Prayer for Deliverance

Lord Jesus, you are my Deliverer. What does the altar look like in my life right now? Would you help me name the deliverance afoot in my own life, perhaps in my family, maybe in my church at this time? Deliver me from my good intentions to make an altar, which will become unhelpful sentiments, and into the actual reality of making a real altar. Would you show me the shape of the altar I might construct in my life at this time? I won't lament altars missed in the past, but I will look to make up for lost opportunities going forward. Thank you for this altar we see Moses making today—The Lord is My Banner! Let it be so for me too! It will be for my good, for others' gain, and for your glory.

Glory be to the Father and to the Son and to the Holy Ghost.
As it was in the beginning, is now and ever shall be.
World without end. Amen! Amen!

The Questions

Do you have an altar story in your past? Can you begin to visualize the altar coming in your near future?

55

Exodus 18:1–12

Monotheism in the Land of Polytheism

Now Jethro, the priest of Midian and father-in-law of Moses, heard of everything God had done for Moses and for his people Israel, and how the Lord had brought Israel out of Egypt.

After Moses had sent away his wife Zipporah, his father-in-law Jethro received her and her two sons. One son was named Gershom, for Moses said, "I have become a foreigner in a foreign land"; and the other was named Eliezer, for he said, "My father's God was my helper; he saved me from the sword of Pharaoh."

Jethro, Moses' father-in-law, together with Moses' sons and wife, came to him in the wilderness, where he was camped near the mountain of God. Jethro had sent word to him, "I, your father-in-law Jethro, am coming to you with your wife and her two sons."

So Moses went out to meet his father-in-law and bowed down and kissed him. They greeted each other and then went into the tent. Moses told his father-in-law about everything the Lord had done to Pharaoh and the Egyptians for Israel's sake and about all the hardships they had met along the way and how the Lord had saved them.

Jethro was delighted to hear about all the good things the Lord had done for Israel in rescuing them from the hand of the Egyptians. He said, "Praise be to the Lord, who rescued you from the hand of the Egyptians and of Pharaoh, and who rescued the people from the hand of the Egyptians. Now I know that the Lord is greater than all other gods, for he did this to those who had treated Israel arrogantly." Then Jethro, Moses' father-in-law, brought a burnt offering and other sacrifices to God, and Aaron came with all the elders of Israel to eat a meal with Moses' father-in-law in the presence of God.

Consider This

The Bible tells us a lot, yet there is so much the Bible doesn't tell us. We aren't getting the comprehensive daily logs of all the happenings of the Israelites on this journey. We are getting the Holy Spirit–inspired highlights. Cloud by day. Fire by night. Quail in the evening. Manna in the morning. Moses raising his arms with the staff of God and the defeat of the Amalekites.

Moses building and naming an altar "The Lord is my Banner." Moses's in-laws visit.

One of these things is not like the others, right? Why so much about Jethro, the priest of Midian, who pays a visit to Moses? Why might the Holy Spirit, who inspired the writer of the text, want us to know about Moses's in-laws? This is a good principle of Bible study—to ask why certain things are included in the text and why others get left out.

The Gospel of John ends like this: "Jesus did many other things as well. If every one of them were written down, I suppose that even the whole world would not have room for the books that would be written" (21:25). The Holy Spirit is very selective about what gets included in Scripture. Everything is there for a purpose. We must be curious about the purpose.

So why such detail about a visit from the in-laws? I have two observations to offer from today's text.

> He [Jethro] said, "Praise be to the Lord, who rescued you from the hand of the Egyptians and of Pharaoh, and who rescued the people from the hand of the Egyptians."

These times, perhaps like all times in one way or another, were very polytheistic (many gods) times. There were many so-called gods, and Jethro was a priest of one of them. He was the priest of Midian. That is what makes his next comment worthy of note:

> Now I know that the Lord is greater than all other gods, for he did this to those who had treated Israel arrogantly.

Notice the phrase "Greater than all other gods." In these times, which differ from our times only in the names of the false gods, everyone was a polytheist. There is always room for another god in the pantheon of deities. It highlights the political correctness violation of a statement like "Greater than all other gods." Friends, we, the followers of Jesus Messiah, are monotheists (people of one God). All of life is received from, mediated by, and lived through the one true and living God who is Father, Son, and Holy Spirit—one God in three persons—blessed Trinity.

This has me remembering a moment from the COVID-19 global pandemic. I will remember it here while stripping out any names because it demonstrates just how salient this matter remains. One of the leading governmental voices from our nation made the following remark in an interview: "Our behavior has stopped the spread of the virus. God did not stop the spread of the virus."[2] And in case it was considered a misguided stroke of bad judgment or that he really didn't mean what he said, he later said this: "The number is down because we brought the number down. God did not do that. Fate did not do that. Destiny did not do that. A lot of pain and suffering did that."[3]

This statement reveals the widely held conviction that God is, at best, one possible actor among many others, even daring to place human beings on the same level, if not on a higher level, in this instance. Here's a translation of the statement: "Human behavior is greater than all other gods." It's kind of a modern-day Genesis 11–Tower of Babel moment. And this is not a critique of the governmental leader, who is a professing Christian. It is, rather, a reflection of the broadly sweeping spirit of the age in which we live.

Imagine if Jethro had said, "The Israelites were delivered from Pharaoh because Moses delivered them. God did not do that. Fate did not do that. Destiny did not do that. Moses did it." It would be shocking, to say the least. Jethro said a very different thing—and he doubled down on it.

---

2. Decision Magazine Staff, "Cuomo: 'God Did Not Stop the Spread of the Virus,'" *Decision Magazine*, May 1, 2020, https://decisionmagazine.com/cuomo-god-did-not-stop-the-spread-of-the-virus/.
3. "Cuomo: 'God Did Not Stop the Spread of the Virus,'" *Decision Magazine*.

> Now I know that the LORD is greater than all other gods, for he did this to those who had treated Israel arrogantly.

He not only said it and reinforced it, but he sealed it at an altar.

> Then Jethro, Moses' father-in-law, brought a burnt offering and other sacrifices to God, and Aaron came with all the elders of Israel to eat a meal with Moses' father-in-law in the presence of God.

The Prayer for Deliverance

Lord Jesus, you are my Deliverer. You are the one and only true and living God. Search me and reveal my own tendencies to acknowledge, salute, and maybe even unwittingly worship other gods in addition to the one true and living God. I think of the god of money, the god of image and reputation and standing in the community (which is another way of saying the god of what other people think), the god of education, skill, and talent, and so many more. It's not that I would put other gods before you. It's that I would have other gods at all that cuts me to the heart. You alone are God. This is my faith—you alone. Deliver me from my dependence on any other god and into the exclusive trust in you alone. It will be for my good, for others' gain, and for your glory.

Glory be to the Father and to the Son and to the Holy Ghost.
As it was in the beginning, is now and ever shall be.
World without end. Amen! Amen!

The Questions

Are you a practicing polytheist (a person of many gods)? Even an unwitting one? Is the God of heaven and earth in a category of his own? Is the God of heaven and earth the only God in your pantheon—no other categories? Are you learning to live your entire life and to receive all its sources through the one true and living God who is Jesus Christ?

Week 8: Discussion Questions

Hearing the Text

Read Exodus 16:31–18:12.

Responding to the Text

- What did you hear?
- What did you see?
- What did you otherwise sense from the Lord?

Sharing Insights and Implications for Discipleship

Drawing from the Scripture text and daily readings, what did you find challenging, encouraging, provocative, comforting, invasive, inspiring, corrective, affirming, guiding, or warning?

Shaping Intentions for Prayer

Write your discipleship intention for the week ahead.

9

WEEK

Exodus 18:13–20:11

57

Exodus 18:13–27

Can You Receive Help?

The next day Moses took his seat to serve as judge for the people, and they stood around him from morning till evening. When his father-in-law saw all that Moses was doing for the people, he said, "What is this you are doing for the people? Why do you alone sit as judge, while all these people stand around you from morning till evening?"

Moses answered him, "Because the people come to me to seek God's will. Whenever they have a dispute, it is brought to me, and I decide between the parties and inform them of God's decrees and instructions."

Moses' father-in-law replied, "What you are doing is not good. You and these people who come to you will only wear yourselves out. The work is too heavy for you; you cannot handle it alone. Listen now to me and I will give you some advice, and may God be with you. You must be the people's representative before God and bring their disputes to him. Teach them his decrees and instructions, and show them the way they are to live and how they are to behave. But select capable men from all the people—men who fear God, trustworthy men who hate dishonest gain—and appoint them as officials over thousands, hundreds, fifties and tens. Have them serve as judges for the people at all times, but have them bring every difficult case to you; the simple cases they can decide themselves. That will make your load lighter, because they will share it with you. If you do this and God so commands, you will be able to stand the strain, and all these people will go home satisfied."

Moses listened to his father-in-law and did everything he said. He chose capable men from all Israel and made them leaders of the people, officials over thousands, hundreds, fifties and tens. They served as judges for the people at all times. The difficult cases they brought to Moses, but the simple ones they decided themselves.

Then Moses sent his father-in-law on his way, and Jethro returned to his own country.

Consider This

Jethro is one great father-in-law. In yesterday's devotional, he was a powerful prophetic witness to the one true and living God. In today's he is an executive coach!

Wisdom can be hard to come by in the wilderness, but when it comes, it is oh so practical. Moses's father-in-law replied:

> What you are doing is not good. You and these people who come to you will only wear yourselves out. The work is too heavy for you; you cannot handle it alone. Listen now to me and I will give you some advice, and may God be with you.

So the advice is pretty straightforward and doesn't need much explanation. It can be brought down to a single word: *delegate*. Despite how obvious it appears to the onlooker, the need for delegation was not apparent to Moses. That's the observation I want to make here. We all find ourselves so deeply immersed in our particular lives and contexts that it can be hard to see even the most obvious things.

We all need a Jethro or three in our lives. We need people who are close enough to us and know us sufficiently well to feel the freedom and permission to say, "What you are doing is not good." We need the kind of elders in our lives who love us enough both to encourage us and to tell us when we are doing things wrong.

I wonder who among us (present company included) needs to hear this admonition today?

> The work is too heavy for you; you cannot handle it alone.

Are you the kind of person whom others can help? What I'm asking is, can you accept and receive help from others? A lot of people can't. Are you embarrassed by the level of your chaotic mess and don't want to be exposed? Are you too controlling to let someone else come in and exercise their discretion in your situation? Are you too self-sufficient to admit you have a need for help?

We all have great limitations and definite incapacities. That is not the problem. The problem is when we can't own those limitations and incapacities. At this point, they become handicaps on the fulfillment of God's capacities in our lives. Hear me right. We don't limit God. We just handicap our ability to be effective agents of God's capacities in our lives. Jethro spotted that immediately in Moses and gently but directly called it out.

> The work is too heavy for you; you cannot handle it alone.

Okay, I'll go first. I'm the kind of person who thinks I actually can't be helped—that it would be too difficult to bring someone into the depths of my unique ways of ordering and organizing things. I tell myself it would be too difficult to explain it all, and by the time I did, I could have already done it myself. The wilderness is a good place to let the Holy Spirit sort us out on such matters as this and to deliver us from the chaos and into new creation.

The Prayer for Deliverance

Lord Jesus, you are my Deliverer. I am not asking for you to deliver me from my limitations but rather to deliver me from my tendency to try and deny or cover over my limitations. Deliver me from my self-sufficiency, my pride, my unwillingness to trust others, and my need to be in control and manage everything myself. I receive your deliverance into a place of embracing my limitations and even embracing my incapacities and my weaknesses. This is where your strength will become manifest and even magnified through others who bring gifts and capacities to the table. I receive your deliverance from the chaos of my making and into the new creation of your making. It will be for my good, for others' gain, and for your glory.

Glory be to the Father and to the Son and to the Holy Ghost.
As it was in the beginning, is now and ever shall be.
World without end. Amen! Amen!

The Questions

Are you the kind of person others can help? What I'm asking is, can you accept and receive help from others? Who are the Jethros in your life? Who do you serve as a Jethro in their life?

58

Exodus 19:1–8

The Reason for It All

On the first day of the third month after the Israelites left Egypt—on that very day—they came to the Desert of Sinai. After they set out from Rephidim, they entered the Desert of Sinai, and Israel camped there in the desert in front of the mountain.

Then Moses went up to God, and the LORD called to him from the mountain and said, "This is what you are to say to the descendants of Jacob and what you are to tell the people of Israel: 'You yourselves have seen what I did to Egypt, and how I carried you on eagles' wings and brought you to myself. Now if you obey me fully and keep my covenant, then out of all nations you will be my treasured possession. Although the whole earth is mine, you will be for me a kingdom of priests and a holy nation.' These are the words you are to speak to the Israelites."

So Moses went back and summoned the elders of the people and set before them all the words the LORD had commanded him to speak. The people all responded together, "We will do everything the LORD has said." So Moses brought their answer back to the LORD.

Consider This

Today we arrive at a major chapter in the story of God and the story of us. Welcome to Mount Sinai.

If we view the storyline of Scripture (so far) at a high level, we might frame it like this: Creation. Fall. Flood. Babel. Abraham. Isaac. Jacob. Joseph. Egypt. Moses. Plagues. Passover. Red Sea. Sinai. While every word or name denotes an important event in and of itself, collectively these words and names tell the grand story of God.

Our great aspiration must be to know the story inside out and upside down, not so we can be Bible experts, but because this is our story. For us to live out our chapter of the story, we must know the story that has come before. Our memory shapes our imagination. The people of God remember their way into the future.

Accordingly, Mount Sinai is shorthand for the Ten Commandments, which is shorthand for the giving of the Law to Moses for the people of God. Few events are more pivotal in the history of the world than this. Though a lot had happened since the Israelites left Egypt, they were only three months into the journey when they came to this mountain of monumental magnitude. Now they came to the reason for it all. God decreed this word to the Israelites, and Moses declared it to them:

> You yourselves have seen what I did to Egypt, and how I carried you on eagles' wings and brought you to myself. Now if you obey me fully and keep my covenant, then out of all nations you will be my treasured possession.

There had been drama and trauma, hardship and difficulties and, through it all, provision and protection. All of this can be neatly captioned under the extraordinarily messy category of deliverance.

God delivered the Israelites from Egypt into the wilderness and onward to the promised land for a relationship with himself—for their good, for others' gain, and for his glory. Let's run the replay in slow motion:

> I carried you on eagles' wings
> and brought you to myself,
> Now if you obey me fully
> and keep my covenant,
> then out of all nations
> you will be my treasured possession.

Remember, this is God speaking to his people—even to us. Let's slow it down to frame by frame.

I c-a-r-r-i-e-d you
on eagles' wings
and brought you
to myself.

Did you see it? That's plan A. Finally, we are back to plan A.

> *I brought you to myself.* (emphasis added)

He didn't bring us out for what we could do for him. He brought us out for himself. This is about God. And because this is about God, this is about a fierce, jealous, overwhelming, protective, providing, all-consuming kind of love.

God simply asks us to listen to (obey) him and keep the covenant. And then he tells us what will happen as a result of this:

> Although the whole earth is mine, you will be for me a kingdom of priests and a holy nation.

God's plan was to make himself known to the rest of the world through the way he loved and lived in relationship with this particular and peculiar group of people. This was the plan all along, and it would be the plan going forward: a kingdom of priests and a holy nation. If we fast-forward to the closing sections of the Scriptures, this same language focuses on the church: "But you are a chosen people, a royal priesthood, a holy nation, God's special possession, that you may declare the praises of him who called you out of darkness into his wonderful light" (1 Peter 2:9).

For us to become the fullness of his presence in the world, he will transform our sin-sick, broken nature to become like his love-filled, holy nature. This was the point of Mount Sinai. This is why the Law was revealed. And the gateway into this gifted life is simple loving obedience:

> Now if you obey me fully and keep my covenant.

And look what we said:

> The people all responded together, "We will do everything the LORD has said."

Of course, we will do everything the Lord has said. Why? Because

> *I carried you on eagles wings and brought you to myself.* (emphasis added)

It makes you want to know what God will say to us on Mount Sinai, doesn't it? Stay tuned!

The Prayer for Deliverance

Lord Jesus, you are my Deliverer. You brought us to yourself. Yes, you brought me to yourself. I want to let that soak in. You carried me on eagles' wings, and you brought me to yourself. Lord Jesus, you paid a debt you did not owe because I owed a debt I could not pay. You rescued me from darkness, delivered me from death, and brought me out of chaos and into your new creation. And you did all of this so you could bring me to yourself. I want to receive deliverance now from everything that keeps me from you and receive deliverance into the kind of obedience and covenant-keeping that is the promised land of a relationship with you. It will be for my good, for others' gain, and for your glory.

Glory be to the Father and to the Son and to the Holy Ghost.
As it was in the beginning, is now and ever shall be.
World without end. Amen! Amen!

The Questions

Have you realized yet, in a personal and particular way, that God has carried you on eagles' wings and brought you to himself? Would you ask him to reveal this to you or to refresh the revelation—to restore you to the prominence of "first love"?

59

Exodus 19:9–15

Consecration Versus Casual Religion

The Lord *said to Moses, "I am going to come to you in a dense cloud, so that the people will hear me speaking with you and will always put their trust in you." Then Moses told the* Lord *what the people had said.*

And the Lord *said to Moses, "Go to the people and consecrate them today and tomorrow. Have them wash their clothes and be ready by the third day, because on that day the* Lord *will come down on Mount Sinai in the sight of all the people. Put limits for the people around the mountain and tell them, 'Be careful that you do not approach the mountain or touch the foot of it. Whoever touches the mountain is to be put to death. They are to be stoned or shot with arrows; not a hand is to be laid on them. No person or animal shall be permitted to live.' Only when the ram's horn sounds a long blast may they approach the mountain."*

After Moses had gone down the mountain to the people, he consecrated them, and they washed their clothes. Then he said to the people, "Prepare yourselves for the third day. Abstain from sexual relations."

Consider This

The word of the day today is *consecrate.*

> And the Lord said to Moses, "Go to the people and consecrate them today and tomorrow. Have them wash their clothes and be ready by the third day, because on that day the Lord will come down on Mount Sinai in the sight of all the people."

What does the word *consecrate* mean to you? The Hebrew word is *qadash*, and it means to set apart something or someone as holy unto the Lord. Why would God want the people to be consecrated? There is only one reason—because God is holy.

"Holy! Holy! Holy!" roar the voices of the angels and the archangels and the elders and the living creatures gathered around the throne of God. They never stop shouting, "Holy! Holy! Holy! is the Lord God Almighty, who was, and is, and is to come" (Revelation 4:8).

"Holy, holy, holy is the LORD Almighty; the whole earth is full of his glory" (Isaiah 6:3) called the six-winged seraphim to one another around the throne of God.

"Holy! Holy! Holy! Lord God Almighty . . . God in three persons, blessed Trinity," goes the great hymn.

"Holy! Holy! Holy! Lord, God of power and might. Heaven and earth are full of your glory," declares the ancient rite spoken around the Lord's Table all over the world.

God is holy. Yet we live in an age with a thin and sentimental vision of God. The Bible says much about God, but it doesn't want us to miss this: God is holy. How have we come to speak of and approach God so casually? There is only one explanation: We have lost sight of his truest nature, of the character that defines all his qualities—God is holy.

God is love, to be sure, but the character and quality of his love is holiness. It is not just another wispy projection of human love. No, the love of God is holy love. It is of another order and comes from another place. The Spirit of God is called "the Comforter," yet we must be reminded that he is called "the Holy Spirit," and he comes like a fire. God's holiness burns with the blaze of ten thousand suns. Indeed, as the writer of Hebrews reminds us, "Our 'God is a consuming fire'" (12:29). Did you catch the extreme nature of the instructions?

> Be careful that you do not approach the mountain or touch the foot of it. Whoever touches the mountain is to be put to death. They are to be stoned or shot with arrows; not a hand is to be laid on them. No person or animal shall be permitted to live.

How long has it been since you meditated on the holiness of God? It has been too long for me. Perhaps, like you, I am aware and understand the concept of the holiness of God, but it is far from top of mind in my daily life. My view of God tends to lean toward the more approachable and embracing features of God. The problem with this is that when I lose immediate awareness of the holiness of God, my relationship with God becomes casual. From here I slowly but surely begin to see God as the mirror image of myself. Holiness is just the opposite—seeing myself in the mirrored image of God.

> And the LORD said to Moses, "Go to the people and consecrate them today and tomorrow."

Consecration is the move to offer oneself wholeheartedly to God. Consecration prepares the way for personal transformation, and personal transformation opens the way for public demonstration.

Far from a ramped-up religion of striving, which is so often signified by earnestness and zeal, consecration is the pathway of humility and surrender.

The Prayer for Deliverance

Lord Jesus, you are my Deliverer. I join the cries of heaven's throngs: "Holy! Holy! Holy!" I receive your deliverance from a casual relationship with almighty God and into an awakened and ever-awakening way of consecrated life. Holy! Holy! Holy! Would you awaken me to your holiness? And would you forgive me for getting the closing words of my prayer backward? I repent, which is to say, I reverse myself in now saying, It will be for your glory, for others' gain, and for my good.

Glory be to the Father and to the Son and to the Holy Ghost.
As it was in the beginning, is now and ever shall be.
World without end. Amen! Amen!

The Questions

Do you enter into the prayer of consecration with me each day on the Wake-Up Call? Perhaps you might try listening if you do not already do so. It can be so easy to skip past it otherwise or just quickly read the words. I'm asking, what is your experience with this consecration work every day? How might it be more real?

60

Exodus 19:16–25

Meeting with God Is the Only Thing That Matters

On the morning of the third day there was thunder and lightning, with a thick cloud over the mountain, and a very loud trumpet blast. Everyone in the camp trembled. Then Moses led the people out of the camp to meet with God, and they stood at the foot of the mountain. Mount Sinai was covered with smoke, because the Lord *descended on it in fire. The smoke billowed up from it like smoke from a furnace, and the whole mountain trembled violently. As the sound of the trumpet grew louder and louder, Moses spoke and the voice of God answered him.*

The Lord *descended to the top of Mount Sinai and called Moses to the top of the mountain. So Moses went up and the* Lord *said to him, "Go down and warn the people so they do not force their way through to see the* Lord *and many of them perish. Even the priests, who approach the* Lord*, must consecrate themselves, or the* Lord *will break out against them."*

Moses said to the Lord*, "The people cannot come up Mount Sinai, because you yourself warned us, 'Put limits around the mountain and set it apart as holy.'"*

The Lord *replied, "Go down and bring Aaron up with you. But the priests and the people must not force their way through to come up to the* Lord*, or he will break out against them."*

So Moses went down to the people and told them.

Consider This

There is so much going on in today's text, yet one thing especially mattered. Visualize the scene: Thunder. Lightning. Thick clouds descending. Loud trumpet blasting. Billowing smoke. Fiery furnace. Mountain shaking violently. People trembling.

So, did you catch the one thing? Because of so many things going on, it can be easy to miss the one thing actually happening. The one thing is not only the most important thing; it is really the only thing:

> Then Moses led the people out of the camp to meet with God.

The one thing—meeting with God.

The giving of the Law on Mount Sinai can be described in many ways, and mostly it is described as simply the Ten Commandments, but in its deepest and most important essence, it is something else: a meeting with God.

Years back, our awakening company, Seedbed, planned a conference called the New Room Conference, and our team made a crucial decision. We decided our conference would not have a theme—that it would be about only one thing: meeting with God. Sure, we'd have speakers and music and snacks and breakouts just like other conferences, but the overarching, underlying, permeating point of everything we do would be meeting with God. We all agreed—we could pull off the most amazing conference ever, but if we did not meet with God, it would be for naught. We could miss a lot of cues, provide FEMA-level rations, cut the light show and smoke machine, but if we met with God, no one would care about the rest.

Church can be this way. I sometimes wonder why we require so much amenity to meet with God. We have massive sound systems to simulate the thunder, all kinds of flashy lighting to simulate the lightning, and, yes, we even have smoke machines to simulate God's presence. I sometimes wonder if this masks the real absence of a true meeting with God. Don't hear me wrong. I don't think there's anything wrong with loud music and lights and even smoke—until there is.

Consider the notion of having a quiet time or doing devotions. Do we conceive of these activities as a meeting with God, or have they just become things we do every day, faithful habits, or worse, boxes we check? I wonder if some dimension of repentance might include waking up from our predictable devotional patterns and getting back to the core essence of what they are really all about: meeting with God.

This is why I started doing the daily podcast version of the Wake-Up Call. I wanted to take the written word as delivered in email and expand the experience of a shared meeting with God. I sing hymns every day and offer exhortations. I am not going through the motions. This is an invitation. When you join me, we are meeting with God. We are moving in response to the presence of the Lord. I know it may not be for everybody, but if you haven't tried it, I wish you would. Wake-Up Call is on all major podcasting platforms (Apple, Spotify, etc.).

Then Moses led the people out of the camp to meet with God.

Maybe the invitation is to step away from the familiarity of the camp so that we might refind that meeting. Might shaking off our coziness help us recover the sense of God's holiness? Let's give David the last word on the subject today:

> As the deer pants for streams of water,
> so my soul pants for you, my God.
> My soul thirsts for God, for the living God.
> When can I go and meet with God? (Psalm 42:1–2)

The Prayer for Deliverance

Lord Jesus, you are my Deliverer. I receive your deliverance from casual and even cozy religion and into face-to-face meetings with you. "As the deer pants for streams of water, so my soul pants for you, my God. My soul thirsts for God, for the living God. When can I go and meet with God?" (Psalm 42:1–2). Breathe awakening into me, Lord. I open myself to you with all I have. Meet with me, Lord Jesus. It will be for your glory, for others' gain, and for my good.

> Glory be to the Father and to the Son and to the Holy Ghost.
> As it was in the beginning, is now and ever shall be.
> World without end. Amen! Amen!

The Questions

Do you see yourself as having a meeting with Jesus every day? Or are you just doing quiet time? See the difference? Are you staying with the movement of consecration in your life today? How does the encouragement in today's devotional build on that of yesterday? How are you responding?

61

Exodus 20:1–7

On Delighting in the Law of God

> *And God spoke all these words:*
>
> "I am the Lord your God, who brought you out of Egypt, out of the land of slavery.
>
> "You shall have no other gods before me.
>
> "You shall not make for yourself an image in the form of anything in heaven above or on the earth beneath or in the waters below. You shall not bow down to them or worship them; for I, the Lord your God, am a jealous God, punishing the children for the sin of the parents to the third and fourth generation of those who hate me, but showing love to a thousand generations of those who love me and keep my commandments.
>
> "You shall not misuse the name of the Lord your God, for the Lord will not hold anyone guiltless who misuses his name."

Consider This

The Ten Commandments summarize all 613 laws God gave to Moses. Jesus boiled down the Ten Commandments (indeed the whole Law) into a singular command: "'Love the Lord your God with all your heart and with all your soul and with all your strength and with all your mind'; and, 'Love your neighbor as yourself'" (Luke 10:27).

We see how the Ten Commandments break into two groupings, with the first four dealing with our relationship with God and the final six dealing with our relationship with our neighbors.

We should be clear at the outset that the commandments are not about becoming law-abiding citizens, as is commonly thought. They are about becoming covenant-keeping worshipers.

Have you noticed how the most important words in the Ten Commandments, indeed in the whole of the Law, are often excluded from the commandments when we see them inscribed in public places and even in Christian literature? These words are often missing:

> I am the LORD your God, who brought you out of Egypt, out of the land of slavery.

The Ten Commandments do not begin with commandments. The Law does not begin with laws. It begins with relationship. "I am Yahweh," he says. "I am the God who heard your cries and who brought you out of Egypt, out of the cruel slavery under which you suffered."

"I am God. I delivered you." This is the most primitive taproot of our entire faith and cannot be overstated. If our faith does not come down to something as simple as "I am yours, and you are mine," we are missing the essence of the Christian faith.

Far from mere rules and regulations, these commandments are the very wisdom of God. Martin Luther once wrote, "This much is certain: those who know the Ten Commandments perfectly know the entire Scriptures and in all affairs and circumstances are able to counsel, help, comfort, judge, and make decisions in both spiritual and temporal matters."[1]

I don't know the Ten Commandments perfectly. I think I know them approximately. So why don't I know them perfectly? Probably because my New Testament bias, which is deeper than I want to admit,

---

1. Robert Kolb and Timothy J. Wengert, eds., *The Book of Concord: The Confessions of the Evangelical Lutheran Church* (Fortress, 2000), 382.

still considers the Old Testament as somehow preempted despite still being the Word of God. And probably because I can look up the Ten Commandments anytime I want. I mean, why know anything perfectly anymore, right? We have Google, for crying out loud!

Over the last several years, I have come to frequent Psalm 1, which opens as follows:

> Blessed is the one
> who does not walk in step with the wicked
> or stand in the way that sinners take
> or sit in the company of mockers. (v. 1)

It is easy to agree with, isn't it? Who wants to do these things? Notice that the psalmist first tells us who the blessed are not. Next, he tells us who the blessed are:

> but whose delight is in the law of the Lord,
> and who meditates on his law day and night. (v. 2)

The clear inference is that those who do not delight in the law of the Lord and meditate on it day and night are the ones who turn out to walk in step with the wicked, stand in the way of sinners, and sit in the seat of mockers.

After many walks through Psalm 1, it finally hit me. I don't think I have actually meditated on the law of God. Somehow it never occurred to me to meditate on the Ten Commandments. So how is it I can claim to have delighted in the law of God? I can't.

I have been in active repentance ever since.

The Prayer for Deliverance

Lord Jesus, you are my Deliverer, I love your Law. I want to delight in it. I will follow the psalmist's lead in declaring:

> The law of the Lord is perfect,
> refreshing the soul.

The statutes of the LORD are trustworthy,
making wise the simple.
The precepts of the LORD are right,
giving joy to the heart.
The commands of the LORD are radiant,
giving light to the eyes.
The fear of the LORD is pure,
enduring forever.
The decrees of the LORD are firm,
and all of them are righteous.

They are more precious than gold,
than much pure gold;
they are sweeter than honey,
than honey from the honeycomb. (Psalm 19:7–10)

Teach me to meditate on your Law day and night that I might become the vision you delight to see, "like a tree planted by streams of water, which yields its fruit in season and whose leaf does not wither—whatever they do prospers" (Psalm 1:3). It will be for your glory, for others' gain, and for my good.

Glory be to the Father and to the Son and to the Holy Ghost.
As it was in the beginning, is now and ever shall be.
World without end. Amen! Amen!

The Questions

What has been your relationship with the law of the Lord? Do you salute and revere it? Or have you found your way to delight and meditation? Can you remember the Ten Commandments?

62

Exodus 20:8–11

From Religious Observance to Relationship Revival

"Remember the Sabbath day by keeping it holy. Six days you shall labor and do all your work, but the seventh day is a sabbath to the Lord your God. On it you shall not do any work, neither you, nor your son or daughter, nor your male or female servant, nor your animals, nor any foreigner residing in your towns. For in six days the Lord made the heavens and the earth, the sea, and all that is in them, but he rested on the seventh day. Therefore the Lord blessed the Sabbath day and made it holy."

Consider This

Sabbath was likely the most remarkable reality in the life of a former Hebrew slave. Every six days former slaves would get a day off from work. It fact, they were actually mandated by the God of the universe to rest.

Interestingly, the Sabbath command mandates six days to work and one day to rest, and it does so for everyone: parents and children, employees, Israelite or not, even the animals—which says something remarkable about God.

This is what Yahweh is like. He created an entire twenty-four-hour period of time when everything ceases. He declared it is a "sabbath to the Lord your God," yet it is not even for himself. Jesus said clearly, "The Sabbath was made for man, not man for the Sabbath" (Mark 2:27).

Why did God do this? The first word of the command is "Remember." And, finally, "For in six days the Lord made the heavens and the earth, the sea, and all that is in them, but he rested on the seventh day." Have you considered that God made human beings on the sixth day of creation, and the first thing they did was rest?

And here's another operative principle of Sabbath-keeping: Sabbath rest is not functional or utilitarian rest. It is not resting from work, nor is it resting up for work. It is resting into relationship with God and others.

To remember the Sabbath and keep it holy means to enter into the rest of God, which is a completely different kind of time-and-space reality than anything else.

We have made at least three major errors over the millennia when it comes to Sabbath-keeping. First, we have considered it optional in light of the work of Jesus and the New Testament. Second, we have misconstrued "to keep it holy" as meaning to keep it religious and otherwise painful. Third, despite incredible words like *remember*, *blessed*, and *holy*, all the energy has gone into rigorously and legalistically defining the meaning of the word *work*.

On it you shall not do any work.

What constitutes work? How far can a person walk on the Sabbath without it counting as work? Breaking off heads of grain to eat was counted as work. To this day, in the city of Jerusalem, elevators in buildings are programmed to open on every floor—as pushing a button would count as work. Enormous legalisms have built up like barnacles over the command throughout the centuries—and this for Christian observance.

Many people in the kingdom prime season of life will remember many rules around their childhood about what they could and could not do on Sunday. Blue laws abounded. My grandfather told us stories about not being allowed to go swimming on Sunday.

One of my happiest memories of my young family life was Sabbath-keeping. Every Saturday night, we would gather as a family around a small oil lamp that we only lit during Sabbath. Tiffani and I would gather our four small children, light the oil lamp, and together say this rhyming prayer we composed for the occasion:

> God give us your peace and cause us to rest.
> We cease from our labor; we seek for your best.
> Embracing each other, we walk in your ways.
> We thank you for giving this new Sabbath day.

For the next twenty-four hours, we enjoyed a very different kind of day than the other six had been. We built the day around four key movements: ceasing (what the word *shabbat* actually means), resting, feasting, and embracing. We played games. We enjoyed sumptuous potluck meals with friends. We lingered after church. We took naps. We didn't wash clothes or dishes or anything else on our six-day to-do list during those twenty-four hours. It was glorious, and it changed our lives and our family. I miss that so much these days.

I'm not sure there exists a more life-giving and holistic practice to sow and nourish the awakened life into a home (at any stage) than Sabbath-keeping. I want to get my Sabbath groove back. I'm wondering who out there might like to go that way with me.

The Prayer for Deliverance

Lord Jesus, you are my Deliverer. I receive your deliverance from the disorientation that comes from never resting, which is another name for voluntary slavery. I receive your deliverance into the wise order of Sabbath, of six days of work and one day of rest. I receive your deliverance from Sabbath-keeping as legalistic religion and spiritual striving and into Sabbath-keeping as a day of righteousness, peace, and joy in the Holy Spirit. Yes, Lord, we receive your deliverance from Sabbath as an observance to Sabbath as a relationship revival. It will be for your glory, for others' gain, and for my good.

Glory be to the Father and to the Son and to the Holy Ghost.
As it was in the beginning, is now and ever shall be.
World without end. Amen! Amen!

The Questions

What have been your experiences with Sabbath-keeping? What might a reboot look like?

Week 9: Discussion Questions

Hearing the Text

Read Exodus 18:13–20:11.

Responding to the Text

- What did you hear?
- What did you see?
- What did you otherwise sense from the Lord?

Sharing Insights and Implications for Discipleship

Drawing from the Scripture text and daily readings, what did you find challenging, encouraging, provocative, comforting, invasive, inspiring, corrective, affirming, guiding, or warning?

Shaping Intentions for Prayer

Write your discipleship intention for the week ahead.

10
WEEK

Exodus 20:12–23:30

64

Exodus 20:12

Flipping the Honor Script

> "Honor your father and your mother, so that you may live long in the land the LORD your God is giving you."

Consider This

The focus of the covenant takes a turn here from the relationship to God to the relationship with others. Do you see the problem with this compartmentalized thinking? "Takes a turn" is not the right phrase.

Let's try it this way: *The focus of the covenant broadens here from our relationship with God to include our relationships with others.* We want to think of these relationships as separate realities, in separate airtight compartments, like putting the meat in one Tupperware container and the vegetables in another. The truth? They are all in the same container and have direct correlation with one another.

Let's be clear—our relationship with God and our relationships with one another are distinctive relationships, yet they are all bound up together in the same seamless space. Said differently, our relationship with God includes our relationships with one another. It's why the Bible says things like, "Whoever claims to love God yet hates a brother or sister is a liar. For whoever does not love their brother and sister, whom they have seen, cannot love God, whom they have not seen" (1 John 4:20).

Translation: If our relationship with God doesn't directly show up in our relationships with one another, our relationship with God is broken.

Naturally, the first place or context of relationship we have is in the home. This is why the covenant seamlessly broadens to:

> Honor your father and your mother, so that you may live long in the land the LORD your God is giving you.

The covenant unfolds in an ever-expanding peace—peace with God, peace in Sabbath, peace in the family, and peace in the community.

One more observation about the text of the day. It's one of my what-ifs. What if honoring your mother and your father is not about them? What if it is about you? Honoring parents, while being for them, is not about them. It is about us, our honor, and, ultimately, it is about God's honor. After all, according to the text, when we honor our parents, they receive honor, but we are the ones who receive the blessing. To honor another person means to confer your honor upon them. In the world, we honor people because we find them honorable. In the kingdom of God, we honor people because God has found us honorable.

Many adults find themselves in a place, looking back on their lives, where they feel as though their parents have not honored them in some form or another. It's real. Parents have made unthinkable mistakes and brought dishonor on entire family lines.

Do we honor them? We do if our honor is for them but not about them. We do if our honor is about us and about God. We do if we desire to receive blessing from the Lord, even if it means giving honor in exchange for dishonor. Returning good for bad sounds a lot like Jesus to me.

Here's some more good news. Some reading this will feel like it's too late to honor their parents because they have passed on. It's not. Even if you could not come to a place of honoring them in life, you can still honor them in death. It may be a challenge, but the cross always is.

In closing, I would be remiss to miss this opportunity to honor my mother and father. All that I am and ever will be I owe to them and, in that seamless way I referenced earlier, to God, yet there is no debt whatsoever. It has been all gift. They are the absolute best, most unselfish, generous, gracious, loving, incredible people I know.

The Prayer for Deliverance

Lord Jesus, you are my Deliverer. Thank you for the gift of our parents, even the ones who were less than we hoped they would be. Help us honor them in life and in death, that we may be blessed and live long in the land. I receive your deliverance from my broken way of thinking that leads me to honor my parents or not based on whether I think they are honorable. I receive your deliverance into the mindset that extends honor to my parents based on the way you have honored me—even though I did not deserve your honor. Show me how I can honor my parents in life and in death. I now receive your healing of my family lineage and the reversal of generational curses into generational blessings. It will be for your glory, for others' gain, and for my good.

> Glory be to the Father and to the Son and to the Holy Ghost.
> As it was in the beginning, is now and ever shall be.
> World without end. Amen! Amen!

The Questions

How have you and are you honoring your parents? What holds you back from this?

65

Exodus 20:13–17

The Heart of the Matter

"You shall not murder.

"You shall not commit adultery.

"You shall not steal.

"You shall not give false testimony against your neighbor.

"You shall not covet your neighbor's house. You shall not covet your neighbor's wife, or his male or female servant, his ox or donkey, or anything that belongs to your neighbor."

Consider This

Why aren't these five laws enough?

I remember early in my law school days, one of my professors made a sage comment. He said, "We can assess the morality of a nation by the number of laws it has recorded in its books."

Why can't those be enough? They are sufficiently broad. Why do we assume that if the law is not written down, the activity must not be illegal? Why do we always look for the loophole to get around the law? Every loophole requires another law to close it.

Jesus took another approach to the law on at least two levels. First, he articulated the great positive law of the comprehensive love of God, neighbor, and self. Where there is love, there is no need for law. In fact, the breaking of the law is the failure of love. Law is not about us but about others. Second, he moved us to understand the law at the level of the heart rather than at the level of behavior.

> You have heard that it was said to the people long ago, "You shall not murder, and anyone who murders will be subject to judgment." But I tell you that anyone who is angry with a brother or sister will be subject to judgment. (Matthew 5:21–22)

> You have heard that it was said, "You shall not commit adultery." But I tell you that anyone who looks at a woman lustfully has already committed adultery with her in his heart. (Matthew 5:27–28)

The law is not about behavior but about the heart. Far before the law is broken, the heart is broken. It raises my final point about the law.

Some years ago, I had the privilege of meeting and getting to know the preacher to the papal household (under John Paul II and beyond), Father Raniero Cantalamessa. He surprisingly accepted our invitation to come to Wilmore, Kentucky, to minister among us when I served as dean of the chapel at Asbury Seminary. He is one of my favorite teachers in the kingdom of God—especially on the Holy Spirit. In a lecture on Pentecost, he spoke this striking word, "The Law was given so the Spirit may be desired. The Spirit was given so the Law might be obeyed."

Isn't that exactly what Ezekiel was saying in this extraordinary word of prophecy?

> I will give them an undivided heart and put a new spirit in them; I will remove from them their heart of stone and give them a heart of flesh. Then they will follow my decrees and be careful to keep my laws. They will be my people, and I will be their God. (Ezekiel 11:19–20)

This passage brings us to the heart of the matter—which is that the law is a matter of heart and spirit. To break the law is to divide (or to break) one's heart. We all know the difference between the letter of the law and the spirit of the law. We must have the Spirit of God in order to obey the spirit of the law, and we must obey the spirit of the law in order to live wholeheartedly.

I must have a new heart and a right spirit—both of which come from the Holy Spirit. This brings us to the prescience of David's broken-hearted prayer, uttered in the contrite aftermath of breaking practically all ten of the Ten Commandments.

> Create in me a pure heart, O God,
> and renew a steadfast spirit within me.
> (Psalm 51:10)

The Prayer for Deliverance

Lord Jesus, you are my Deliverer. I receive your deliverance from a hard heart of stone. I receive your deliverance into a soft heart of flesh, a heart that leaps to listen and trust and obey. Father, thank you that by your Spirit you give us an undivided heart; you remove from us our heart of stone and give us a heart of flesh. We have your Spirit, Lord, yet we must have more of your Spirit; or rather, your Spirit must have more of us. Work on me and in me and through me at the level of my heart. As the psalmist prays, "I will run in the way of your commandments when you enlarge my heart" (Psalm 119:32 ESV). It will be for your glory, for others' gain, and for my good.

Glory be to the Father and to the Son and to the Holy Ghost.
As it was in the beginning, is now and ever shall be.
World without end. Amen! Amen!

The Questions

Have you entered into the heart-level discipleship of the Spirit? Are you ready to get beneath the behavioral level of life and into the matters of brokenness and healing? Are you seeing the brokenness of the letter of the law legalism and the wholeness of trusting obedience? Are you grasping the connections between law and heart and spirit?

66

Exodus 20:18–21

On Fearing God Without Being Afraid of God

When the people saw the thunder and lightning and heard the trumpet and saw the mountain in smoke, they trembled with fear. They stayed at a distance and said to Moses, "Speak to us yourself and we will listen. But do not have God speak to us or we will die."

Moses said to the people, "Do not be afraid. God has come to test you, so that the fear of God will be with you to keep you from sinning."

The people remained at a distance, while Moses approached the thick darkness where God was.

Consider This

There is being afraid of God, and then there is the fear of God.

Being afraid of God describes the reaction of persons who come into God's unmitigated presence and do not know God's nature. The fear of God describes the posture of persons who know the enormity of God's holiness yet trust in the extravagance of God's goodness.

In today's devotional, the Israelites are bouncing between these two places. The wilderness can be like that. One day it is cloud by day and fire by night, manna in the morning and quail in the evening, and the next it's thunder, lightning, and something akin to volcanic fire on the mountain.

The Israelites kept their distance and asked Moses,

> Speak to us yourself and we will listen. But do not have God speak to us or we will die.

Notice that Moses did not want them to be afraid of God, yet he wanted them to live in the "fear of God." It's plain here:

> Moses said to the people, "Do not be afraid. God has come to test you, so that the fear of God will be with you to keep you from sinning."

It feels like a contradiction—don't be afraid of God, yet live in the fear of God—but it's not. It comes back to these two sides of the same coin—holiness and love. God is holy love, and in the end, these are not two things. Holy love is one thing. It is both awe-inspiringly terrifying and breathtakingly good. God splits the sea, drowns an enemy army of cruel tormentors, and provides breakfast.

Every encounter with God is a test designed to give us experienced understanding. We must all depend completely on God's mercy without presuming on his grace. Doing so is impossible unless we actually know God. Knowing about God is not enough. Relating to God through an intermediary like Moses is not workable. We must know God directly. The goal of this way of life is to live in the fear of God without being afraid of God.

We live in the fear of God and in the embrace of God at the same time. On the one hand, we approach God humbly, and on the other, we approach him confidently. Are we growing in our awareness of the true nature of God, or does our vision of God remain skewed? This is why staying close to the Scriptures is essential. Without the witness of

Scripture to the true God, we re-create God in our own image about as fast as it takes to say "golden calf."

I was driving down the interstate recently when I spotted a bumper sticker that said, "Sin Now. Pray Later." This sentiment denies both holiness and love. Let's close today with the bumper sticker that fellow needed (we all need it!). Warning—it will take a large sticker:

> If we deliberately keep on sinning after we have received the knowledge of the truth, no sacrifice for sins is left, but only a fearful expectation of judgment and of raging fire that will consume the enemies of God. Anyone who rejected the law of Moses died without mercy on the testimony of two or three witnesses. How much more severely do you think someone deserves to be punished who has trampled the Son of God underfoot, who has treated as an unholy thing the blood of the covenant that sanctified them, and who has insulted the Spirit of grace? For we know him who said, "It is mine to avenge; I will repay," and again, "The Lord will judge his people." It is a dreadful thing to fall into the hands of the living God. (Hebrews 10:26–31)

The Prayer for Deliverance

Lord Jesus, you are my Deliverer. Father, you are holy, and you are love, and how perfectly have you revealed yourself to us through your Word and your Spirit. And how beautifully you show us the fullness of Word and Spirit in your Son, Jesus. The miracle we struggle to believe is this—as we see your fullness in Jesus Christ, we marvel that you can grant that same fullness to us in him. Bring us breakthrough this week in our understanding of you and of ourselves. We want to live in the fear of you without being afraid of you. It will be for my good, for others' gain, and for your glory. In Jesus's name. Amen.

> Glory be to the Father and to the Son and to the Holy Ghost.
> As it was in the beginning, is now and ever shall be.
> World without end. Amen! Amen!

The Questions

Do you struggle to perceive and experientially appreciate God's holiness or God's love? How does seeing these two things as one thing help you? Not the same thing, mind you, yet the one thing?

67

Exodus 20:24–26

Eight Learnings from the Wilderness So Far

> *"Make an altar of earth for me and sacrifice on it your burnt offerings and fellowship offerings, your sheep and goats and your cattle. Wherever I cause my name to be honored, I will come to you and bless you. If you make an altar of stones for me, do not build it with dressed stones, for you will defile it if you use a tool on it. And do not go up to my altar on steps, or your private parts may be exposed."*

Consider This

In case you're not familiar with the old acronym KISS, let me enlighten you. It stands for Keep it simple, stupid. And I hear that in the opening words of today's text:

> Make an altar of earth for me.

Translation: Keep it simple, stupid.

Throughout the exodus journey, God did extraordinary things yet kept those things very simple. Here are eight extraordinary and profoundly simple learnings we've acquired so far:

1. God hears the prayers and cries of his people and remembers his covenant with them.

2. God delivers us from evil, from slavery, from oppression, and from the power of Pharaoh and every otherworldly and heavenly principality.
3. God provides for our needs with daily bread and every other dimension of provision, though he will allow us to hunger and thirst at times.
4. God guides us on the path of pilgrimage, cloud by day and fire by night. He leads us in the way of his will and according to his wisdom.
5. God fights through us and with us and for us, defeating our enemies and his in the wilderness.
6. God instructs us according to his Word. He speaks his Word to us concerning how he would have us live before him and others.
7. God is holy, and he wants a holy people for himself and his purposes on the earth.
8. God is love, and he wants only this from us: Love for himself and love for others. It really is that simple.

When you think about it, the Ten Words (or Commandments) are all about keeping things simple, aren't they? And because God knows we will break all ten and then some, in anticipation, he said this:

> Make an altar of earth for me and sacrifice on it your burnt offerings and fellowship offerings, your sheep and goats and your cattle.

And because God knows our propensity to make the simple complicated—to introduce all sorts of sophistication to things he intended to keep very basic—in anticipation, he said this:

> If you make an altar of stones for me, do not build it with dressed stones, for you will defile it if you use a tool on it.

If an altar of earth is good, then an altar of diamonds and gold must be better, right? Wrong!

KISS—Keep it simple, stupid.

Make an altar of earth for me.

One of the things I appreciated about John Wesley is the way he emphasized what he called "plain scriptural Christianity." He often spoke of "primitive faith." Primal faith is plain and unadorned, albeit very powerful. (And, yes, I recognize that making everything plain and unadorned can create the same broken reality in the opposite direction.) I wonder how our faith has become adorned with all manner of decoration, attire, and accoutrements. I wonder what it would mean to get back to primitive faith, to plain scriptural Christianity. Might we have such an opportunity before us now?

Make an altar of earth for me.

The Prayer for Deliverance

Lord Jesus, you are my Deliverer. Thank you for your persistent mind and heart to pursue relationship with us. Would you train us in the simplicity of how we might respond to your initiative? We are so filled with our own initiative, even noble religious initiative, that we easily miss what you are doing in our midst. Awaken us to the primitive and plain faith of our ancestors. Enliven us by your Spirit to the re-creating power of your Word. Come, Holy Spirit, and strip away the layers and levels of adornment and amenity we have constructed so that we might be alive again to the fullness of you. It will be for your glory, for others' gain, and for my good.

Glory be to the Father and to the Son and to the Holy Ghost.
As it was in the beginning, is now and ever shall be.
World without end. Amen! Amen!

The Questions

What are you learning in this wilderness journey? Which of the eight learnings do you most resonate with now? What is your number 9?

How is your life and life with God being pared back, stripped away, and brought back to the primitive edge?

68

Exodus 21:12–14; 22:5; 23:2

The Lord Is in the Details

> *"Anyone who strikes a person with a fatal blow is to be put to death. However, if it is not done intentionally, but God lets it happen, they are to flee to a place I will designate. But if anyone schemes and kills someone deliberately, that person is to be taken from my altar and put to death. . . .*
>
> *"If anyone grazes their livestock in a field or vineyard and lets them stray and they graze in someone else's field, the offender must make restitution from the best of their own field or vineyard. . . .*
>
> *"Do not follow the crowd in doing wrong. When you give testimony in a lawsuit, do not pervert justice by siding with the crowd."*

Consider This

A funny phrase often deployed in contracts law is "The big print giveth, but the little print taketh away."

Some people think that way about the biblical law—like there are the Big Ten, and then there's the minutia. It's easy to think, *Well, most of this no longer applies, so what's the point of studying it?* My take is that the Word of God always reveals the wisdom of God, and the wisdom of God always points us toward the will of God.

Another phrase often bandied about in courtrooms and board rooms is, "The devil is in the details." Exodus 21, 22, and 23 reveal just the opposite: The Lord is in the details. That said, rather than spending weeks, I want to offer a brief story and comment.

One evening when our family was out on a walk through the neighborhood, we approached some neighbors in their front yard. My oldest son (who was about seven at the time) walked up to their friendly Labrador retriever, whom he often greeted. This time when he reached out to pet the dog, it snapped at him, sinking its canines deep into his arm. He still has the bite scar to prove it. It traumatized David and shocked us all—especially the owner.

I immediately remembered an obscure learning from law school. They called it the One Bite Rule. In most places, if a dog bites someone for the first time, the owner is not liable for the injury. However, if the dog bites someone after this, the owner is liable for the damages from the personal injury. Where does this kind of wisdom come from? Well, Exodus 22, of course!

> If a bull gores a man or woman to death, the bull is to be stoned to death, and its meat must not be eaten. But the owner of the bull will not be held responsible. If, however, the bull has had the habit of goring and the owner has been warned but has not kept it penned up and it kills a man or woman, the bull is to be stoned and its owner also is to be put to death. (Exodus 21:28–29)

Shall we call it the "One Gore Rule"? The Law then goes on to make provision for the payment of damages instead of the loss of the owner's life and goes further to deal with the scenario if the loss of life occurred with a son or daughter or a slave.

Take some time and read these chapters of what can be so easily dismissed as "no longer binding" or "arcane minutia," and you will find scores of antecedents and precursors to present-day property law, personal injury law, and criminal law. The Word of God reveals the wisdom of God, which points the way to the will of God. No, modern-day courts do not cite statutes from Exodus, though they stand on the foundations given by God and inscribed by Moses on Mount Sinai.

At a later time, I politely shared the law and suggested to the owner of the dog that he would be wise to consider euthanizing the dog, though I didn't insist on it. Sure enough, several years later, I learned the dog had found another victim—the son of a good friend of mine living in a different city—biting him on the face this time. I informed them that they had the dog and its owners "dead to rights."

The Prayer for Deliverance

Lord Jesus, you are my Deliverer. Thank you for the way we see the wisdom and the will of God imparted in the Law given to Moses on Mount Sinai. Thank you for both the depth of justice and the breadth of mercy articulated in the statutes. Thank you for revealing the depth of your care for all people by investing yourself in the details of our everyday lives. We receive your deliverance for our broken ways of executing justice without mercy—which is not just. We receive your deliverance from our broken ways of extending mercy without justice—which is not merciful. We receive your deliverance into the indivisible union of justice and mercy, which we behold in your life, death, and resurrection. Thank you for the cross, where you took our just penalty on yourself and transformed it into the mercy of eternal salvation. May our lives reflect such miraculous love. It will be for your glory, for others' gain, and for my good.

Glory be to the Father and to the Son and to the Holy Ghost.
As it was in the beginning, is now and ever shall be.
World without end. Amen! Amen!

The Questions

What has been your level of attention or indifference to and posture toward the multiplicity of statutes following the Ten Commandments?

69

Exodus 23:20–30

Learning the Landscape of Salvation and Deliverance

"See, I am sending an angel ahead of you to guard you along the way and to bring you to the place I have prepared. Pay attention to him and listen to what he says. Do not rebel against him; he will not forgive your rebellion, since my Name is in him. If you listen carefully to what he says and do all that I say, I will be an enemy to your enemies and will oppose those who oppose you. My angel will go ahead of you and bring you into the land of the Amorites, Hittites, Perizzites, Canaanites, Hivites and Jebusites, and I will wipe them out. Do not bow down before their gods or worship them or follow their practices. You must demolish them and break their sacred stones to pieces. Worship the Lord *your God, and his blessing will be on your food and water. I will take away sickness from among you, and none will miscarry or be barren in your land. I will give you a full life span.*

"I will send my terror ahead of you and throw into confusion every nation you encounter. I will make all your enemies turn their backs and run. I will send the hornet ahead of you to drive the Hivites, Canaanites and Hittites out of your way. But I will not drive them out in a single year, because the land would become desolate and the wild animals too numerous for you. Little by little I will drive them out before you, until you have increased enough to take possession of the land."

Consider This

We are learning a lot about salvation and deliverance on this journey through Exodus. With the following contrasts, I will show you how they are not the same thing.

- Salvation: The transfer of ownership from Pharaoh to God—from the identity of slaves to the identity of sons and daughters.

- Deliverance: The realized experiential journey from slavery to freedom, which comes from the healing of our deepest identity through the transformation of our brokenness.
- Salvation: The transactional transfer from the kingdom of darkness, death, and chaos to the kingdom of light, life, and new creation.
- Deliverance: The transformational journey and process from darkness to light, from death to life, and from chaos to new creation.
- Salvation: Lord, you took me out of Egypt.
- Deliverance: Now take Egypt out of me.

The Israelites got out of Egypt's ownership overnight. It would take years before they were free of the impacts and effects of Egypt's oppression. Today's text gives us some solid guidance on the transformational process of deliverance.

> See, I am sending an angel ahead of you to guard you along the way and to bring you to the place I have prepared. Pay attention to him and listen to what he says.

We do not deliver ourselves. It is not self-help or self-improvement or trying harder to be better. Jesus is our Deliverer. God decrees deliverance by his Word. We must then declare the decree of deliverance over our world by the Word through the Spirit.

> If you listen carefully to what he says and do all that I say, I will be an enemy to your enemies and will oppose those who oppose you.

Though salvation happens in an instant, deliverance takes time. Salvation is by grace through faith and requires only our receiving it. Deliverance is by grace through faith and requires our involved participation to see it through.

> I will send my terror ahead of you and throw into confusion

> every nation you encounter. I will make all your enemies turn their backs and run. I will send the hornet ahead of you to drive the Hivites, Canaanites and Hittites out of your way.

Deliverance is the transformational journey and experienced outcome of "working out one's salvation with fear and trembling" as God works in us "to will and to act in order to fulfill his good purpose." It requires our participation. It is the Holy Spirit–empowered process whereby Jesus displaces our sin by his righteousness, our brokenness by his wholeness, and our emptiness by his fullness. Deliverance is the ongoing and often protracted battle of confronting and tearing down demonic strongholds of darkness, death, and chaos, the breaking of generational curses, the healing of brokenness, afflictions, addictions, and infirmities, and the driving out of everything that opposes the Word, will, and ways of God.

> Therefore, my dear friends, as you have always obeyed—not only in my presence, but now much more in my absence—continue to work out your salvation with fear and trembling, for it is God who works in you to will and to act in order to fulfill his good purpose. (Philippians 2:12–13)

There is one more bit in today's text we must highlight.

> Little by little I will drive them out before you, until you have increased enough to take possession of the land.

Deliverance takes time and, as a result, requires patience and perseverance. We are being retrofitted for ever-increasing glory. We have seasons of intense battle and breakthrough followed by what feels like lengthy seasons of waiting and even regression at times. Everything will come against deliverance, especially discouragement. It is why we must keep this watchword ever before us:

> Encourage one another daily, as long as it is called "Today," so that none of you may be hardened by sin's deceitfulness. (Hebrews 3:13)

The Prayer for Deliverance

Lord Jesus, you are my Deliverer. I now declare the word you have decreed:

> The Lord is the Spirit, and where the Spirit of the Lord is, there is freedom. And we all, who with unveiled faces contemplate the Lord's glory, are being transformed into his image with ever-increasing glory, which comes from the Lord, who is the Spirit. (2 Corinthians 3:17–18)

And as you have decreed in your Word, I also now declare:

> [Your] divine power has given us everything we need for a godly life through our knowledge of [you] who called us by [your] own glory and goodness. Through these [you] have given us [your] very great and precious promises, so that through them we may participate in the divine nature, having escaped the corruption in the world caused by evil desires. [Empower us now to] make every effort to add to [our] faith goodness; and to goodness, knowledge; and to knowledge, self-control; and to self-control, perseverance; and to perseverance, godliness; and to godliness, mutual affection; and to mutual affection, love. For if [we] possess these qualities in increasing measure, they will keep [us] from being ineffective and unproductive in [our] knowledge of our Lord Jesus Christ. (2 Peter 1:3–8)

It will be for your glory, for others' gain, and for my good.

> Glory be to the Father and to the Son and to the Holy Ghost.
> As it was in the beginning, is now and ever shall be.
> World without end. Amen! Amen!

The Questions

How is your understanding of the Lord's work for, in, and through you growing? How might you articulate the particular work of deliverance afoot in your life just now? What are the particular barriers you face and feel? How do you receive encouragement? Are you in a discipleship group yet?

Week 10: Discussion Questions

Hearing the Text

Read Exodus 20:12–23:30.

Responding to the Text

- What did you hear?
- What did you see?
- What did you otherwise sense from the Lord?

Sharing Insights and Implications for Discipleship

Drawing from the Scripture text and daily readings, what did you find challenging, encouraging, provocative, comforting, invasive, inspiring, corrective, affirming, guiding, or warning?

Shaping Intentions for Prayer

Write your discipleship intention for the week ahead.

11
WEEK

Exodus 24:1–32:6

71

Exodus 24:1–8

Paving the Road to Hell (and Heaven)

Then the Lord said to Moses, "Come up to the Lord, you and Aaron, Nadab and Abihu, and seventy of the elders of Israel. You are to worship at a distance, but Moses alone is to approach the Lord; the others must not come near. And the people may not come up with him."

When Moses went and told the people all the Lord's words and laws, they responded with one voice, "Everything the Lord has said we will do." Moses then wrote down everything the Lord had said.

He got up early the next morning and built an altar at the foot of the mountain and set up twelve stone pillars representing the twelve tribes of Israel. Then he sent young Israelite men, and they offered burnt offerings and sacrificed young bulls as fellowship offerings to the Lord. Moses took half of the blood and put it in bowls, and the other half he splashed against the altar. Then he took the Book of the Covenant and read it to the people. They responded, "We will do everything the Lord has said; we will obey."

Moses then took the blood, sprinkled it on the people and said, "This is the blood of the covenant that the Lord has made with you in accordance with all these words."

Consider This

If my count is correct, today's text marks the third time the Israelites have verbally and vocally expressed their intentions of obedience, stating some version of the following:

> Everything the Lord has said we will do.

As we are now within days of recounting the catastrophic failure known to history as "The Golden Calf," it seems apropos to remember the old adage "The road to hell is paved with good intentions."

But what about the road to heaven?

It would make sense to say something like, "The road to heaven is paved with loving obedience." If only it were true. You want the truth? It's a hard one. Brace for it: The road to heaven is paved with blood.

Remember the Passover? "The blood will be a sign for you on the houses where you are, and when I see the blood, I will pass over you" (Exodus 12:13).

And, of course, you saw it in today's text as the "young men" sacrificed "young bulls."

> Moses took half of the blood and put it in bowls, and the other half he splashed against the altar. . . . Moses then took the blood, sprinkled it on the people.

The salvation and deliverance wrought by a Holy God is a bloody mess. But why blood? "For the life of a creature is in the blood, and I have given it to you to make atonement for yourselves on the altar; it is the blood that makes atonement for one's life" (Leviticus 17:11).

In the spirit of primitive Christianity and primal faith, let's strip it back to the foundation: Sin is death. Blood is life.

But how is sin death? Sin destroys our relationship with God. An unreconciled relationship with God is death. The Bible does not mince words: "For the wages of sin is death, but the gift of God is eternal life in Christ Jesus our Lord" (Romans 6:23).

Sin is death. Blood is life. Atonement (at-one-ment) is reconciliation with God. Therefore, only blood can atone for sin—restoring the relationship between sinful people and a holy God.

So, back to where we began today: The road to hell is paved with good intentions.

And, yes, the road to heaven is paved with loving obedience—not ours, but Jesus's. "For just as through the disobedience of the one man the many were made sinners, so also through the obedience of the one man the many will be made righteous" (Romans 5:19).

And, yes, the road to heaven is paved with blood—not the blood of animals anymore but the blood of Jesus.

> For God was pleased to have all his fullness dwell in him, and through him to reconcile to himself all things, whether things on earth or things in heaven, by making peace through his blood, shed on the cross. (Colossians 1:19–20)

The road to heaven is paved with blood.

The Prayer for Deliverance

Lord Jesus, you are my Deliverer. I receive your deliverance from sin to righteousness, from darkness to light, from death to life, and from chaos to new creation—indeed, from hell to heaven—all of which has come by your blood. I receive your blood sacrifice for my sins, your death in my place, and your resurrection as my eternal life. I do not claim this as a distant hope but receive it as a present reality. Awaken me to the unparalleled power of the blood of Jesus—nothing but the blood of Jesus. It will be for your glory, for others' gain, and for my good.

> Glory be to the Father and to the Son and to the Holy Ghost.
> As it was in the beginning, is now and ever shall be.
> World without end. Amen! Amen!

The Questions

What is your level of real appreciation for the blood of Jesus? Does it remain primarily at the level of your theological or conceptual understanding, or has it seized your core being? Have you come to grips with the fact that neither your good intentions nor your good actions will be enough for your salvation and deliverance from sin and death?

72

Exodus 25:1–9

On the Difference Between Fundraising and Fund-Receiving

The Lord said to Moses, "Tell the Israelites to bring me an offering. You are to receive the offering for me from everyone whose heart prompts them to give. These are the offerings you are to receive from them: gold, silver and bronze; blue, purple and scarlet yarn and fine linen; goat hair; ram skins dyed red and another type of durable leather; acacia wood; olive oil for the light; spices for the anointing oil and for the fragrant incense; and onyx stones and other gems to be mounted on the ephod and breastpiece.

"Then have them make a sanctuary for me, and I will dwell among them. Make this tabernacle and all its furnishings exactly like the pattern I will show you."

Consider This

We come now to the building of the tabernacle—the place set apart for God to dwell in the midst of his people. There is so much to say, and I will say more as we move along, but the one thing I want to point out at the outset is the way something is built is as (or perhaps more) important as the thing being built for God. This is doubly so when it comes to the way such things are funded. Today's text reveals some clear wisdom.

> The Lord said to Moses, "Tell the Israelites to bring me an offering. You are to receive the offering for me from everyone whose heart prompts them to give."

I hate fundraising. I suspect you hate it too. There's an entire industrial complex out there built up around raising funds. The emphasis is on people or organizations "raising" funding from other people. Sure, it is being done "for God" and in God's name and so often for the sake of a godly mission, but I think it misses the mark.

The text seems to articulate a different approach from "fundraising." I would call it "fund-receiving." Look closely at the text again.

1. *"Tell the Israelites to bring me an offering"*: This endeavor was between the people and God, not the people and the organization or ministry. Moses was not asking the Israelites to support the cause or fund the budget. He was leading them to engage with God.
2. *"You are to receive the offering for me"*: The organization or ministry receives the offering for God, not for the organization. It seems like a subtle nuance. It is not.
3. *". . . from everyone whose heart prompts them to give"*: Moses was not asking for everyone to "do their part." We get the impression Moses was not going to send endless appeals to wear down the Israelites. There is a difference between God prompting a person's heart toward giving and Moses prompting them.
4. "These are the offerings you are to receive from them": Moses laid out with specificity the offering to be received. Note, though, that the blueprints for the tabernacle had not yet been given.

A few days later, the Israelites exhibited quite a different approach to such things. Do the words "golden calf" ring a bell?

> When the people saw that Moses was so long in coming down from the mountain, they gathered around Aaron and said, "Come, make us gods who will go before us. As for this fellow Moses who brought us up out of Egypt, we don't know what has happened to him." (Exodus 32:1)

Notice the contrasting approach at work here:

> Aaron said to them, "Take off the gold earrings that your wives, your sons and your daughters are wearing, and bring them to me." (Exodus 32:2)

I will let you do the math from here.

The Prayer for Deliverance

Lord Jesus, you are my Deliverer. I receive your deliverance from the money-centered enterprise of the golden calf and all its conscripted economy. I receive your deliverance into the God-centered world of the tabernacle with all its gracious provision. I receive your deliverance from the tiring approach of conscription and into the gracious reality of offering. Put my heart in touch with your prompting alone and grant me an expansive generosity by your Spirit. Remind us all that everything belongs to you—the cattle on a thousand hills and, yes, the hills too. Make us stewards of the manifold grace of God, keeping us ever mindful that where our hearts are, our treasure will be also. It will be for your glory, for others gain, and for my good.

Glory be to the Father and to the Son and to the Holy Ghost.
As it was in the beginning, is now and ever shall be.
World without end. Amen! Amen!

The Questions

What contrasts do you see between the approach taken with the tabernacle and that taken with the golden calf? List as many as you can discern.

73

Exodus 26:1–6; 27:20–21; 28:1–5

Why Those Curtains Are to Die For!

"Make the tabernacle with ten curtains of finely twisted linen and blue, purple and scarlet yarn, with cherubim woven into them by a skilled worker. All the curtains are to be the same size—twenty-eight cubits long and four cubits wide. Join five of the curtains together, and

do the same with the other five. Make loops of blue material along the edge of the end curtain in one set, and do the same with the end curtain in the other set. Make fifty loops on one curtain and fifty loops on the end curtain of the other set, with the loops opposite each other. Then make fifty gold clasps and use them to fasten the curtains together so that the tabernacle is a unit. . . .

"Command the Israelites to bring you clear oil of pressed olives for the light so that the lamps may be kept burning. In the tent of meeting, outside the curtain that shields the ark of the covenant law, Aaron and his sons are to keep the lamps burning before the Lord *from evening till morning. This is to be a lasting ordinance among the Israelites for the generations to come. . . .*

"Have Aaron your brother brought to you from among the Israelites, along with his sons Nadab and Abihu, Eleazar and Ithamar, so they may serve me as priests. Make sacred garments for your brother Aaron to give him dignity and honor. Tell all the skilled workers to whom I have given wisdom in such matters that they are to make garments for Aaron, for his consecration, so he may serve me as priest. These are the garments they are to make: a breastpiece, an ephod, a robe, a woven tunic, a turban and a sash. They are to make these sacred garments for your brother Aaron and his sons, so they may serve me as priests. Have them use gold, and blue, purple and scarlet yarn, and fine linen."

Consider This

Curtains.

God cares about the curtains.

Don't ever tell me that God is not in the details. He cares about the curtains.

Exquisitely cares.

Ten curtains. All the same size. Twenty-eight cubits long by four cubits wide. (By my math, with conversions, it came to about 240 square feet per curtain [2,400 square feet in all].) They were to be joined together into two groups of five. Not just any old blackout curtains from Target would do. These were custom curtains. They were to be made of finely twisted linen in blue, purple, and scarlet yarn, and they were to have cherubim woven into them by a skilled worker.

After that, loops were to be made for the curtains, presumably so they could be held up by rods. The craftsmen were to make one hundred loops, fifty for each set of five curtains. But that was not ten loops for each curtain. No, they were to put fifty loops on the curtain at one end of the first set and then fifty loops on the other end curtain of the second set and to make sure those loops were on opposite sides of each other. Oh, yes, and they were to make the loops from blue material—not the trendy beige, but blue. (And the Hebrew word likely identified some specific shade of blue—like perhaps indigo.)

Now, the craftsmen couldn't forget they needed fifty clasps so they could close and fasten those finely crafted cherubim-woven curtains with the exquisitely stitched blue loops. And those clasps had to be made from solid gold because they would be hung in the presence of the almighty God of heaven and earth.

Curtains matter to God.

Why all this exquisite care about these otherwise seemingly insignificant details?

Because the people were dealing with a holy God—a divine being who is wholly other than human beings, though he created them in his image. This God is not common, not casual, and not contaminated by sin.

The curtains mattered because God's people were creating a space unlike any other space on the earth. It was a place where the holy God could draw near to and meet with unholy people. It was a place of overlap—the overlap of realms long separated, the heavens and the earth. It would serve as a portal of sorts—a most holy place unlike any other place in the cosmos, where mortals could behold the eternal, where a person could dare to breathe the rarified air of "on earth as it is in heaven" and dare to sing the ancient verse, "As it was in the beginning, is now and ever shall be. World without end. Amen! Amen!"

Curtains matter so much to God that he himself became the curtain.

> Therefore, brothers and sisters, since we have confidence to enter the Most Holy Place by the blood of Jesus, by a new and living way opened

for us through the *curtain*, that is, his body, and since we have a great priest over the house of God, let us draw near to God with a sincere heart and with the full assurance that faith brings, having our hearts sprinkled to cleanse us from a guilty conscience and having our bodies washed with pure water. (Hebrews 10:19–22, emphasis added)

That's why curtains matter and oil matters and clothes matter. And if these curtains and oil and clothes matter most, might all curtains and oil and clothes matter more?

And, yes, those curtains are to die for!

The Prayer for Deliverance

Lord Jesus, you are my Deliverer. I receive your deliverance from seeing and approaching you as casual and common and otherwise believing all the hullabaloo about curtains was overkill. Forgive me. I receive your deliverance into approaching you as holy beyond any degree of holiness I could ever even conceive of and into a measure of gratitude for your Son and his blood atonement for me beyond anything I can presently fathom. Thank you that the very physical body of Jesus became the curtain of all curtains, and at the moment of his death, the curtain in the temple tore from top to bottom. Deliver me into the fullness of the open curtain like never before, by the blood of Jesus into the most holy place of his presence, which is now available everywhere and all the time. Thank you for the cross. It will be for your glory, for others' gain, and for my good.

Glory be to the Father and to the Son and to the Holy Ghost.
As it was in the beginning, is now and ever shall be.
World without end. Amen! Amen!

The Questions

What do you make of all this detail about curtains? Are you as wowed as I am?

74

Exodus 29:44–46; 30:25–30

Waking Up to the Presence of God

"So I will consecrate the tent of meeting and the altar and will consecrate Aaron and his sons to serve me as priests. Then I will dwell among the Israelites and be their God. They will know that I am the Lord *their God, who brought them out of Egypt so that I might dwell among them. I am the* Lord *their God. . . .*

"Make these into a sacred anointing oil, a fragrant blend, the work of a perfumer. It will be the sacred anointing oil. Then use it to anoint the tent of meeting, the ark of the covenant law, the table and all its articles, the lampstand and its accessories, the altar of incense, the altar of burnt offering and all its utensils, and the basin with its stand. You shall consecrate them so they will be most holy, and whatever touches them will be holy.

"Anoint Aaron and his sons and consecrate them so they may serve me as priests."

Consider This

In this passage, we come again to one of the most significant terms in the Bible.

Consecrate.

This is what people do when God draws near. God is holy—a divine being from another realm, of another multi-infinity of orders of magnitude. But notice how the text opens:

> So I will consecrate the tent of meeting and the altar and will consecrate Aaron and his sons to serve me as priests.

God is so completely other than us that there is nothing we can do to prepare to be in his presence. He has to make a way. That's what God was saying and doing in today's text.

We do not consecrate ourselves.

We cannot consecrate ourselves.

> *So I will consecrate.*

Almighty, holy, uncreated, unapproachable, I-Am-That-I-Am God does the consecrating. We present ourselves for consecration, but it is God who consecrates.

That's what we are doing here. We are not having quiet time. We are entering into a holy rite of consecration. We are winning the day. I frequently say to our church, "If you want to win the day, you have to win the morning."

Then I add, "If you want to win the week, you have to win Sunday."

And winning the morning is all about consecration. I recognize that people read and pray at different times of day, but if I'm the doctor (and I'm not) and I'm writing the prescription, I'm saying, "Take the medicine in the morning." The morning is for consecration. Consecration opens the door into the vast cathedral of the Word of God, which is the house of transformation—the place of beholding and becoming. And transformation opens the door into the fields of the world, longing for the demonstration—hungry for the seeds of grace and love; of justice with mercy; of blessing and encouragement.

> So I will consecrate the tent of meeting and the altar and will consecrate Aaron and his sons to serve me as priests.

Consider joining me daily by reciting this transformational prayer of consecration.

> Wake up, sleeper,
> rise from the dead,
> and Christ will shine on you. (Ephesians 5:14)

Abba, I belong to you.
I lift up my heart to you.
I set my mind on you.
I fix my eyes on you.
I offer my body to you as a living sacrifice.

Today I receive afresh in my inmost being—the sanctuary of your Spirit—the transforming gift of your Son, our Lord, Jesus Christ.

Praying in the name of the Father, and the Son, and the Holy Spirit. Amen.

To be clear, we are not consecrated by this prayer or by anything else we do. We are consecrated by God, by the blood of Jesus, through the curtain, which is Christ's body.

The Prayer for Deliverance

Lord Jesus, you are my Deliverer. I receive your deliverance from casual religion and into real consecration. And I receive your deliverance from rigorous striving, which is so often the turn I mistakenly make trying to escape my casual approach. I receive your deliverance into the simple, humble faith of a consecrated life. Abba, I belong to you. It will be for your glory, for others' gain, and for my good.

Glory be to the Father and to the Son and to the Holy Ghost.
As it was in the beginning, is now and ever shall be.
World without end. Amen! Amen!

The Questions

How are you resonating (or not) with my vision for what we previously called "quiet time" or "morning devotions"? Are you living into this daily movement of consecration, transformation, and demonstration? Do you approve of and accept the proposed edits to the consecration prayer?

75

Exodus 31:1–6

The Holiness of Art and Artists

> *Then the LORD said to Moses, "See, I have chosen Bezalel son of Uri, the son of Hur, of the tribe of Judah, and I have filled him with the Spirit of God, with wisdom, with understanding, with knowledge and with all kinds of skills—to make artistic designs for work in gold, silver and bronze, to cut and set stones, to work in wood, and to engage in all kinds of crafts. Moreover, I have appointed Oholiab son of Ahisamak, of the tribe of Dan, to help him. Also I have given ability to all the skilled workers to make everything I have commanded you."*

Consider This

Bezalel.

I don't recall any place in the Bible thus far where we see words like this:

> I have filled him with the Spirit of God.

Bezalel, son of Uri, son of Hur, of the tribe of Judah.

It looks like the first person the completely other, uncreated, I-am-who-I-am, holy, and living God has determined to fill with the Spirit of God is not a prophet or preacher, a priest or a teacher, a king or a military leader, a shepherd, a farmer, or a fisherman, but—wait for it—an artist.

I want you to grasp the full effect of this:

> I have filled him with the Spirit of God, with wisdom, with understanding, with knowledge and with all kinds of skills.

Picture the Israelites in the middle of the wilderness. Before them is their first building project. It is not a courthouse nor a Manna-Mart Super Center nor a sandal repair shop; it is a tabernacle with a sophisticated set of instructions for making everything from exquisite curtains to priestly apparel. And the first person on the call list is an artist. The job description—straight from heaven:

> to make artistic designs for work in gold, silver and bronze,
> to cut and set stones,
> to work in wood, and
> to engage in all kinds of crafts.

This is brilliant. God called an artist. And lest we miss the significance of that little word we so often see translated to English as "see," if it even gets translated at all—the better rendering is "behold."

> [Behold], I have chosen Bezalel.

Behold. To behold is to see beyond sight. Me thinks of beholding as a participation in divine perceptivity.

This same little Hebrew word appears first in Genesis 1—no less than eight times, the last of which says:

> And God saw everything that he had made, and behold, it was very good. And there was evening and there was morning, the sixth day. (Genesis 1:31 ESV)

God creates, and God beholds. As divine image-bearers, we do the same. That's what we were made for.

And that's precisely what artists do. Artists have a sense of vision beyond eyesight. They see what can't be seen, and they bring it into visibility through acts of creation so we can see it too. They behold, and in creating something for us to see, they train us to behold—to see beyond our limited sight.

Behold—the first art project in the kingdom of God is an installation of creativity that will point us not to the artist nor to the art, but to God himself. This is the divine calling of holy artists—to forge and fashion the vision of "on earth as it is in heaven" through every medium imaginable by all manner of creative work. I think I may have stumbled onto a definition of worship from the back side.

What if all work was approached in this same way? When work is done as worship—which is to say, from a place of beholding—it causes all work to rise to the level of art. It becomes a thing to "behold," which points us to the God of glory. There is a word for this kind of awakening: *renaissance*.

There's a bit of an art meets tabernacle (aka Seed House) meets small-town Arkansas unfolding in my village—a rural renaissance of sorts. My son David, whom I believe to be one of the Bezalels of our time, has joined me in Gillett, Arkansas. He's working on a piece of art on the exodus (called Ex Deus) that we will be sharing soon.[1] It will be something to behold!

The Prayer for Deliverance

Lord Jesus, you are my Deliverer. I receive your deliverance from my failure to notice. I'm moving so fast and often am so consumed by my own concerns that I fail to notice the signs of your glory. I receive your deliverance into a new and fresh capacity to behold, to see what you are seeing. And forgive me for dismissing the artists. Forgive us as your church for pushing the artists and their art to the margins. We pray for and anticipatorily receive a new generation of Bezalels—of all ages. Fill them with the Spirit of God, with wisdom, with understanding, with knowledge, and with all kinds of skills—to create and to make things that cause us to behold you. It will be for your glory, for others' gain, and for my good.

Glory be to the Father and to the Son and to the Holy Ghost.
As it was in the beginning, is now and ever shall be.
World without end. Amen! Amen!

The Questions

Do you know any Bezalels these days? How are you encouraging them? Are you a Bezalel in exile (or hiding)? How can we encourage you? How are you growing in your capacity to behold?

---

1. Visit "The Daily Seed Company," https://www.jdwalt.com/, for more information.

76

Exodus 32:1–6

When People Take Control

When the people saw that Moses was so long in coming down from the mountain, they gathered around Aaron and said, "Come, make us gods who will go before us. As for this fellow Moses who brought us up out of Egypt, we don't know what has happened to him."

Aaron answered them, "Take off the gold earrings that your wives, your sons and your daughters are wearing, and bring them to me." So all the people took off their earrings and brought them to Aaron. He took what they handed him and made it into an idol cast in the shape of a calf, fashioning it with a tool. Then they said, "These are your gods, Israel, who brought you up out of Egypt."

When Aaron saw this, he built an altar in front of the calf and announced, "Tomorrow there will be a festival to the Lord.*" So the next day the people rose early and sacrificed burnt offerings and presented fellowship offerings. Afterward they sat down to eat and drink and got up to indulge in revelry.*

Consider This

My caption over this section of Scripture, rather than calling it "The Golden Calf," is "The People Take Control."

When people take control, they get something that looks, smells, and quacks like the real thing, but it couldn't be further from it. So, how do you tell when people are taking control? I see four tells in today's text:

Tell #1 of control is the canary in the coal mine: Impatience.

> When the people saw that Moses was so long in coming down from the mountain,

Tell #2 is a distancing from the leader:

> As for this fellow Moses who brought us up out of Egypt, we don't know what has happened to him.

Tell #3 is the shift from an offering of funds to an assessment of fees.

> Aaron answered them, "Take off the gold earrings that your wives, your sons and your daughters are wearing, and bring them to me."

When people take control, we see pressure-filled conscription rather than heartfelt giving.

Tell #4 is the blatant disregard for the Word of God.

> He took what they handed him and made it into an idol cast in the shape of a calf, fashioning it with a tool.

Not only did God forbid the making of idols in the form of anything, but he forbade the use of any tool—even on the altars he authorized the Israelites to make for worshiping him.

Everything is wrong here, especially this:

> Then they said, "These are your gods, Israel, who brought you up out of Egypt."

In their minds, they weren't making an alternate God at all. They were simply making a visible representation of the God of Israel. So why does God so strictly forbid this practice? Because the hands of the ones who make the representations of gods soon become the self-appointed hands of the gods themselves. Idolatry is another name for control.

> When Aaron saw this, he built an altar in front of the calf and announced, "Tomorrow there will be a festival to the LORD."

This must have looked, smelled, and felt exactly like church to these worshipers.

> So the next day the people rose early and sacrificed burnt offerings and presented fellowship offerings.

They thought they were worshiping God, only later to realize they had magnified themselves. Look where their worship led them:

> Afterward they sat down to eat and drink and got up to indulge in revelry.

True worship leads to self-sacrificial living. Idolatry (or false worship) leads to self-indulgence. True worship leads to heartfelt repentance. Idolatry (or false worship) leads to sinful revelry.

Remember how all of this began? The unwillingness of the people to wait patiently on the Lord. They needed to be in control of the timeline and the outcomes. One of the hallmark signs of our need to be in control is our impatience and unwillingness to wait.

Control is the Achilles' heel of so many people, especially leaders. A leader who must be in control is actually no leader at all—they lead us only into lostness.

Are you a controlling person? Do you excuse that tendency to control in the name of some desired end or outcome? I want to say to you gently yet boldly: It is not okay to be a controlling person. This is unhealed brokenness, and it does great damage to everyone around you. Whether it be a home or a business or a church—though outward appearances seem intact—the inside reality is as empty as that golden calf.

Consider this a merciful intervention. Repent while there is still time.

Remember, control is just another name for idolatry.

The Prayer for Deliverance

Lord Jesus, you are my Deliverer. We think we left golden calves in ancient times. Wake us up to see that they are all around us all the time. Help us realize that what is built by control and conscription is just another form of an idol, something that looks like the real thing but is far from it. Forgive us for excusing our controlling nature as just who we are. Unearth the roots beneath our need to control and heal the broken and fearful hearts within us. Give us the grace to repent, releasing our need to control people and things and outcomes, trusting you with all things. I receive your deliverance from my controlling nature and tendencies, which is a core dimension of my broken, sinful nature. I receive your deliverance into the freedom of trusting completely in you. I receive your deliverance from worry and into a trust-filled waiting. I receive your deliverance from making things happen and into letting your will unfold in your way and in your timing. It will be for your glory, for others' gain, and for our good.

Glory be to the Father and to the Son and to the Holy Ghost.
As it was in the beginning, is now and ever shall be.
World without end. Amen! Amen!

The Questions

What is your appetite for control? Do you need to be in control of people, organizations, situations, outcomes, image, and other things? What brokenness in you underlies this need? Did someone somewhere in your past take control over you? What are you afraid of?

Week 11: Discussion Questions

Hearing the Text

Read Exodus 24:1–32:6.

Responding to the Text

- What did you hear?
- What did you see?
- What did you otherwise sense from the Lord?

Sharing Insights and Implications for Discipleship

Drawing from the Scripture text and daily readings, what did you find challenging, encouraging, provocative, comforting, invasive, inspiring, corrective, affirming, guiding, or warning?

Shaping Intentions for Prayer

Write your discipleship intention for the week ahead.

12
WEEK

Exodus 32:7–33:23

78

Exodus 32:7–14

On Loving People Anyway

Then the Lord said to Moses, "Go down, because your people, whom you brought up out of Egypt, have become corrupt. They have been quick to turn away from what I commanded them and have made themselves an idol cast in the shape of a calf. They have bowed down to it and sacrificed to it and have said, 'These are your gods, Israel, who brought you up out of Egypt.'

"I have seen these people," the Lord said to Moses, "and they are a stiff-necked people. Now leave me alone so that my anger may burn against them and that I may destroy them. Then I will make you into a great nation."

But Moses sought the favor of the Lord his God. "Lord," he said, "why should your anger burn against your people, whom you brought out of Egypt with great power and a mighty hand? Why should the Egyptians say, 'It was with evil intent that he brought them out, to kill them in the mountains and to wipe them off the face of the earth'? Turn from your fierce anger; relent and do not bring disaster on your people. Remember your servants Abraham, Isaac and Israel, to whom you swore by your own self: 'I will make your descendants as numerous as the stars in the sky and I will give your descendants all this land I promised them, and it will be their inheritance forever.'" Then the Lord relented and did not bring on his people the disaster he had threatened.

Consider This

God heard the prayers of the Israelites, but it was Moses he knew personally. By this point, God was severely disappointed in the Israelites. Did you notice how, in verse 7, he referred to them in conversation with Moses as "your people"? That was intentional. He even went so far as to say that Moses was the one who brought them up out of Egypt. In verse 9, he called them "these people."

Contrast that with how God referred to them back in Exodus 19: "'Now therefore, if you will indeed obey my voice and keep my covenant, you shall be my treasured possession among all peoples, for all the earth is mine; and you shall be to me a kingdom of priests and a holy nation.' These are the words that you shall speak to the people of Israel" (vv. 5–6 ESV).

Here's what arrests me. The Israelites all witnessed the plagues, the Passover, the Red Sea, the cloud by day and fire by night, the water from the rock, the defeat of the Amalekites. They saw the thick clouds, the thunder and lightning, and the billowy black smoke and heard the blaring trumpet blast. Despite all of this, they seemingly had no fear of God. In fact, after all this, they were the ones running low on patience.

The real story here is God's waning patience with the Israelites.

> "I have seen these people," the Lord said to Moses, "and they are a stiff-necked people."

This is the one thing you never want God to say about you. What does it mean to be stiff-necked? It means to be stubborn, willful, high-handed, imperious, and, at times, even supercilious. (I threw that last one in there for the logophiles among us!). Stiff-necked is the twin brother of controlling. They are not identical twins, mind you, but fraternal twins. A controlling nature and a stiff-necked disposition work in concert. The way a controlling person keeps control is through some form of being stiff-necked.

Here's the most dangerous thing about being a stiff-necked person: Of all the things you are certain of the most, you are most certain you are not a stiff-necked person. This makes one impervious to repentance. Here's how God feels about that:

> Now leave me alone so that my anger may burn against them and that I may destroy them.

Notice something special in today's text. God ever so subtly provoked Moses into his school of prayer. Observe the spirit of godly intercession rising up in Moses, the man of God:

> But Moses sought the favor of the Lord his God.

I can't say I have ever thought of prayer in this fashion—of seeking the favor of God. I mostly assume I have the favor of God. Repentance #1 for me.

> "Lord," he said, "why should your anger burn against your people, whom you brought out of Egypt with great power and a mighty hand?"

Pay attention to the pronouns here. Moses corrected God's grammar, referencing the Israelites as "your" people that "you" brought up out of Egypt. It is as though Moses was saying, "God, this is your rodeo, not mine." He even questioned God's anger. This is bold intercession. Next, he made an honor/shame appeal before God.

> Why should the Egyptians say, "It was with evil intent that he brought them out, to kill them in the mountains and to wipe them off the face of the earth"?

He followed this with a piercingly straightforward petition—a demand even:

> Turn from your fierce anger; relent and do not bring disaster on your people.

And if that weren't enough, Moses closed his appeal by reminding God of his Word and covenant.

> Remember your servants Abraham, Isaac and Israel, to whom you swore by your own self: "I will make your descendants as numerous as the stars in the sky and I will give your descendants all this land I promised them, and it will be their inheritance forever."

Just wow! After breaking this down, it occurred to me that God had outwitted Moses. Was this whole thing a test for Moses? Would Moses abandon God's people, or would Moses dare to take up God's own interest in his people? The most amazing thing about God in the face of controlling idolaters and stiff-necked people? He loves us anyway.

God is looking for this in us—someone who will not give up on God's people even when it seems that God has given up on them. God is looking for someone who will love them anyway.

And isn't that the secret of intercession—not our reluctant tolerance of people whom we don't prefer, but participating in the movement of the unswerving, relentless, jealous love of Jesus (who indwells us) for them?

Moses loved them anyway. Will I? Will you?

The Prayer for Deliverance

Lord Jesus, you are my Deliverer. Thank you for this powerful exchange you had with Moses on Mount Sinai. In the midst of the people's outright rebellion, you discipled Moses after your own heart. Train my heart to love like this and believe like this and not to let go of your people. Remind me of how you have done the same thing for me. I receive your deliverance from my easy willingness to walk away from people who have hurt or offended me. I receive your deliverance into your mind and heart to "love them anyway." I receive your deliverance from my reluctant tolerance of difficult people and into your transformational love for them. I receive your deliverance from my prayers and into your praying. It will be for your glory, for others' gain, and for our good.

Glory be to the Father and to the Son and to the Holy Ghost.
As it was in the beginning, is now and ever shall be.
World without end. Amen! Amen!

The Questions

Do you know any stiff-necked people? How are you doing at loving them anyway? How do you relate to this way of intercession on display in today's text? Would you dare to sign up for this course? Jesus stands ever ready to indwell and train you.

79

Exodus 32:30–35

What Sin Really Is

The next day Moses said to the people, "You have committed a great sin. But now I will go up to the Lord*; perhaps I can make atonement for your sin."*

So Moses went back to the Lord *and said, "Oh, what a great sin these people have committed! They have made themselves gods of gold. But now, please forgive their sin—but if not, then blot me out of the book you have written."*

The Lord *replied to Moses, "Whoever has sinned against me I will blot out of my book. Now go, lead the people to the place I spoke of, and my angel will go before you. However, when the time comes for me to punish, I will punish them for their sin."*

And the Lord *struck the people with a plague because of what they did with the calf Aaron had made.*

Consider This

The next day Moses said to the people, "You have committed a great sin. But now I will go up to the Lord; perhaps I can make atonement for your sin."

What is sin anyway? And why must sin be atoned for? We think we know until we are asked. It is easy to provide a religious answer, but the wilderness invites us to dig deeper into the essence of sin and atonement. Be warned: This entry is a thinker.

I thought of sin over the course of my life as a personal failure, I failed to live up to a standard, behaved badly, or otherwise "did it again." In other words, I defined sin in a self-referenced fashion. I am coming to understand the essence of sin—even the way I am defining sin—as living in a self-centered way or revolving life around myself (a.k.a. self-ish-ness).

To demonstrate how deep this goes, let's consider how we might define the opposite of sin. Is it to be sinless, or to behave according to expectation, or to be obedient to God? If we define sin as selfishness, then the opposite would be self-less-ness or unselfishness. See the problem there? The very effort to define the opposite condition of sin still finds itself caught in the gravity of self. It leads to defining sin in behavioral categories around individual success or failure, which leads to a pervasive framework of pride and shame (aka self-righteousness and self-loathing).

We need to shift the center of gravity in our lives from self to something else. Naturally, we consider the opposite of a self-centered life to be an others-oriented life. This is where we come up against our big problem, being trapped in the brokenness of our self-referenced way of life so that even our best efforts to be oriented around others easily become a veiled effort to benefit ourselves.

In other words, even my unselfish efforts rarely go beyond my self-interest in some way, shape, or form (i.e., to increase my self-esteem or to gain the esteem of others). It is impossible to overestimate the pervasive permeation of the self-referenced structure of our lives. This is the law of sin. Sin is not bad behavior. That is what sin looks like, but that's not what it is under the surface. Sin is the pervasive permeation of a human being who is comprehensively referenced and strategically structured around himself or herself.

Consider the eternal words of the apostle Paul, about the law of sin no less:

> So I find this law at work: Although I want to do good, evil is right there with me. For in my inner being I delight in God's law; but I see another law at work in me, waging war against the law of my mind and making me a prisoner of the law of sin at work within me. What a wretched man I am! Who will rescue me from this body that is subject to death? (Romans 7:21–24)

Paul testified to the powerful, inescapable gravity of sin—the pervasive structure of a self-centered life. One cannot behave or even repent one's way out of this reality. We must be delivered from it. I have good news:

> Thanks be to God, who delivers me through Jesus Christ our Lord! (Romans 7:25)

And there it is: deliverance. The only way we can move from self-centeredness to others-centeredness is to be delivered by the greatest Other in the history of others, Jesus Christ our Lord. Becoming Other-centered is the secret to becoming others-centered, which is the outcome of being delivered from self-centeredness. It is to be free.

We need to understand sin as fundamentally relational (not individual), which is why the first impulse of a sinner is to hide from "the Other" (aka God) and from others. We must come to understand that all sin is all at once against God, other people, and ourselves. In other words, while sin is always committed by an individual, its effect is always to desecrate three relationships—my relationship with God, my relationship with myself, and my relationship with other people. Finally, we must come to understand that we do not become free from sin by trying harder not to sin but by living according to the law of love (i.e., the greatest commandment)—the life-giving law of the Spirit.

There, I said it. The opposite of sin is not sinless. It is love. Sin is not primarily an individual moral failure. It is the failure to love God and neighbor.

> There is now no condemnation for those who are in Christ Jesus, because through Christ Jesus the law of the Spirit who gives life has set you free from the law of sin and death. (Romans 8:1–2)

Now we can start to understand the meaning of atonement. The way we understand sin will dictate the way we understand atonement. Atonement is an act of love. Because sin is the failure of love, only love can atone for sin. Herein is the meaning of the celebrated text: "But God demonstrates his own love for us in this: While we were still sinners, Christ died for us" (Romans 5:8).

The Prayer for Deliverance

Lord Jesus, you are my Deliverer. As I think about the worship of the golden calf, the great sin committed by the Israelites, it strikes me that all sin is great sin. I confess my ways of wanting to minimize my sin and then to dismiss it. Worse, I confess that I am blind to the way my sin hurts you and others and even myself. I need the deeper understanding that precedes the deeper deliverance. I receive your deliverance from my thin and thoughtless understanding of sin and what it is and how it works. I receive your deliverance into the wisdom of God and particularly the Word of God, that I might understand sin rightly. I receive your deliverance from my own self with all its sophisticated, self-referenced, and self-centered structures and ways. I receive your deliverance by your great act of love in the atonement of the cross. I receive the life-giving law of the Spirit coming from your death to sin and your resurrection to life. Teach and train me to behold the Lamb of God who takes away the sin of the world. It will be for your glory, for others' gain, and for our good.

Glory be to the Father and to the Son and to the Holy Ghost.
As it was in the beginning, is now and ever shall be.
World without end. Amen! Amen!

The Questions

How does this challenge your view of sin? How have you primarily thought about sin in the past? What if you began to think of sin not so much as the behavioral failure of self but the relational failure of love for God and others? What might change?

80

Exodus 33:1–6

The Seven Worst Words in the Bible

Then the LORD said to Moses, "Leave this place, you and the people you brought up out of Egypt, and go up to the land I promised on oath to Abraham, Isaac and Jacob, saying, 'I will give it to your descendants.' I will send an angel before you and drive out the Canaanites, Amorites, Hittites, Perizzites, Hivites and Jebusites. Go up to the land flowing with milk and honey. But I will not go with you, because you are a stiff-necked people and I might destroy you on the way."

When the people heard these distressing words, they began to mourn and no one put on any ornaments. For the LORD had said to Moses, "Tell the Israelites, 'You are a stiff-necked people. If I were to go with you even for a moment, I might destroy you. Now take off your ornaments and I will decide what to do with you.'" So the Israelites stripped off their ornaments at Mount Horeb.

Consider This

> But I will not go with you.

Those are easily seven of the most distressing words in the whole Bible. They are the outcome and impact of sin. Internalize them a bit and let them settle over you.

> But I will not go with you.

God promises the Israelites the grace and help of a delivering angel and all the blessings of the promised land, but he opts out of going himself. Is this some kind of punishment? No. It is actually an enormous mercy.

> But I will not go with you, because you are a stiff-necked people and I might destroy you on the way.

The presence of a holy God in the midst of a sinful people is a recipe for disaster. It is as though God were saying, "Better that you go without me and live than go with me and die."

It brings us back to our conversation about sin. We all have a lot of unlearning and relearning to do when it comes to our understanding of sin. I will speak for myself. I thought about sin in the same way I think about crime. With a crime, all the focus is around the accused and the law. What did they do? How did they break the law? What was their intent? What was their motive? How should they be punished?

In thinking this way, we tend to regard mercy as a get-out-of-jail-free card and grace as an expungement of the crime from our record. And this is the gospel truth, as far as it goes. It just stops way too soon. Why? Note the focus of this analysis: me, myself, and I. Sin is defined as my failure, so salvation gets defined as my pardon and my freedom.

But what about the effects and impacts of my sin?

With sin, our tendency is to focus on the breaking of the law and how we get over our problem of having broken it. Almost no thought is given to this question: How did it break the Lawgiver? Why does my sin grieve the heart of God? Even less thought goes into this question: How does my sin destroy my relationship with God? How does my sin damage other people's relationship with God, not to mention how does my sin harm other people?

When people like you and me, who mostly live in the United States, read the Bible, particularly as it speaks on sin and atonement, our question is: How do we stay out of the doghouse or jail or, worse, hell—which is another way of saying *eternal jail*? I believe God wants us to read the Bible with this primary question: How do we live in the presence of the one true, holy, and loving God in the wilderness?

The grace of God is not that he pardons our sin and keeps us out of hell-jail. The grace of God is that he loves us so much he desires us in his presence all the time, constantly, now and forever, world without end, amen. It's why the blood of Jesus speaks a better word. It's why the cross is not a transactional escape from death. It is life itself.

The life, death, resurrection, and ascension of Jesus is not a transactional eternal benefits package. He is the forever embodied divine union of the holiness of God and the love of God. His life means death to the foes of God, and his death means life to the friends of God—those being absolutely anyone, without exception, who will follow Jesus in his baptism of the Father's love and receive the gift of the Spirit of holiness.

This is the resurrection life of the body of Christ—a people enveloped by the promises of God, saturated by his presence and filled with the power of his love, the holiness of which makes demons flee and raises the dead, even me.

But I digress. Or maybe not.

God seemed to give the Israelites just what they wanted—the promised land without the problem of his presence.

> Go up to the land flowing with milk and honey. But I will not go with you, because you are a stiff-necked people and I might destroy you on the way.

Notice their response. They grieved.

> When the people heard these distressing words, they began to mourn and no one put on any ornaments.

The Israelites did not want God's promise without his presence. They decided on that day that the presence of God was even greater than his promises. And that, my friends, is the whole nutshell.

From the garden of Eden to the present day, the essence of all sin is this: We want the promises of God without the presence of God. This is the miraculous mystery of the atonement of Jesus Christ—God would suffer unimaginable pain to keep his promise and gift us with his presence anyway.

> But I will not go with you.

These are easily the seven worst words in the Bible.

In the end, God's greatest promise turns out to be his presence.

The Prayer for Deliverance

Lord Jesus, you are my Deliverer. I receive your deliverance from a self-oriented, self-referenced, self-protecting way of life. I receive your deliverance into a life completely oriented around your presence. I confess my own tendency to want your promises more than I desire your presence. I receive your deliverance into the reality of Psalm 27:4, which says,

> One thing I ask from the LORD,
> this only do I seek:
> that I may dwell in the house of the LORD
> all the days of my life,
> to behold the beauty of the LORD
> and to seek him in his temple.

I want to desire your presence more than anything else. I'm not there yet, but I want to be there. I know you want that too. What blows my mind the most is that you desire to be in my presence. It will be for your glory, for others' gain, and for our good.

> Glory be to the Father and to the Son and to the Holy Ghost.
> As it was in the beginning, is now and ever shall be.
> World without end. Amen! Amen!

The Questions

Have you ever considered that the Lord desires to be in your presence? How might that change things? Do you find yourself pursuing the promises and benefits of the Lord more than the gift of his presence? Do you want your whole life to be oriented around the presence of the Lord?

81

Exodus 33:7–11

On Becoming a Tent of Meeting

Now Moses used to take a tent and pitch it outside the camp some distance away, calling it the "tent of meeting." Anyone inquiring of the Lord would go to the tent of meeting outside the camp. And whenever Moses went out to the tent, all the people rose and stood at the entrances to their tents, watching Moses until he entered the tent. As Moses went into the tent, the pillar of cloud would come down and stay at the entrance, while the Lord spoke with Moses. Whenever the people saw the pillar of cloud standing at the entrance to the tent, they all stood and worshiped, each at the entrance to their tent. The Lord would speak to Moses face to face, as one speaks to a friend. Then Moses would return to the camp, but his young aide Joshua son of Nun did not leave the tent.

Consider This

I love this text! And here are seven reasons why.

1. Moses created sacred designated space for prayer and gave it a name: the "tent of meeting." Have you ever created this dimension of space for prayer? Would you consider it?
2. Anyone could go to the tent of meeting if the purpose was to "inquire of the Lord." What a great phrase. Our prayers tend toward asking God for many things, but how often are we specifically inquiring of the Lord about the matters of our times, the curiosities of our circumstances, and the puzzling dilemmas of our days? That's a weakness for me.
3. This tent was set apart. It was "outside of the camp." I picture a steady stream of people coming and going to do business with the Lord. It reminds me of the prayer mountains the South

Korean church is known for.[1] This tent was different from the prayer room in my home. It required a deeper intention and more decided action to go "outside of the camp." The text tells us it was "outside of the camp" and that it was "some distance away." (If you have an extra few minutes today, run down Mark 1:35; Luke 5:16; 6:12; and 22:41–42 for more inspiration.)

4. Moses modeled this practice not just to perform the role of a model but because it was the very source of his life. When people saw it happen, it arrested their attention, and they rose to their feet. The witness of true holiness is palpable. Everyone knew that Moses's holiness did not come from himself or his practices or even his prayer life. It came from the Lord, who abided in the cloud.
5. Verse 11 never gets old:

> The LORD would speak to Moses face to face, as one speaks to a friend.

In those days, this privilege was beyond rare. Unheard of would be more like it. For us, this is the common gift of the grace of God in Jesus Christ. Now hear this: "I no longer call you servants, because a servant does not know his master's business. Instead, I have called you friends, for everything that I have learned from my Father I have made known to you" (John 15:15).

The problem is not that it is common but that we take words like these so casually. To the extent we are not utterly stunned and blown away by texts like these—to that extent, we are asleep. The good news is that awakening is ever near to the holy discontented who will come to grips with this.

6. When someone, anyone, lives into and out of an authentic friendship with Jesus and really gives themselves to him, it becomes a clarion call to worship to thousands and ultimately millions. "Whenever the people saw the pillar of cloud stand-

---

1. Christopher Peters, "Surprised by a Smile on Kwanglim's Prayer Mountain," Seedbed, May 11, 2013, https://seedbed.com/surprised-by-a-smile-on-kwanglims-prayer-mountain/.

ing at the entrance to the tent, they all stood and worshiped, each at the entrance to their tent." Notice how even now, thousands of years later, this story awakens something deep within us, inspiring us to rise up and worship this God.

7. "Then Moses would return to the camp, but his young aide Joshua son of Nun did not leave the tent." People in our lives are always watching, taking note of the things we may take for granted. From time to time, the Lord will entrust us with a young aide, a Joshua-type, who will not only pay attention but will double down their focus on what they glean from our lives.

   We get a glimpse here of spiritual parenting, and there is an absolute dearth of it in our time. It's no one's fault. The reason most of us aren't coming alongside younger believers is because no one came (with any intention) alongside us. What we need is a generation who will step forward as first-generation spiritual parents, who will step out of their comfort zone and stumble awkwardly at times into a new kind of relationship.

It would be easy now to press hard on the need to go and create a new and special place of prayer, a "tent of meeting" somewhere, some distance beyond your house. And maybe if we lived in the days of Moses, that would be in order. But we live in the day of the Lord Jesus Christ, in the age of the Holy Spirit, which leads us to this breakthrough implication: I am the tent of meeting. You are the tent of meeting. We are the tent of meeting. We don't need to go and make the tent of meeting to be some physical structure somewhere other than here. Places matter, and structures are good and fine, but they are not the point. Because Jesus's body became the curtain, our body and our bodies together become the most holy place—the very dwelling place of God.

Everywhere we go, we carry the tent of our physical body with us. That said, sometimes (it was often for Jesus), we need to walk the path some distance away and outside of the camp to host the tent meeting. Are you reading me, friends? You and I and us together are mobile tabernacle houses of prayer. If we make this shift from a tent of meeting being a physical structure outside of us to the tent of meeting being our very bodies—the implications will be mind-blowing.

The Prayer for Deliverance

Lord Jesus, you are my Deliverer. I receive your deliverance from my casual sleepiness in prayer. I also receive your deliverance from striving harder after a deeper prayer life. What I want is to receive your deliverance into your way of often withdrawing to lonely and out-of-the-way places to abide in friendship with God. I am a tent of meeting, Lord—a place where we can meet together face-to-face as a person talks to his or her friend. Lord Jesus, it is such a marvel that you would call me friend. Forgive me for neglecting our friendship. I don't mean to. Awaken me again, in yet a new way, to the depths of friendship with you. What could be better than that? It will be for your glory, for others' gain, and for our good.

Glory be to the Father and to the Son and to the Holy Ghost.
As it was in the beginning, is now and ever shall be.
World without end. Amen! Amen!

The Questions

Which of the seven points speaks to, encourages, or challenges you the most today? Or is it the unnumbered eighth point—that your body is the tent of meeting? What are the implications of your physical body being/becoming the tent of meeting with the Lord? How might it help you to go beyond the camp to host the meeting?

82

Exodus 33:12–17

Moving from Resignation to Surrender

Moses said to the Lord, "You have been telling me, 'Lead these people,' but you have not let me know whom you will send with me. You have said, 'I know you by name and you have found favor with me.' If you are pleased with me, teach me your ways so I may know you and continue to find favor with you. Remember that this nation is your people."

The Lord replied, "My Presence will go with you, and I will give you rest."

Then Moses said to him, "If your Presence does not go with us, do not send us up from here. How will anyone know that you are pleased with me and with your people unless you go with us? What else will distinguish me and your people from all the other people on the face of the earth?"

And the Lord said to Moses, "I will do the very thing you have asked, because I am pleased with you and I know you by name."

Consider This

Moses knew it was beyond a long shot by now. He'd gone to bat one too many times for the Israelites. Though he did his absolute best, he missed cues, made mistakes, lost his cool more than once, and wanted to give up several times; he knew he had not been enough. He wanted to salvage the job, get these former slaves into the promised land, and maybe retire.

Despite so many miraculous things, Moses knew the mission had been a bust. It felt like a bridge too far at this point. In fact, as we enter into today's text, Moses seemed resigned to finish the job without God.

> Moses said to the Lord, "You have been telling me, 'Lead these people,' but you have not let me know whom you will send with me.'"

In the past, Moses appealed to God on the basis of God's power, God's mercy, and God's reputation. He reminded God of his own covenant promise with Abraham, Isaac, and Jacob. And God had answered.

This day was different. We see in Moses a clear spirit of resignation. He was not quitting; he just knew he couldn't go it alone. He needed help, and he wanted the details so he could get his mission over with. He was willing to limp across the finish line and fade off into the sunset.

So many of us know this feeling. We got off the trail. We missed the boat. We fell from grace. We made a critical error in judgment, went to sleep at the wheel, or even had some kind of moral failure. And those two words—don't get me started. Who hasn't committed moral failure? It's the bare threshold definition of sin, for crying out loud. People don't commit moral failure. They succumb to weakness in their brokenness. It doesn't make it okay, just understandable. They don't need to be shamefully exposed but graciously covered by the unswerving mercy of God in Jesus Christ.

In this moment, Moses made the most significant decision of his life. He got in touch with his heart, and he abandoned himself to God.

> You have said, "I know you by name and you have found favor with me." If you are pleased with me, teach me your ways so I may know you and continue to find favor with you. Remember that this nation is your people.

Moses staked everything on his relationship with God.

In response, he and we get the pure gospel. Here it is. Brace yourself for the best news you have ever heard.

> The LORD replied, "My Presence will go with you, and I will give you rest."

Try to imagine Moses hearing these words from God. Truth is, he didn't seem to hear it at all.

> Then Moses said to him, "If your Presence does not go with us, do not send us up from here. How will anyone know that you are pleased with me and with your people unless you go with us? What else will distinguish me and your people from all the other people on the face of the earth?"

Moses! Are you listening? Did you even hear what Yahweh, the God of heaven and earth, just said to you?

> My Presence will go with you, and I will give you rest.

Clearly, this seemed too good to be true for Moses. Same with us. We are conditioned to disbelieve anything that seems too good to be true. And the truth is, there is only one thing in life too good to be true that is actually true: the Word of God. God is so good, he adds this:

> And the LORD said to Moses, "I will do the very thing you have asked, because I am pleased with you."

I'm going to press now. Let's go deep into the promised land, aka the gospel. When Jesus was baptized at the Jordan River, at the very place of the crossing of the Israelites, he received a gospel word from the Father. It is the same word God speaks over all who follow Jesus into his baptism. He said, "[Your name here], you are my son/daughter. You are my beloved. I am pleased with you."

We, you and me, desperately need to hear this re-forming word in the depths of our being—over and over and over again until we finally hear it and then over and over and over again until we finally dare to believe it. This is the core of the core of our core identity. God is pleased with us, and there is nothing we can do about it. Because we didn't earn it, we can't unearn it. It is God's gift of amazing grace. The only thing God asks of us is to follow Jesus out of these waters and into the life of his promised presence. He wants relationship.

Can I translate these words to their most practical level today:

You are my son/daughter = I love you.
You are my beloved = I like you.
With you, I am well pleased = And I'm proud of you.

Watch how the text ends today:

> And I know you by name.

The Prayer for Deliverance

Lord Jesus, you are my Deliverer. I receive your deliverance from a vague and general sense of your love for us and into a personal, "you know me by name," deep and ever-deepening awareness of your love for, delight in, and pleasure in me. I receive your deliverance from a spirit of weak resignation and into a way of abandoned surrender into your arms. Thank you for knowing me by name. I want to know you more by name. I want to talk to you as a friend talks to a friend. I want to be done with casual religion and move into the country of real faith, primal faith, plain, unadorned, heart-level faith. It will be for your glory, for others' gain, and for our good.

> Glory be to the Father and to the Son and to the Holy Ghost.
> As it was in the beginning, is now and ever shall be.
> World without end. Amen! Amen!

The Questions

Do you struggle with a spirit of weak resignation—giving up hope of winning or even running well—just trying to get through the race? Do you really believe this amazing grace of the gospel shared today? What holds you back? Will you dare to speak these words of God over yourself aloud today? How about tomorrow and the next day too?

83

Exodus 33:18–23

The Journey from Hiding to Hiddenness

> *Then Moses said, "Now show me your glory."*
>
> *And the LORD said, "I will cause all my goodness to pass in front of you, and I will proclaim my name, the LORD, in your presence. I will have mercy on whom I will have mercy, and I will have compassion on whom I will have compassion. But," he said, "you cannot see my face, for no one may see me and live."*
>
> *Then the LORD said, "There is a place near me where you may*

stand on a rock. When my glory passes by, I will put you in a cleft in the rock and cover you with my hand until I have passed by. Then I will remove my hand and you will see my back; but my face must not be seen."

Consider This

Then Moses said, "Now show me your glory."

The lesson? God will reveal the glory of heaven, which is his presence, to all who are willing to be hidden in him on earth. Hiddenness is one of the essences of humility.

Moses was hidden from birth. He was hidden in a small ark of reeds and pushed out on the Nile River. Later he was hidden in the wilderness for forty years, herding his father-in-law's sheep. Of all the people in the world, this is who God chose for this assignment. Later in this wilderness, the Bible is careful to tell us, "(Now Moses was a very humble man, more humble than anyone else on the face of the earth)" (Numbers 12:3).

Here's the kicker: Moses turned out to be one of the most well-known people who has ever lived. It brings me to the second part of my learning here. The antithesis of hiddenness is fame. The opposite of fame is not obscurity but hiddenness. We live in an age the core value of which is fame. When people do not have a deep inner validation as a person, they clamor for adulation on the surface.

Self-importance is one of the darker values of social media (or its misuse). Look at me. I am somebody. We are all made for the glory of God, but short of that, we will accrue all manner of glory for ourselves. And the worst permutation of this happens when people accrue glory for themselves in the name of God. It's why "famous saint" is an oxymoron (or at least a non sequitur).

These are such massive constructs of thought I can hardly wrap my mind around them. Hiddenness does not mean hiding. Hiddenness is the gift of God to the humble ones who have traded in their own quest for glory for the pursuit of beholding the glory of Another.

For a long time in my life, I wanted to be famous. I believe God continues to save and deliver me from this desire. He has shown me something infinitely better than being famous. It is being known—not well known, but known well, deeply known. I want to be known by God and by my family and friends (whom I consider you to be). I want to be known simply and completely as I most truly am. And that's how I want to know God and others. I think that's what we all want. The thirst for fame is simply the broken longing to be known.

> When my glory passes by, I will put you in a cleft in the rock and cover you with my hand until I have passed by. Then I will remove my hand and you will see my back; but my face must not be seen.

This was a one-of-a-kind event here, reserved for Moses alone. What if I told you there is a better word for us—an even richer vision?

> For God, who said, "Let light shine out of darkness," made his light shine in our hearts to give us the light of the knowledge of God's glory displayed in the face of Christ. (2 Corinthians 4:6)

We can see the face of God and live. In fact, the tables have turned. No one can really live who does not see the face of Jesus Christ. And the most marvelous thing of all is the way his face can be reflected in our very faces. Others can see him when they look at us.

The Prayer for Deliverance

Lord Jesus, you are my Deliverer. I receive your deliverance from my quest for self-actualization, for the realization of what I think is my best and highest self and usefulness in the world. I receive your deliverance into the actualization of my baptism, my old self and sinful nature being buried with Jesus in his death, and my new creation being raised to life with Jesus in his resurrection. Now I receive your deliverance into the actualization of this reality: "I have been crucified with Christ and I no longer live, but Christ lives in me. The life I now live in the body, I live by faith in the Son of God, who loved me and gave himself for me" (Galatians 2:20). Now I receive your deliverance into the actualization of this reality: "For you died, and your life is now hidden with Christ in God" (Colossians 3:3). It will be for God's glory, for others' gain, and for our good.

Glory be to the Father and to the Son and to the Holy Ghost.
As it was in the beginning, is now and ever shall be.
World without end. Amen! Amen!

The Questions

What do you think about this contrast between being famous and being known? How about the connection between humility and hiddenness? How about the notion of being delivered from the quest for self-actualization and into baptismal actualization?

Week 12: Discussion Questions

Hearing the Text

Read Exodus 32:7–33:23.

Responding to the Text

- What did you hear?
- What did you see?
- What did you otherwise sense from the Lord?

Sharing Insights and Implications for Discipleship

Drawing from the Scripture text and daily readings, what did you find challenging, encouraging, provocative, comforting, invasive, inspiring, corrective, affirming, guiding, or warning?

Shaping Intentions for Prayer

Write your discipleship intention for the week ahead.

13
WEEK

Exodus 34:1–40:38

85

Exodus 34:1–7

Between a Rock and a God Place

> *The* Lord *said to Moses, "Chisel out two stone tablets like the first ones, and I will write on them the words that were on the first tablets, which you broke. Be ready in the morning, and then come up on Mount Sinai. Present yourself to me there on top of the mountain. No one is to come with you or be seen anywhere on the mountain; not even the flocks and herds may graze in front of the mountain."*
>
> *So Moses chiseled out two stone tablets like the first ones and went up Mount Sinai early in the morning, as the* Lord *had commanded him; and he carried the two stone tablets in his hands. Then the* Lord *came down in the cloud and stood there with him and proclaimed his name, the* Lord*. And he passed in front of Moses, proclaiming, "The* Lord*, the* Lord*, the compassionate and gracious God, slow to anger, abounding in love and faithfulness, maintaining love to thousands, and forgiving wickedness, rebellion and sin. Yet he does not leave the guilty unpunished; he punishes the children and their children for the sin of the parents to the third and fourth generation."*

Consider This

The expensive theological term for encounters such as the one described in today's Scripture passage is *theophany*, and the Bible is filled with them—from Jacob's dream of the ladder coming down to earth, to young Samuel's encounter with the voice of God calling in the night, to the annunciation to Mary, to Jesus on the Mount of Transfiguration, on and on we could go. These encounters with the manifest presence of God narrate our shared story.

Let's begin by remembering where we left off in yesterday's devotional:

> Then the Lord said, "There is a place near me where you may stand on a rock. When my glory passes by, I will put you in a cleft in the rock and cover you with my hand until I have passed by. Then I will

> remove my hand and you will see my back; but my face must not be seen." (Exodus 33:21–23)

Reminder: We aren't tourists on a vacation to the Holy Land. We are pilgrims on a journey into the mystery of the holiness of God. Don't hear me wrong. At times pilgrims do ride tour buses. You know—those buses with nice air-conditioning and large, tinted windows on both sides. They can cover miles of territory in a day, and much of the time passengers are gazing out the window at the countryside as the guide points things out.

Tour buses make lots of short stops where people get out and walk around sites, snapping photos, visiting gift shops, and otherwise learning all the things. Today's excursion is more than that. Today is why we came. More than walking around and grabbing a brochure and a snack, we will take off our shoes and get down low to the ground. With our ear to the ground we'll listen for the seismic reverberations of the ancient, ever-radiating Word of God.

In Genesis 3, after their fall from glory, the man and the woman hid from God. This time Moses was hidden by God in the cleft of the rock. A cleft is a crevice—a split in a rock face—a small cave-like opening. Let's go inside the cleft and stand there with Moses. He has the two stone tablets inscribed with the Law with him.

> Then the LORD came down in the cloud and stood there with him and proclaimed his name, the LORD.

In other words, he said, "Yahweh." (When you see Lord spelled with small caps—LORD—in your Bible, think "Yahweh.") It has been described as the very sound of breath. In the Hebrew Bible, the Lord says "Yahweh" twice. Then he goes on to elucidate the fullness of what his name means.

> the compassionate and gracious God, slow to anger, abounding in love and faithfulness, maintaining love to thousands, and forgiving wickedness, rebellion and sin.

In case you read that too quickly, let's try it this way. Wherever you are reading this, find a way to get nearer the ground. Stand then bow your body downward, kneel, or prostrate yourself, whatever you can do to signal to yourself that the Lord is passing by. Now speak these words aloud so your ears can hear them just as Moses's ears heard them:

> the compassionate and gracious God, slow to anger, abounding in love and faithfulness, maintaining love to thousands, and forgiving wickedness, rebellion and sin.

This is our God. This is why we came. This is the encounter we never get over. This is not a God to hide from but to be hidden in. His presence is healing because his nature is love.

As much as I would like to end here, we need to hear verse 7.

> Yet he does not leave the guilty unpunished; he punishes the children and their children for the sin of the parents to the third and fourth generation.

God's deepest nature is love, yet his character is holy. As we have noted before, the wrath of God is not some kind of angry emotion. The wrath of God is what happens when the holiness of God meets up with anyone unprepared for his presence.

This is why and how Jesus saves. He hides us in the cleft of his heart—his life, death, resurrection, and ascension. I love how Paul frames the invitation to abide in the Rock of Ages:

> Since, then, you have been raised with Christ, set your hearts on things above, where Christ is, seated at the right hand of God. Set your minds on things above, not on earthly things. For you died, and your life is now hidden with Christ in God. When Christ, who is your life, appears, then you also will appear with him in glory. (Colossians 3:1–4)

I remember growing up in my small-town Methodist church, on

the front row between my meemaw and peepaw, and hearing them sing loud and slightly off-key, "Rock of ages cleft for me. Let me hide myself in Thee."

The Prayer for Deliverance

Lord Jesus, you are my Deliverer. I receive your deliverance from my false notions and images of who God is and what God is like. I receive your deliverance into the truth about God and into becoming the image-bearer who is growing more and more into his likeness. Let me reflect and refract the very nature of God in this world—the compassionate and gracious God, slow to anger, abounding in love and faithfulness, maintaining love to thousands, and forgiving wickedness, rebellion and sin. It will be for God's glory, for others' gain, and for our good.

> Glory be to the Father and to the Son and to the Holy Ghost.
> As it was in the beginning, is now and ever shall be.
> World without end. Amen! Amen!

The Questions

> The Lord, the Lord, the compassionate and gracious God, slow to anger, abounding in love and faithfulness, maintaining love to thousands, and forgiving wickedness, rebellion and sin.

What does it mean to you today that this is the core nature of the God of heaven and earth? What does that change for you?

86

Exodus 34:8–14

How Might God Experience Your Worship?

Moses bowed to the ground at once and worshiped. "LORD," he said, "if I have found favor in your eyes, then let the LORD go with us. Although this is a stiff-necked people, forgive our wickedness and our sin, and take us as your inheritance."

Then the LORD said: "I am making a covenant with you. Before all your people I will do wonders never before done in any nation in all the world. The people you live among will see how awesome is the work that I, the LORD, will do for you. Obey what I command you today. I will drive out before you the Amorites, Canaanites, Hittites, Perizzites, Hivites and Jebusites. Be careful not to make a treaty with those who live in the land where you are going, or they will be a snare among you. Break down their altars, smash their sacred stones and cut down their Asherah poles. Do not worship any other god, for the LORD, whose name is Jealous, is a jealous God."

Consider This

Moses bowed to the ground at once and worshiped.

This, of course, was in response to his encounter with Yahweh in yesterday's devotional. "The LORD, the LORD, the compassionate and gracious God, slow to anger, abounding in love and faithfulness, maintaining love to thousands, and forgiving wickedness, rebellion and sin" (Exodus 34:6–7).

Let me test a working hypothesis with you as we get started today. Here it is: God is as real to you as your worship is real to him.

I will take that a step further. We talk a lot about our experience of God. But do we consider how God experiences us? That's what I love about today's opening words.

Moses bowed to the ground at once and worshiped.

Slightly invasive question: When is the last time you did that—bowed down to the ground and worshiped God?

Most of us believe in God. But how real is God to you—in your everyday experience? Back to my working hypothesis: God is as real to you as your worship is real to him.

So, how real do you think your worship is to God? What about at church? What about in private? I'm not asking if your worship of God is physically demonstrative. It doesn't have to be physically demonstrative to be real, but the Bible does reveal worship most often as a physically embodied posture, like raising one's hands or bowing down or prostrating oneself on the ground.

Moses bowed to the ground at once and worshiped.

Consider these lines from Psalm 95:

> Come, let us bow down in worship,
>   let us kneel before the LORD our Maker;
> for he is our God
>   and we are the people of his pasture,
>   the flock under his care. (vv. 6–7)

For half of my life, I was content to let my worship exist in my heart as a generalized sense of felt gratitude and sometimes affection aimed generally in God's direction. I suspect God experiences this at about the level I do—real but kind of vague. If I'm honest, that is how I reacted to some of the most stunning words in all of Scripture yesterday.

I don't in any way mean to question your worship or your sincerity before God. I'm just asking you to consider it. Might it be true that God is as real to you as your worship is real to him?

While faith is a matter of the heart, the life of faith is lived out and expresses itself in the body. Our bodies will invariably tell the story of our hearts.

Moses bowed to the ground at once and worshiped.

The Bible teaches us that our hearts are deceitful above all things (see Jeremiah 17:9). Our bodies though—our movements, our actions—do not lie. They tell the story of our hearts. And I think the way our bodies worship, perhaps more than anything else, tells that story.

Moses bowed to the ground at once and worshiped.

We communicate through two primary languages: our spoken words and our bodies (hence the term *body language*). We don't have a body. We are a body. The implications of that last sentence are staggering. By a simple act of will, we can decide to say something to God with our bodies today, right now. And those words influence, even transform, the quality of faith in your heart.

Today, now, I want you to consider a movement of worship with your body.

Moses bowed to the ground at once and worshiped.

The Prayer for Deliverance

Lord Jesus, you are my Deliverer. I receive your deliverance from a vague, general, disembodied way of worshiping you. I receive your deliverance from my indifference as it comes to how you might experience my worship of God. I receive your deliverance into an experiential, fully embodied way of worshiping you. I receive your deliverance into a way of worship wherein I care how you experience my worship. Teach and train my body to worship you. I find myself waiting for some kind of feeling or emotional experience to lead me to physical and embodied worship. But I know that it can be the other way around, too, that my bowed body or my lifted hands or my prostrated posture can actually change my spirit. Give me the grace and the courage today, even if I am all by myself, to be stretched—in my body—to worship you. It will be for your glory, for others' gain, and for our good.

Glory be to the Father and to the Son and to the Holy Ghost.
As it was in the beginning, is now and ever shall be.
World without end. Amen! Amen!

The Questions

What is your comfort level with the embodied (even demonstrative) physical worship of God—raising hands, bowing low, and so on? How about with your physical expressions at football games? What might your unwillingness to express any physically embodied dimension of worship say about your heart?

87

Exodus 34:15–28

It's All About Worship

"Be careful not to make a treaty with those who live in the land; for when they prostitute themselves to their gods and sacrifice to them, they will invite you and you will eat their sacrifices. And when you choose some of their daughters as wives for your sons and those daughters prostitute themselves to their gods, they will lead your sons to do the same.

"Do not make any idols.

"Celebrate the Festival of Unleavened Bread. For seven days eat bread made without yeast, as I commanded you. Do this at the appointed time in the month of Aviv, for in that month you came out of Egypt.

"The first offspring of every womb belongs to me, including all the firstborn males of your livestock, whether from herd or flock. Redeem the firstborn donkey with a lamb, but if you do not redeem it, break its neck. Redeem all your firstborn sons.

"No one is to appear before me empty-handed.

"Six days you shall labor, but on the seventh day you shall rest; even during the plowing season and harvest you must rest.

"Celebrate the Festival of Weeks with the firstfruits of the wheat harvest, and the Festival of Ingathering at the turn of the year. Three

times a year all your men are to appear before the Sovereign Lord, the God of Israel. I will drive out nations before you and enlarge your territory, and no one will covet your land when you go up three times each year to appear before the Lord your God.

"Do not offer the blood of a sacrifice to me along with anything containing yeast, and do not let any of the sacrifice from the Passover Festival remain until morning.

"Bring the best of the firstfruits of your soil to the house of the Lord your God.

"Do not cook a young goat in its mother's milk."

Then the Lord said to Moses, "Write down these words, for in accordance with these words I have made a covenant with you and with Israel." Moses was there with the Lord forty days and forty nights without eating bread or drinking water. And he wrote on the tablets the words of the covenant—the Ten Commandments.

Consider This

I warned you at the start that this is a different kind of Bible study. So don't worry about how I will work through all of today's verses. Reading a big chunk of Scripture is good for us. I love how God addresses even the smallest things like yeast and then gardening and the offering of not just firstfruits but "the best of the firstfruits."

He doesn't just reference Sabbath-keeping here but says to keep the Sabbath even during seasons of plowing and harvesting—when it seems insane. Remember yesterday's observation? "God is as real to us as our worship is real to him." These commands, the Law, are not about laws but about the Lawgiver; not about the rules, but about the worship of the Ruler.

Almost every command on today's list has to do with the worship of God. Notice that he repeats making treaties with other nations twice in the span of four verses.

> Be careful not to make a treaty with those who live in the land where you are going, or they will be a snare among you.

What's wrong with making a treaty with a foreign nation? Nothing. The problem is with their gods.

> for when they prostitute themselves to their gods and sacrifice to them, they will invite you and you will eat their sacrifices.

All about worship:

> Do not make any idols.

All about worship:

> Celebrate the Festival of Unleavened Bread.

All about worship:

> The first offspring of every womb belongs to me, including all the firstborn males of your livestock, whether from herd or flock.

All about worship:

> No one is to appear before me empty-handed.

You get the point. All of life is all about worship. We were made to worship. Worship is first, middle, and last, all about living a comprehensive life of bonded and secure attachment to God. The truth is, we are all pretty good worshipers. Addicts are some of the most voracious worshipers on the planet.

The question is not whether we worship; it's who or what we worship. Whatever or whoever it is that we order our lives around to make them work—that is our God.

Worship is about security—personal security, family security, community security, national security. Whatever we turn to and attach ourselves to for security—that is who or what we worship. For most it is money. For many it is image and physical appearance. For others it is reputation. Only Jesus Christ can deliver true security.

Everyone and everything else that promises security in this life or in the life to come is a false god. God is adamant about these commands and this covenant, not because he needs our worship but because he wants us to be free.

The wilderness clarifies our worship. It would take the Israelites another forty years to learn the biggest lesson of the wilderness—that slavery is not a place or a condition—it's an identity. Worship matters so much to God and to us because it is the very path to freedom. In fact, the right worship of the true and living God is freedom itself.

Let's give Paul the last word today from his brilliant word to the Corinthians.

> Now the Lord is the Spirit, and where the Spirit of the Lord is, there is freedom. And we all, who with unveiled faces contemplate the Lord's glory, are being transformed into his image with ever-increasing glory, which comes from the Lord, who is the Spirit. (2 Corinthians 3:17–18)

The Prayer for Deliverance

Lord Jesus, you are my Deliverer. I receive your deliverance from my attachment to anyone or anything other than you in my attempt to find any measure of any kind of security. I receive your deliverance into a deep and bonded attachment to you as my 100 percent life provider—my complete source of security and wholeness and wellness, even flourishing. Heal the wounds from my broken attachments to other things and people. Restore me to wholeheartedness, even in the details and small things. It will be for God's glory, for others' gain, and for our good.

> Glory be to the Father and to the Son and to the Holy Ghost.
> As it was in the beginning, is now and ever shall be.
> World without end. Amen! Amen!

The Questions

What is your level of insecurity, and in what places does it show up, and to what or whom do you attach in order to alleviate it? How are you growing in a bonded attachment to God, who is your only true source of security?

88

Exodus 34:29–35

The Two Letters That Changed Everything

When Moses came down from Mount Sinai with the two tablets of the covenant law in his hands, he was not aware that his face was radiant because he had spoken with the LORD. When Aaron and all the Israelites saw Moses, his face was radiant, and they were afraid to come near him. But Moses called to them; so Aaron and all the leaders of the community came back to him, and he spoke to them. Afterward all the Israelites came near him, and he gave them all the commands the LORD had given him on Mount Sinai.

When Moses finished speaking to them, he put a veil over his face. But whenever he entered the LORD's presence to speak with him, he removed the veil until he came out. And when he came out and told the Israelites what he had been commanded, they saw that his face was radiant. Then Moses would put the veil back over his face until he went in to speak with the LORD.

Consider This

Did you pick up on what's going on in today's text? When Moses returned from his time on the mountain with the Lord, his face radiated with the glory of God.

Here's what I love about the passage:

He was not aware that his face was radiant because he had spoken with the Lord.

Like when you spend a few hours outside in the early summer and your face gets sunburned, often it takes someone pointing out the burn before you realize it: "Boy, you got a lot of sun on your face today, didn't you?"

Moses spent time in God's presence, and as a consequence, his face reflected the glory of God. To reflect means to throw back light, heat, or sound without absorbing it. Moses's face was radiant, yet it was not radiating. That's what it's like when a person gets sunburned. Their face is radiant with the sun, yet it is not radiating the sun. The sun would actually have to be inside of you in order for you to radiate with its radiance. I'm sure you see where this is heading.

See how Paul reflected on this passage from his New Testament point of view.

> We are not like Moses, who would put a veil over his face to prevent the Israelites from seeing the end of what was passing away. But their minds were made dull, for to this day the same veil remains when the old covenant is read. It has not been removed, because only in Christ is it taken away. Even to this day when Moses is read, a veil covers their hearts. (2 Corinthians 3:13–15)

Once Moses became aware that his face was reflecting the glory of God, he also realized it was an ever-fading reality. Moses seemed to take a certain prestige or status in the glory of his face. He did not want the Israelites to know it was fading away. He went from not being aware of it to needing to protect it. To this end, he covered his face with a veil. And this veil, in time, became a barrier between the Israelites and God.

Another word for *veil*, which has immediate relevance, is *mask*. It is a false front—a fake image—something to bolster our appearance or to make us look or seem better than we actually are. And to a greater or lesser degree, we all do it (or we have done it in the past). Something deep within us has convinced us that if people really knew us, they wouldn't like us, so we pretend to be something or someone else.

The lesson here I can't quite grasp has something to do with the way the invulnerability of a leader creates a dangerous vulnerability for those who follow him or her. The essence of invulnerability is hiding. Moses was not hiding from God, but perhaps he was trying to hide something from the people. Maybe the invulnerability of a spiritual leader dulls the spiritual senses of all who follow them.

Bottom line: Veils between us and God and us and one another aren't good for the prospering of our souls. Let's keep thinking that one through.

Perhaps the most critical difference between the Old Testament and the New Testament comes down to two letters. In the Old Testament, God is with us. In the post-Pentecost New Testament, God is within us.

Two letters: From with to with-*in*.

Watch for the two letters in this text: "For God, who said, 'Let light shine out of darkness,' made his light shine in our hearts to give us the light of the knowledge of God's glory displayed in the face of Christ" (2 Corinthians 4:6).

So, how does one move from God with me to God within me? By turning to the Lord Jesus, receiving the Holy Spirit, and beholding the glory of the Lord. This is the place where I mysteriously find my real life inside of the miracle of becoming like you. This is the place where the ten words become my living truth: The bush was on fire. It did not burn up.

Paul explained how this transformation happens.

> But when one turns to the Lord, the veil is removed. Now the Lord is the Spirit, and where the Spirit of the Lord is, there is freedom. And we all, with unveiled face, beholding the glory of the Lord, are being transformed into the same image from one degree of glory to another. For this comes from the Lord who is the Spirit. (2 Corinthians 3:16–18 ESV)

This is where we move from reflecting the glory from the surface to radiating the glory from deep within. This is the miracle. It is not a sunburn but a heart on fire. And it is available to all of us all of the time.

Let's close with 2 Corinthians 3:12 and really take it to heart: "Therefore, since we have such a hope, we are very bold."

The Prayer for Deliverance

Lord Jesus, you are my Deliverer. I receive your deliverance from the veils or masks I wear—especially the religious ones. I want to be done with hiding. Deliver me from the layers of image management I have been doing for so long that I don't even know I'm doing it. I receive your deliverance into the simplicity, beauty, and fullness of your image in me. Deliver me into the depths of my true identity, which comes from your presence in me—even from one degree of glory to the next. Thank you for this one small word that makes all the difference in the universe: in. Jesus Christ in me. The Holy Spirit in me. Take me into the school of beholding and becoming, where I will learn the patience of the slow burn of transformational glory—where the bush is on fire but is not consumed. It will be for your glory, for others' gain, and for our good.

Glory be to the Father and to the Son and to the Holy Ghost.
As it was in the beginning, is now and ever shall be.
World without end. Amen! Amen!

The Questions

Have you discovered the miracle of the two letters that change everything? What is your "with-in" story? How have you and do you find yourself trying to appear better or different than you really are? Are you ready to be done with image management and to dive deep into identity transformation?

89

Exodus 39:32–43

On the Process of Deliverance and the Pilgrimage of Worship

So all the work on the tabernacle, the tent of meeting, was completed. The Israelites did everything just as the LORD commanded Moses. Then they brought the tabernacle to Moses: the tent and all its furnishings, its clasps, frames, crossbars, posts and bases; the covering of ram skins dyed red and the covering of another durable leather and the shielding curtain; the ark of the covenant law with its poles and the atonement cover; the table with all its articles and the bread of the Presence; the pure gold lampstand with its row of lamps and all its accessories, and the olive oil for the light; the gold altar, the anointing oil, the fragrant incense, and the curtain for the entrance to the tent; the bronze altar with its bronze grating, its poles and all its utensils; the basin with its stand; the curtains of the courtyard with its posts and bases, and the curtain for the entrance to the courtyard; the ropes and tent pegs for the courtyard; all the furnishings for the tabernacle, the tent of meeting; and the woven garments worn for ministering in the sanctuary, both the sacred garments for Aaron the priest and the garments for his sons when serving as priests.

The Israelites had done all the work just as the LORD had commanded Moses. Moses inspected the work and saw that they had done it just as the LORD had commanded. So Moses blessed them.

Consider This

> Then the LORD said to Moses, "Go to Pharaoh and say to him, 'This is what the LORD says: Let my people go, so that they may worship me.'" (Exodus 8:1)

So here we are at the end of the long and winding journey of Exodus in the next to the last chapter of the book and the next to the last entry in the series, and finally we come to the setting up of the tabernacle. One would think—based on the original decree of deliverance calling the people to worship—that we might have begun with the construction of the tabernacle. So why here at the end, instead of at the beginning, are we finally getting to the construction of the tabernacle?

> So all the work on the tabernacle, the tent of meeting, was completed.

Perhaps because deliverance is a process and worship is a pilgrimage. Deliverance is a process of cataclysmic revelation. Worship is a pilgrimage of catalytic response. Perhaps it is because true worship must originate in the heart and not from the building and all its adornments and accoutrements. First must come the heart of worship and only then the house of worship.

Perhaps it is because once worship gets shifted even a degree of a degree off of its proper object, who is I AM THAT I AM, worship itself becomes the subject. And we know what happens when worship is the subject. It becomes all about the songs and the style and the music and the instruments and the lights and the cameras and the action and the worship leaders and the preachers and what they are wearing and not wearing, and on and on we could go and have gone. All the while worship is not all about any of these things. It is all about you, Jesus.

Perhaps God waited so long to set up the tabernacle in order to give the necessary time, sequence, and scope so the tabernacle could first be constructed in the human heart. And perhaps God gave such specific and detailed instructions on the construction of the tabernacle and all its contents to save us from any and all of these things that tend to keep worship from becoming the subject of all our preferential debates and distractions. It is ironic how from time to time we may need to be delivered from our mistaken notion and misguided practice of worship.

Years back, the British worship leader Matt Redman called his church to a lengthy season of gathering for worship where they would have no music and sing no songs. He realized their worship had become about the music rather than God. As the period of weeks came to a close, he wrote the song we know as "The Heart of Worship."

The Prayer for Deliverance

Lord Jesus, you are my Deliverer. I receive your deliverance. And I offer you my worship. Make my heart a tabernacle for your presence. And grace my life to keep it so. It will be for your glory, for others' gain, and for our good.

Glory be to the Father and to the Son and to the Holy Ghost.
As it was in the beginning, is now and ever shall be.
World without end. Amen! Amen!

The Questions

How are you seeing and understanding the relationship between deliverance and worship? More importantly, how are you practicing and living out this relationship? Have you personally witnessed the way worship becomes about so many other things than God? How are you keeping the tabernacle of your heart revived and refreshed?

90

Exodus 40:34–38

Back to Plan A

Then the cloud covered the tent of meeting, and the glory of the Lord *filled the tabernacle. Moses could not enter the tent of meeting because the cloud had settled on it, and the glory of the* Lord *filled the tabernacle.*

In all the travels of the Israelites, whenever the cloud lifted from above the tabernacle, they would set out; but if the cloud did not lift, they did not set out—until the day it lifted. So the cloud of the Lord *was over the tabernacle by day, and fire was in the cloud by night, in the sight of all the Israelites during all their travels.*

Consider This

And so we come to the end of the epic of Exodus, with the glory of the Lord filling the tabernacle.

Do you remember how we began? I was with my friend Mike on the anniversary of a tragic day in his past and all that it had led to when he said, "I guess my life is now on plan B."

The journey from the land of slavery to the land of promise must pass through the wilderness. The wilderness is a place of teaching, testing, and transformation. And through these processes, it is a place of divine deliverance. All the old means and modes of the control matrix of slavery are gone. The outward shackles fall off only to reveal their inner strongholds in our hearts and minds.

The wilderness teaches us a whole new order and a completely new and different way of life. We have been delivered from the empire of Pharaoh to the kingdom of God. We must learn the gracious intricacies of covenant-keeping rather than the onerous yoke of rule-following. Our relationship is not with the rules but with the Ruler himself—following him via cloud by day and fire by night. The wilderness teaches us the trust of daily bread—manna in the morning, quail in the evening. Indeed, the wilderness teaches us that when we follow the Ruler, seeking his kingdom and his righteousness, everything else falls into place.

The end of Exodus is really the beginning. Everything so far has led to this point. From the day our forebears were exiled from the garden of Eden, the slow gears of redemption have rolled on, leading us to this encounter in the wilderness: the tabernacling of God in the midst of his people.

The eternal will of the Father in the garden is now being revealed in the untamed wild of the wilderness. We are now delivered from plan B back into plan A. It will not be all smooth sailing from here. We will need ongoing deliverance, but God who delivers us dwells in our midst—indeed, in our very bodies.

> Then the cloud covered the tent of meeting, and the glory of the LORD filled the tabernacle. Moses could not enter the tent

> of meeting because the cloud had settled on it, and the glory of the LORD filled the tabernacle.

In like fashion, in the fullness of time, Jesus Christ, the Word of God, came into the wilderness of this world. There could be no more profound revelation in the entirety of Scripture than John 1:14, "The Word became flesh and made his dwelling among us. We have seen his glory, the glory of the one and only Son, who came from the Father, full of grace and truth."

The translation "made his dwelling" fails to capture it. The Greek word is *skay-no-o* (phonetic spelling). It means, quite literally, "He pitched his tent and tabernacled among us." Jesus is the tabernacle of God—in human flesh, just like you and me. And do you remember his calling to us? "Follow me."

> In all the travels of the Israelites, whenever the cloud lifted from above the tabernacle, they would set out; but if the cloud did not lift, they did not set out—until the day it lifted.

And then came the day of Pentecost, when the glory of the Spirit of God—the one who filled the tabernacle, the one who filled the Son of God in perfection—came and filled followers of Jesus.

Yes, my friends, you are the tabernacle of God—the dwelling place of the Holy Spirit—personally and communally.

May the God and Father of our Lord Jesus Christ awaken us more and more to this reality and lead us into the destiny for which we were made.

The Prayer for Deliverance

Lord Jesus, you are my Deliverer. I receive your deliverance from plan B back to plan A. I receive your deliverance from burned out to on fire but not burning up. I receive your deliverance from a distant sense of your presence with me to an abiding sense of your presence tabernacling within me. Thank you for the glory of the exodus and the goodness of deliverance and the greatness of Jesus—joy of every longing heart. It will be for your glory, for others' gain, and for our good.

Glory be to the Father and to the Son and to the Holy Ghost.
As it was in the beginning, is now and ever shall be.
World without end. Amen! Amen!

The Questions

There is no testimony without a test.

To that end, I have an invitation for you today. How have your life and faith been tested? How have you grown? How has God—Father, Son, and Holy Spirit—revealed himself to you? How have you been stretched in your response to the Word of God and the Spirit of God? Was there a particular entry or revelation or concept through which God engaged you in an impactful way, and if so, how?

Are you filled with the fullness of the Holy Spirit? Are you ready for even more? What will be your next steps on the journey? How might you move to the edges of your comfort zone? What about a step beyond that?

Week 13: Discussion Questions

Hearing the Text

Read Exodus 34:1–40:38.

Responding to the Text

- What did you hear?
- What did you see?
- What did you otherwise sense from the Lord?

Sharing Insights and Implications for Discipleship

Drawing from the Scripture text and daily readings, what did you find challenging, encouraging, provocative, comforting, invasive, inspiring, corrective, affirming, guiding, or warning?

Shaping Intentions for Prayer

Write your discipleship intention for the week ahead.

Conclusion

Many years ago, as legend has it, the Prince of Asburias, the next in line for the Spanish throne, was condemned to spend his life in solitary confinement in a Madrid prison cell. For thirty-three years this would-be king languished in his jail cell. He had access to one book the entire time: the Holy Bible. Throughout these years, he read it from cover to cover hundreds of times, finally dying in the cell. After his death, officials discovered some etchings made on the wall next to where his bed sat. He had used a nail to scratch out four notations on the soft stone walls of the cell. What marvelous mysteries they expected to find in these etchings. Instead, here is what they found:

1. "The eighth verse of the ninety-seventh psalm is the middle verse of the Bible."
2. "Ezra 7:21 contains all the letters of the alphabet except the letter *J*."
3. "The ninth verse of the eighth chapter of Esther is the longest verse in the Bible."
4. "No word or name of more than six syllables can be found in the Bible."

This story shows us how one can read the Bible and completely miss the meaning, how reading the greatest truth in the history of truth can become an adventure in missing the point, even reduced to a trivial pursuit.

Here are a few trivia-oriented but perhaps less trivial observations.

1. The Bible contains 727,993 words in the NIV.
2. The book of Exodus is the fifth longest book of the Bible, coming in at 28,413 words.

3. By comparison, the shortest book of the Bible is 3 John at 323 words.

In response to those 28,413 words of Exodus, I have added tens of thousands of my own words to hopefully interpret and make application for our lives. But here's the bottom line: As helpful as my words may be to this end, when placed alongside the words of Scripture, my words are trivial in comparison. Lest we forget the sobering declaration of the prophet, "The grass withers and the flowers fall, but the word of our God endures forever" (Isaiah 40:8), let the reader be assured, my words fall somewhere in between the grass and the flowers.

That said and in the interest of a conclusion, I thought it best—rather than add more of my words to the mix—to summarize the book of Exodus with its own words. I have combed through each entry and pulled from the associated biblical text a few words or a phrase, which when read together in sequence, capture the storied flow of the book. And in keeping with our trivial pursuit, this summary of the fifth longest book in the Bible, coming in at 28,413 words, comes to a mere and quite digestible 532 words.

If You See That the Baby Is a Boy, Kill Him
She Hid Him for Three Months
So the Girl Went and Got the Baby's Mother
He Sat Down by a Well
During That Long Period
The Far Side of the Wilderness
The Bush Was on Fire . . . It Did Not Burn Up
Take Off Your Shoes . . .
So Now, Go.
Who Am I?
I Will Be with You
I AM WHO I AM
Now Go; I Will Help You
So He May Worship Me
Let My People Go!
I Am the LORD
I Will Harden Pharaoh's Heart
Just as the LORD Had Said
The LORD Makes a Distinction
It Was a Night of Watching by the LORD
Commemorate This Day
So God Led the People Around by the Desert Road
By Day . . . in a Pillar of Cloud and by Night in a Pillar of Fire
Tell the Israelites to Turn Back
All Pharaoh's Horses and Chariots, Horsemen and Troops

The LORD Will Fight for You
Raise Your Staff and Stretch Out Your Hand
The Cloud Brought Darkness to One Side and Light to the Other
During the Last Watch of the Night
Not One of Them Survived
But the Israelites Walked
I Will Sing to the LORD
The Desert of Shur
What Are We to Drink?
I Am the LORD Who Heals You
Twelve Springs and Seventy Palm Trees
The Whole Community Grumbled
I Will Rain Down Bread from Heaven
You Are Not Grumbling Against Us, but Against the LORD
The Israelites Did as They Were Told
Some of Them Paid No Attention to Moses . . . Maggots
So the People Rested on the Seventh Day
To Be Kept for the Generations to Come
But the People Were Thirsty
Is the LORD Among Us or Not?
As Long as Moses Held Up His Hands
Moses Built an Altar
I, Your Father-in-Law Jethro, Am Coming to You
The Work Is Too Heavy for You
They Came to the Desert of Sinai
Go to the People and Consecrate Them
Then Moses Led the People out of the Camp to Meet with God
And God Spoke All These Words
Remember the Sabbath Day
Honor Your Father and Your Mother
You Shall Not
They Trembled with Fear
Make an Altar of Earth
However, If It Is Not Done Intentionally
Little by Little I Will Drive Them Out
We Will Do Everything the LORD Has Said
You Are to Receive the Offering for Me
Make the Tabernacle with Ten Curtains
So I Will Consecrate
Behold, I Have Chosen Bezalel
Moses Was So Long in Coming Down
And They Are a Stiff-Necked People
Perhaps I Can Make Atonement for Your Sin
But I Will Not Go with You
Now Moses Used to Take a Tent
Because I Am Pleased with You and I Know You by Name
Now Show Me Your Glory
The LORD, the LORD, the Compassionate and Gracious God

Moses Bowed to the Ground at Once and Worshiped

Be Careful . . . Write Down These Words

His Face Was Radiant

So All the Work on the Tabernacle . . . Was Completed

The Glory of the LORD Filled the Tabernacle

Glory be to the Father and to the Son and to the Holy Ghost.
As it was in the beginning, is now and ever shall be.
World without end. Amen! Amen!

JOHN DAVID (J. D.) WALT JR.
Easter 2025